SAM CLEMENS
OF HANNIBAL

Sam Clemens

OF HANNIBAL

BY DIXON WECTER

SENTRY EDITION

1961

The Riverside Press Cambridge

HOUGHTON MIFFLIN COMPANY

BOSTON

The Riverside Press

CAMBRIDGE · MASSACHUSETTS
PRINTED IN THE U.S.A.

4336

PREFACE

IN THE AUTUMN of 1946, Dixon Wecter was appointed editor of The Mark Twain Estate by the trustees of that estate — Clara Clemens Samossoud, Thomas G. Chamberlain, and the Central Hanover Bank of New York. His editorship was third in the line of succession since Mark Twain's death. Albert Bigelow Paine served as the first editor, Bernard DeVoto as the second. In the four years that followed his appointment, Dixon Wecter developed a long-range publication program designed to make thorough use of that great wealth of material preserved by Mark Twain in the collection known as The Mark Twain Papers. Those Papers were consigned to his custody at the Huntington Library, where he was Chairman of the Research Staff, and were then moved to the Library of the University of California at Berkeley when he accepted the Byrne Chair of United States History at that institution, in the fall of 1949.

For Harper and Brothers, Dixon Wecter edited "Report from Paradise," a collection of Mark Twain's celestial writing, as yet unpublished. In 1949 he prepared *Mark Twain to Mrs. Fairbanks* in which he used much unpublished Twain material to annotate the collection of letters owned by the Huntington Library. In 1950, he edited *The*

Love Letters of Mark Twain, a collection owned by Mark Twain's daughter, Clara Clemens Samossoud.

But the major project Dixon Wecter planned was a biography — a truly definitive biography. There has been a plethora of writing about Mark Twain — biographies and demi-biographies included — but no biographer save Paine had access to the all-important Mark Twain Papers. And Paine's gullibility and personal prudery forever contrived to distort the focus of his lens on his protagonist.

Readying himself for the writing of this all-time biography, Dixon Wecter steeped himself in Twainiana, criss-crossed the country to know every setting meaningful in Mark Twain's life. One hot July, Dixon Wecter even sailed down the Mississippi River, with *Life on the Mississippi* and transcripts of Mark's river notebooks in hand. His was the delight of hearing the leadsman call out "mark twain" — safe water — and of going aground on Stack Island, which had menaced pilot Sam Clemens a century before.

Plans for the biography grew to two-volume proportions, and the writing of it was begun. In June 1950, the first section of the biography completed first-draft, Dixon Wecter set out for the Mother Lode country to refresh his knowledge of Mark's rollicking Nevada-California days. On that trip Dixon Wecter died very suddenly. *Sam Clemens of Hannibal* is, then, the first portion of that projected biography — an entity in itself, a recounting of the most significant and least known of all the years in Mark Twain's seventy-five.

In preparing a book for posthumous publication, the editor assembles a poignant list of names of those who have helped and counseled. To the Mark Twain Estate Trustees and to Frank MacGregor I would like to tell my especial thanks for long-term guidance and for permission to use so rich a treasure of unpublished and published Mark Twain material. To Paul Brooks, Robert Penn Warren, and Bernard DeVoto my thanks for wise advice. If this book could bear a dedication it would be to Van der Veer Varner. My thanks to Lamar McLeod, Helen Gray, Margaret Kahn, and Jane Carroll for their help in the preparation of this book, and to Donald Coney, Librarian of the University of California at Berkeley, for his co-operation. And finally, thanks to the true friends who interested themselves in this project.

ELIZABETH WECTER

CONTENTS

OF CONTENTS

SAM CLEMENS
OF HANNIBAL

CHAPTER ONE

"DAMN THE ANCESTORS"

LIKE HIS Connecticut Yankee, Mark Twain sometimes reflected upon heredity, "a procession of ancestors that
stretches back a billion years to the Adam-Clam or grass-
hopper or monkey from whom our race has been so tediously
and ostentatiously and unprofitably developed." As a democrat Mark tended to make sport of genealogy, and its prac-
titioners who often sit apart from the toil and challenge of
the present under the shade of a spreading family tree. His
copy of Suetonius's *Lives of the Caesars,* a favorite book,
bears a marginal comment upon the historian's mention of
a certain Flavius Clemens, "a man below contempt for his
want of energy." Mark observes: "I guess this is where our
line starts. It will end with another kind of line, probably." [1]

To an inquisitor from Arkansas in 1902 Mark confessed:
"I am helpless when it comes to genealogies. While my
mother was alive she always kept the run of them, and I
referred inquirers to her with full confidence; but now I
have nowhere to turn. My father was John M. Clemens,
but back of him — or even around him — I am in the dark."
His father's own disdain for lineage Mark portrayed in an
unpublished sketch in which John Clemens, cast as "Judge
Carpenter," yearns to "lie down in the peace and the quiet

and be an ancestor, I do get so tired of being posterity," and, more vehemently, cries "Damn the ancestors" while asserting he "would rather be a dog's ancestor than a lieutenant-governor's posterity." [2]

Nevertheless in his *Autobiography* Mark Twain the perennial romantic alluded to vague traditions of Elizabethan pirates and slave traders, a regicide judge who allegedly became English ambassador to Spain and brought into the clan a Castilian wife and her infusion of exotic blood, and a colonial Clemens who was a friend of the Fairfaxes and had settled first in Maryland and then in Virginia. Mark was especially fond of the regicide judge — whom he persistently miscalled Geoffrey and fabricated into an ambassador to Spain merely by reason of his having traded there — because in signing the death warrant of Charles I he "did what he could toward reducing the list of crowned shams of his day." [3] Here was an ancestor in whom both the romantic and the democrat could take pride, at least if one did not inquire too closely into the career of this London merchant-judge, whom his fellow Roundheads later expelled from Parliament for "having been frail with his female servant at Greenwich," and who begged vainly for mercy in 1660 when the Restoration sent him to the gallows.[4]

Beyond question this Gregory Clement had a son named James, a Quaker who emigrated to Long Island in 1670, founding an American family that produced at least one Samuel Clement early in the eighteenth century.[5] But no certain link with Mark Twain's grandfather, Samuel B. Clemens of Virginia, has been forged, although the name is common enough in colonial records of the Old Dominion.[6] Mark's retort discourteous to Paul Bourget — that while an American may sometimes fill idle time in "trying to find out who his grandfather was," on the other hand a Frenchman "can turn in and see if he can't find out who his father was" — has a literal bearing on his own case, and the mystery enshrouding even the place and date of this grandfather's birth.[7]

More rewarding to the seeker after early records is the ancestry of Mark Twain's paternal grandmother, Pamela Goggin Clemens. The earliest known progenitor is a Kentish tradesman of Tudor times named Christopher Reynolds, born about 1530, whose grandson of the same name, born at Gravesend, England, in the year of the King James version of the Bible, settled in Isle of Wight County, Virginia, some time prior to drawing up his will in 1654. He sired a third Christopher, whose daughter Elizabeth in 1704 married a young Quaker named Charles Moorman. The Moormans had reached Virginia in the third quarter of the seventeenth century — despite the act of 1660 which embodied Governor Berkeley's ire against the "unreasonable and turbulent sort of people called Quakers," when any shipmaster bringing a member of that persecuted sect into Virginia risked a fine of £100, while the immigrant himself was liable to imprisonment without bail until he abjured his religion or posted security for speedy departure.[8] Such testing, as usual, failed of its purpose. Among the Virginia farming stock from which Mark Twain sprang, the Quaker faith was held not only by the Moormans but also the Reynoldses and the Clarks. The forebears who united these Quaker strains may have left a family heritage not unconnected with their famous descendant's bias toward pacifism, his sturdy anti-authoritarianism and anti-clericalism, his horror of debt, and his instinctive sympathy for all underdogs and minorities against cruelty and bullying in any form.

The first Moorman — by patronymic, "a man of the moors" — to reach America was Charles's grandfather Zachariah, who arrived from England in 1670. Finding in Nansemond County, Virginia, a haven for Quakers, he and his children soon began to prosper. George Fox himself visited Nansemond County in 1672 and held a great meeting there. The grandson Charles acquired considerable tracts of land in Louisa County, and his eldest son Thomas likewise throve in neighboring Albemarle County, not far from the site of Charlottesville — leaving his name upon the map of Virginia in Moormans River, a tributary to the James. He also assured the family's Quaker continuity by marrying, about 1730, Rachel Clark, daughter of a wealthy tobacco planter and Hanover County Justice of the Peace named Christopher Clark, who on joining the Society of Friends had resigned his captaincy in the colonial militia.[9] Upon moving east to Caroline County about 1746, Thomas and Rachel Moorman joined the Golansville Meeting. In later years, Thomas bought a farm of two hundred acres on Tomahawk Creek in Bedford (later Campbell) County, and in the spring of 1765 the aging couple transplanted themselves into the well-known Quaker settlement along the James River near Lynchburg of today. To the South River Meeting they carried a "certificate of removal" from the clerk at Golansville, stating that "Thomas and Rachel Moorman, having removed from under our care and within the verge of your Meeting, requested us for a few lines as a recommendation to you. After due care taken we do not find but that he has settled his worldly affairs to satisfaction and has always been esteemed orderly persons [*sic*] and held in good unity among us. . . ."[10]

Among their thirteen children several, including Mark

Twain's great-grandmother Rachel, were disowned "for marrying out from among us by a hireling priest" — that is, a paid preacher — but others wedded Quaker mates. The Quaker conscience, however, continued to work, being doubtless responsible for the action which Thomas' brother Charles took in manumitting his thirty-three slaves, declaring himself "fully persuaded that freedom is the natural right of all mankind." [11] Nevertheless some slaveholding continued in the family. Rachel Moorman was given as her portion under her father's will, probated on November 25, 1766, "one Negro Girl Jude to her and her Heirs forever one Horse & Sadle one Feather Bed and Furniture." And in the following generations, Mark Twain's grandparents and parents owned slaves, as will be seen.[12] But the spirit of humanity, as well as the uneasy conscience in respect to that "peculiar institution," were to reappear in Mark, who long after the Civil War paid the way of a Negro student through Yale College, as his part of "the reparation due to every black man by every white man."

Rachel's inheritance became her dowry when in 1773 she married Stephen Goggin, Jr. The elder Stephen Goggin, a member of the Anglican Church, left Queen's County, Ireland, for America in 1742, and began to farm on the banks of Flat Creek, a tributary to Roanoke River in Bedford County, Virginia. Here his son Stephen was born in 1752. On the eve of the Revolution — in which Stephen, Jr., served as first lieutenant in the Bedford County Militia — he built for his bride a cabin of hewn logs with a stone chimney, on Goose Creek in that rolling country of peach and apple orchards, tobacco and hay fields, lying under the shadow of the Blue Ridge Mountains. And here on October 31, 1775, was born their daughter Pamelia — or Pamela as she herself spelled the name — Mark Twain's grandmother. Twenty-two years later, upon Pamela's marriage to Samuel B. Clemens, the young couple are said to have shared for a while its four or five rooms with the Goggins. This cabin survived until April 1949, when it was burned by the explosion of a stove that cost the lives of a Negro family long housed there.[13]

"As concerneth length of line and multiplicity of ancestors — in that property I am as poor as Jesus: no grandfather," [14] jotted Mark in an unpublished passage from his notebooks, blandly pruning his family tree. The earliest known trace left by Samuel B. Clemens is the marriage bond dated October 23, 1797, by which he and his surety, Samuel Hancock, bound themselves to Governor Wood of Virginia, in the amount of $150, to be forfeited if any "lawfull cause" prevented "a marriage shortly intended to be had & solemnized between the above bound Samuel Clements and Pamelia Goggin." Attached is the bride's petition to the Clerk of the Bedford County Court: "Sir Please to grant Saml Clemens License to intermarry with me being of lawful age." Her signature is witnessed by Pleasant Moorman Goggin, her younger brother who later became a member of the Virginia Legislature from Bedford County. Six days later, on October 29, the engaged couple were married.[15] Of Samuel Clemens' personal qualities almost nothing is known, although a family tradition recalls his "liking for writing poetry." [16]

The first child of Samuel and Pamela Clemens, born on August 11, 1798, was named John Marshall — after the rising Virginia lawyer from the back country who within three years would become Chief Justice of the United States Supreme Court. As the lad grew up he signed his name John M. Clemens, but family papers show that he was called Marshall by his relatives. The place of birth is given on his tombstone in Mount Olivet Cemetery, Hannibal, Missouri, as Campbell County, Virginia, originally that part of Bedford County lying to the east but detached in 1782. The personal tax records show that Marshall's father was a resident of Campbell County as late as 1801. Nevertheless the other business records that survive — from the years of Marshall Clemens' infancy, through the birth of a brother christened Pleasant in 1800, a sister named Elizabeth in 1801, to another brother in 1803 called (by curious prophetic insight) Hannibal — still associate the parents with Bedford County.[17]

These records also suggest the modest prosperity of the young farming couple. While they may have dwelt with Pamela's parents for a few months after marriage, in the rambling log cabin near Goose Creek, and in the adjoining county of Campbell during the period of Marshall's birth and infancy, they were back in the old neighborhood with the means to possess a home in 1802 — having returned perhaps at the time of Stephen Goggin's death in that year. An indenture dated November 18, 1802, reveals that Daniel and Lucy Brown (both making their mark) conveyed to Samuel Clemens for $1000 a property of nearly four hundred acres lying south of the old homestead and loosely described as "one certain Track of Land Situate in the County of Bedford on both sides of the big Road leading from the Meadows of Goose Creek to hailsford on Stanton River and . . . adjoining the Lands of Sam'l Hancock. . . . " Many years later, on receiving this and other documents from his elder brother Orion, in answer to a request for some of their father's papers, Mark wrote on November 11, 1881, in his usual bantering of Orion: "Think pa did not write the 1802 one — he was only three years old, then." [18] Another paper in this group is a bill of sale dated May 9, 1803, showing that Samuel Clemens of Bedford County purchased for "One hundred and ninty [*sic*] pounds current money of Virginia" a male Negro named Moses and a female called Violet; and in this year his name appears upon the Bedford County personal tax list.

But soon after this date the Clemenses decided to pull up stakes and move westward, where as always the land looked bright. On June 27, 1803, Samuel and Pamela sold to their old friend and neighbor, Samuel Hancock, for £105, a ninety-three-acre tract bounded by oaks and dogwood, adjoining his land, and so pretty clearly part of the Clemenses' home farm.[19] By the summer of 1804 the pioneering couple crossed the Alleghenies into Mason County, where West Virginia now borders upon Ohio, and began to farm on the south bank of the Ohio River, about six miles above its meeting with the Great Kanawha at Point Pleasant. Carved out of the frontier, Mason County was organized in the summer of 1804 and Samuel Clemens was appointed its first Commissioner of Revenue, with the task of listing all taxable property. On October 2 the court granted him fifty days' allowance for his services. He continued to fill this office until the following April, when a successor took over his duties. Meanwhile with much civic energy he had superintended Mason County's first election, served on a jury, and entered surety for a fellow citizen authorized to run a ferry across the Ohio River. In March 1805 — the month in which his last child, Caroline, was born — Samuel Clemens purchased two tracts totaling a hundred and nineteen acres along Ten Mile Creek in this new county which he had done so much to organize.[20]

In the summer of that year, two Quaker cousins of Pamela

Clemens from Campbell County, Thomas and John Hope Moorman, set out on horseback carrying a pocket compass to scout out the Ohio and Illinois country with a view to migration; on August 7, as their diary records, they rode from Point Pleasant "up the Ohio River, six miles to Cousin Parmela [*sic*] Clemens, and rested there two nights and one day." [21] Soon after this visit, probably in the autumn of 1805, tragedy overtook the young couple. Mark Twain's brother Orion Clemens told the story many years later to a local historian, who wrote: "When [John Marshall Clemens] was seven years old his father, Samuel Clemens, rode away one morning before sunrise without kissing him. John M. was much grieved by this unwonted omission. He never again saw his father alive. Mr. Clemens had gone to a house-raising. While pushing a log before him up an inclined plane, the log slipped, carrying him down and fatally crushing him against a stump." [22] A martyr to the neighborliness of the frontier, Samuel B. Clemens thus left five fatherless children, John Marshall being the eldest. And, whether rightly or not, the modern psychologist will fancy in the lad's long-remembered slight from his father a key to the austerity with which he treated his own family, in whose circle no kiss was ever given or received save in the shadow of death. [23]

A spinster cousin of Mark Twain from Louisville, Xantippe Saunders — also a grandchild of Pamela Goggin Clemens, but by her second husband — declared that after Samuel's death his widow was invited by her brother "Jubal Goggin" to move to Kentucky and keep house for him. "Pretty soon after she came here she found in one of her brother's neighbors an old suitor who, soon after she married Clemens, sought relief to his wounded heart in the wilds of Kentucky. Of course he sympathized with her and soon relieved her brother from his burden by marrying her." This was Simon Hancock, originally from Bedford County, Virginia, undoubtedly the nephew of that Samuel Hancock who had signed Samuel Clemens' marriage bond, and who purchased land from the Clemenses when they moved westward.[24] Pamela had no brother named Jubal, but her brother Thomas and her younger sister Polly, who in 1801 had married Alexander Gill, all eventually moved to Adair County, Kentucky. Whether Pamela Clemens and her five children came to that neighborhood with or soon after Thomas Goggin and the Gills is not known.[25]

Possibly two or three years passed between the death of Samuel Clemens and the arrival of his widow with her children in the Western country. Mark Twain's biographer Paine — who incidentally makes no mention of the earlier removal to Mason County — states that John Marshall Clemens, now male head of the house, soon took a job clerking in an iron manufactory at Lynchburg. If true, this detail suggests that Pamela in the first years of her widowhood had returned east some two hundred miles to her relatives in Bedford and Campbell counties. But even in those days void of restrictions upon child labor, it may be doubted that a boy between the ages of seven and ten could qualify as a clerk in a foundry, and more likely is the account based upon Orion's information which describes him clerking in a Lynchburg iron factory "when verging on manhood." Yet Paine is probably right in saying that despite the death of the breadwinner, his family was not left poor — considering the legal documents dated long afterward, settling title to "the slaves & real estate of said Samuel Clemens deceased." [26] But the possession of western Virginia acres and some half-dozen slaves, in the lack of a man to manage them and a permanent *pied à terre,* doubtless bred a sense of incertitude and probably a lack of present cash.

At any rate, in Adair County, Kentucky, on May 21, 1809,[27] Pamela Clemens married her girlhood suitor Simon Hancock — thus solving the problem of a broken home and orphaned children in a way which Thomas Lincoln and Sarah Bush Johnson, and many other Kentucky pioneers, came to adopt. Legal records show Simon Hancock as a buyer of farm lands in Adair County, and "captain of patrollers" in the year he married his old sweetheart.[28] During the next eight years Pamela bore three more children. All of course were brought up together, in this segment of south-central Kentucky known as the Pennyrile — from the local pronunciation of pennyroyal, which grows here as lushly as the bluegrass in more fertile counties to the north. Organized in 1801 with the building of a brick courthouse in the village of Columbia, Adair County became a region of small but fairly prosperous farms, its limestone soil supporting corn, wheat, and tobacco, and its rolling hillsides giving pasture to livestock.

Glimpses of how the Clemens children grew up in the new household of their stepfather can be caught from an account drawn up in 1821, after Mark Twain's father had come of age and assumed the task of administering the Clemens estate.[29] Preserved by Mark himself in a bundle of yellowing family documents, it is headed "Simon Hancock's Claim against Marshall Clemens administrator for Samuel Clemens dec^st." Simon Hancock dates the children's indebtedness to him from the day he married their mother, and begins with the entry, "Support of Marshall Clemens three years at twenty dollars pr year, $60.00." From the age of fourteen, in 1812, Marshall Clemens was evidently self-supporting. Probably the clerking in an iron factory and the night hours which permanently weakened his health — whether demanded by his job, as Orion's correspondent Holcombe states, or by his eagerness to get an education, as Paine assumes — belong to this period in his early teens, when by the standards of a pioneer society he was old enough to shift for himself and seek work in the neighborhood of his mother's Virginia kin. The over-serious nature of Marshall Clemens through the years that followed — ambitious, industrious, austere, corroded by worry and haunted by the specter of poverty — was surely moulded during a boyhood that knew no time for play or humor, and had seemingly scant acquaintance with either affection or family security. This bias, in turn, had its signal effect upon his fourth and most sensitive son, Samuel Langhorne Clemens.

But to return to the bookkeeping of Simon Hancock. Marshall's younger brother Pleasant — bearing an old Virginia Quaker name — who died in November 1811, was charged one year's support and doctors' fees of ten dollars. As for the still younger children, Elizabeth, or Betsy, was indebted for eight years' support, and Hannibal and Caroline eleven each, as well as sums to pay for schooling and supplies, including "slate and arithmetick for Hanibal." In 1817, at the age of sixteen, Betsy removed herself from the dependents' roll, as Marshall had done five years earlier. Her new status was marked by this entry: "To Betsy Clemens one saddle and Bridle and Saddle blanket, and ten dollars in Cash when she started to Virginia, $30.00." Other family records show that she set out to visit her Goggin relatives in Bedford County, and there in Virginia she married Captain John Pollard, veteran of the War of 1812, and set up housekeeping in the old log cabin where her mother had been born.[30]

The total of Simon Hancock's bill for raising his step-children, supporting the young slaves, and meeting other charges against the estate of Samuel Clemens, $884.38, was duly paid by Marshall Clemens before midsummer 1821, save for a small debt which ran until the following January, and was then liquidated by the payment of fifteen dollars in cash and fifty-two dollars offset against the hire for one year of a Negro woman named Betty and a black boy called Reason.[31] The neat signature of Mark Twain's grandmother, Pamela Hancock, attests on January 1, 1821, that she renounces any right or title to her first husband's estate.

The chief assets of this estate were slaves, now numbering ten, and on January 30, 1821, three commissioners, appointed by the Adair County Court to distribute these chattels of flesh-and-blood among the heirs, made their allotment. As his share, Marshall Clemens received a Negro woman named Mariah, a girl Louisa, and a boy Green. He also inherited a mahogany sideboard, which the Clemenses later carried into the West with them as a symbol of better days. Betsy Clemens, far away in Virginia, was given a woman called Daisy and a girl Nancy, her brother signing the indenture for her as "Jno. M. Clemens atty." Hannibal Clemens obtained the slaves named Betty and Reason, whose labor helped to meet Simon Hancock's bill, along with another lad called Silas; and Caroline's portion was two black boys known as Campbell and Andrew.[32] The institution of slavery, transplanted from Virginia a generation earlier, was already proving less profitable in this second-grade farming country of the Pennyrile, so that the more enterprising slaveholders in the 1820's were beginning to thin out — seeking either the rich bluegrass counties northward or else the Cotton Kingdom of the Deep South. This economic factor helps to explain why young Marshall Clemens, his assets chiefly black labor, did not thrive notably here and soon began that series of migrations which were to mark the years ahead.

His initial step toward a career of his own was apprenticeship to the law. He settled in Columbia, Kentucky, to study with an attorney named Cyrus Walker, later prominent at the bar of Macomb, Illinois. Through all the later years of disappointment in this profession, Clemens carefully preserved a document signed on October 29, 1822, by Judge Christopher Tompkins and Judge Joseph Eve — the latter a well-known Circuit justice — attesting that "John M. Clemens . . . having produced to us a certificate, of the County Court of Adair, that he is a young man of honesty, probity, and good demeanour; and it appearing to us, upon a critical examination as to his legal knowledge, that he is duly qualified for the practice," was granted a license to practice in the courts of Kentucky.[33]

The integrity and dignity herein certified were more than formal phrases. His tall spare frame, piercing gray eyes, hair brushed vigorously back, and mouth that rarely smiled and never laughed, belonged to a stern, proud, frugal disposition whose bent determined his life. Almost fanatic in his scruples touching honesty, Marshall Clemens was long remembered as "sternly and irreproachably moral." Despite a high-strung, irritable temper — the result of "shattered nerves," his family believed, in blaming it all upon those early years of night labor and exhaustion — he almost never swore, and then only at white heat. The product of inherited Virginia pride and straitened circumstances, of a stepchildhood and precocious responsibilities, Marshall Clemens was also a true scion of pioneer Kentucky. He belonged to that self-dosing generation of chills and fevers and perennial stomach complaint, whose chronic sickliness went apace with the gaunt physique and wiry constitution, as in Old Hickory himself, whom he is alleged to have resembled. But as befitted his Federalist name, John Marshall Clemens in politics followed "Young Harry of the West" as a firm Henry Clay Whig. In religion he kept aloof from churches and creeds, being regarded in later days as a freethinker or agnostic, yet confounding the godly with his stern Puritan morality. The sturdy individualism of frontier Kentucky, in the generation that spanned the late eighteenth and dawning nineteenth century, had built up a widespread spirit of anticlericalism and grass-roots radicalism — in a region where Tom Paine was the author most widely read, and the typical home-grown intellectual was Dr. Joseph Buchanan, agnostic physician-philosopher. The seeds of skepticism early took root in the self-educated mind of Marshall Clemens — even though his family liked vaguely to think he "inclined to the Campbellites" — as they did in the mind of his celebrated son.[34]

On May 6, 1823, the Adair County Clerk received a marriage bond signed by this serious-minded young man and Thomas Cheek, posting the sum of £50 as security for the marriage "shortly intended to solemnized [*sic*] between the above bound John M. Clemons above the age of twenty one years and Jane Lampton daughter of Benjamin Lampton whose consent was personally given." On that same day they were married.[35]

CHAPTER TWO

THE LAMPTON SIDE

JANE LAMPTON, "said to be one of the most beautiful women in the state at that time," possessed the slow Southern speech, the small delicate hands and feet, and the luxuriant red hair that her son Samuel inherited.[1] Her blithe and social spirit was a strange match for the dour temperament of John Marshall Clemens, while her charm, wit, impulsiveness, erratic spelling, and indifferent housekeeping seemed hardly to comport with his cold, self-disciplined, and orderly ways. Their first-born, Orion, wrote of his mother shortly after her death at the age of eighty-seven:

During her girlhood Jane Lampton was noted for her vivacity and her beauty. To the last she retained her rosy cheeks and fine complexion. She took part in the custom in Kentucky and Tennessee, of going on horseback from house to house during the week from Christmas to New Year. To the music of one or two violins they danced all night, slept a little, ate breakfast, and danced all day at the next house. To the last Mrs. Clemens maintained dancing to be innocent and healthful. Even in the last year of her life she liked to show a company the beautiful step and graceful movement she had learned in her youth. Until within a few years she was so straight she almost leaned backward. Her happy flow of spirits made her a popular favorite where she lived.

Cyrus Walker was a young attorney, just married to a cousin of Mrs. Clemens, and was traveling on his circuit. He took his fees in cash or other articles of value as might suit the convenience of his clients. Once he was returning home with a silk dress pattern, when he heard uproarious laughter in his own house. On entering there was an instant hush. After a good deal of examination and cross-examination he brought out the truth that Jane Lampton, then about 15 years of age, had been imitating his dancing. He wished to see himself as she saw him, but she refused till he offered the silk dress. She then showed him his own awkward dancing. It amused him, and she got the dress.[2]

In the improbable courtship of Jane and John Marshall Clemens, the latter's apprenticeship to the law in the Columbia office of Cyrus Walker, county attorney in 1821 and justice of the peace in 1823, doubtless played its part.[3] But the immediate reason for their mating — according to a story which Jane Lampton Clemens told over sixty years later, after keeping it long locked in her breast — was a fit of pique which had turned the impulsive girl against her real love, a young medical student named Barrett, who had begun to court Jane when she was eighteen. "[He] lived in Columbia [Ky.] eighteen miles away; and he used to ride over to see me," she recalled.

This continued for some time. I loved him with my whole heart, and I knew that he felt the same toward me, though no words had been spoken. He was too bashful to speak — he could not do it. Everybody supposed we were engaged — took it for granted we were — but we were not. By and by there was to be a party in a neighboring town, and he

wrote my uncle telling him his feelings, and asking him to
drive me over in his buggy and let him (Barrett) drive me
back, so that he might have that opportunity to propose.
My uncle should have done as he was asked, without ex-
plaining anything to me; but instead, he read me the letter;
and then, of course, I could not go — and did not. He
(Barrett) left the country presently, and I, to stop the clack-
ing tongues and to show him that *I* did not care, married, in
a pet.[4]

Jane never saw him again. But the sequel which brought
forth the telling of this story took place in her old age in
Iowa — where she lived with Mark's older brother Orion at
Keokuk — after thirty-eight years of widowhood. In the
autumn of 1885 her eyes fell upon Barrett's name in a newspaper among the expected visitors at an old settlers' reunion
in an Iowa town. Intending to ask his forgiveness, she made
the tedious trip — "young again with excitement, interest,
eagerness, anticipation" — but found that Dr. Barrett had
left three hours before, to return to St. Louis. And, as Mark
learned from Orion and Mollie, his wife, she "turned away,
the fire all gone from her, and said, 'Let us go home.'"

This tale — "as pathetic a romance as any that has crossed
the field of my personal experience in a long lifetime," Mark
called it — has been widely doubted as the figment of an
aged mind. Mark himself, after recounting the story in a
letter to William Dean Howells, said of his mother, "Since
then, her memory is wholly faded out and gone."[4] And at
this moment of Jane's life Orion wrote to Mark, "Ma's
reasoning powers remain good, but her memory sometimes
makes bedfellows of strangers, or divorces couples whom God
hath joined together."[5] But a few facts can be garnered to
give partial credence to this tale.

A Richard Barrett lived in neighboring Green County at

the time of Jane's marriage to John M. Clemens, and became a doctor after studying at Transylvania Medical School in Lexington, Kentucky, during the years from 1824 to 1827. He established a tie with Iowa when the company he headed invested heavily at the land sales of 1838 and 1839 at Burlington and Dubuque. Another link in the chain of association is forged by his move to St. Louis in 1840, where he became Professor of Materia Medica at Kemper College. In the mid-forties he built Barret [*sic*] House at Burlington. However, he died in 1860 at Barret House while on a business trip, twenty-five years before Jane's expedition in search of her remembered Dr. Barrett.[6] Mark's account does not specify his mother's destination. Newspaper accounts, however, report that a Tri-State Old Settler's Association reunion was held in Keokuk in late September 1885. An address on pioneer physicians, part of the reunion program, may well have mentioned Barrett's name.[7] Mark's fascination with this saga is evidenced by its reappearance in his dictation of December 1906, and again in "Villagers of 1840–3" — his unpublished roster of Hannibal citizens, some cloaked in pseudonyms, which contains a sketch of John Marshall Clemens as "Judge Carpenter" who "had been married to spite another man." [8]

Undoubtedly the outlines of this romantic tale were blurred by the mists of an aging memory, or obscured in the retelling, but whether or not Jane's marriage to John Marshall Clemens was actually the result of her anger at another man, it is clear enough that theirs was not a true love match. In later years, Mark said:

> All through my boyhood I had noticed that the attitude of my father and mother toward each other was that of courteous, considerate and always respectful, and even def-

erential, friends; that they were always kind toward each other, but that there was nothing warmer; there were no outward and visible demonstrations of affection. This did not surprise me, for my father was exceedingly dignified in his carriage and speech, and in a manner he was austere. He was pleasant with his friends, but never familiar; and so, as I say, the absence of exterior demonstration of affection for my mother had no surprise for me. By nature she was warm-hearted, but it seemed to me quite natural that her warm-heartedness should be held in reserve in an atmosphere like my father's.[9]

And what of Jane Lampton's contribution to the heredity of Mark Twain? Being the annalist of the family, she liked to tell her children about this background. Even Mark Twain, with his unsteady grasp of genealogical fact, never forgot that "my maternal grandmother's maiden name was Margaret Casey; Margaret Casey's mother's maiden name was Montgomery." And apparently he told the biographer Paine how this Jane Montgomery had once outrun a redskin pursuer — an exploit in which he almost certainly confused her with her sister Betsey, as will be seen.[10] The father of these girls, an Irishman named William Montgomery, had settled awhile in Virginia, but moved to Kentucky in the autumn of 1779 and built four log cabins on the headwaters of Green River some twelve miles from Logan's Fort. This fort had been planted four years earlier in the howling wilderness by Montgomery's giant son-in-law Benjamin Logan, noted Indian fighter of the Revolution.

In March, 1780, soon after the big snows of that memorable winter had melted, Indians silently surrounded these four Montgomery cabins by night. At daybreak when William Montgomery, followed by his Negro boy, stepped forth, both

were shot and killed instantly, the boy's head falling back
on the doorsill.

Jane, the daughter, then a young woman . . . sprang to the
door, pushed out the negro's head, shut the door and called
for her brother Thomas' gun. Betsey, her sister, about twelve
years of age, clambered out at the chimney, which was not
higher than a man's head, and took the path to Pettit's
station, distant about two and a half miles. An Indian pursued her for some distance, but being quite active, she was
too fleet for him, and reached the station in safety. From
Pettit's a messenger was immediately dispatched to Logan's
fort.

From some cause or other, probably the call of Jane for
her brother's rifle, which was doubtless overheard by the
Indians, they did not attempt to break into the cabin.[11]

After assaulting another cabin, killing Jane's brother John
and capturing his wife, other women, and children, the
Indians retreated, but were hotly pursued by Logan's party,
routed with bloodshed, and the captives retaken. These
things Mark Twain's great-grandmother Jane remembered
in her old age.[11] Her grave and humorless great-grandson
Orion Clemens wrote, "Though a good Baptist she never
could, while she lived, endure the presence of Indians, because by savages five of her relatives were killed." [12]

Jane Montgomery soon married William Casey, a buckskin rifleman of Logan's Fort and son of a Virginia captain
in the Continental Army. He was a stalwart young hunter,
with sharp black eyes and long black hair, already famous
for his courage.[13] The couple lived at Casey's Station on the
Hanging Fork of Dick's River, not far from Logan's Fort
in Lincoln County, until about 1790, when they led a colony

to wild country fifty miles from any white settlement, in the heart of what became Green, and later Adair, County. Here, on Russell's Creek, near present-day Columbia, Colonel Casey built a blockhouse and stockade, commanded the militia, and won the reputation of leading citizen and chief protector against the Indians, whose forays still made Kentucky a Dark and Bloody Ground. Knowing the traits and habits of the red man as shrewdly as he knew those of the buffalo, the panther, and the bear, Colonel Casey surprised and killed several Indian warriors in forest and canebrake who were stalking him, and once with considerable slaughter stood off a band of fifteen Indians who had ambushed some women and children "pulling" flax in the fields. Benevolent, sincere, honest, civic-minded, he employed a traveling tutor for those early Kentucky settlements and later had a main share in establishing academies in Green and Adair counties. In 1795 he served in the State House as Representative from Green County, in 1799 he was a member of Kentucky's second Constitutional Convention, and beginning in 1800 sat in the State Senate. In 1806 a new county between Adair and Lincoln was christened Casey in his honor.[14]

His eldest daughter, Peggy, Mark Twain's grandmother, in March 1801 married a neighbor, Benjamin Lampton, aged thirty, "sociable and a good singer." [15] His father, William, had crossed from England to Virginia sixty years earlier, and become a small landowner in the northern part of the Piedmont. In 1763 he married Patsy Schooler in Page County, Virginia, and later moved on to Kentucky.[16]

A shadowy tie with the Lambtons, Earls of Durham, fascinated Mark Twain, whose interest in the futile attempts of various American Lamptons to prove their claim to the earldom and the wealth of its collieries left him in later years

with a lively sympathy for a great variety of "claimants" —
Satan, the Golden Calf, Shakespeare-Bacon, Mrs. Eddy, and
the Tichborne pretender Arthur Orton, about whom he
collected no less than six scrapbooks of clippings in 1873.
This bit of Lampton family apocrypha also inspired his
novel *The American Claimant,* and doubtless played its
part in the favorite Mark Twain device of a princeling in
disguise — whether for purposes of romance in *The Prince
and the Pauper,* comedy in the persons of the duke and the
king in *Huckleberry Finn,* drollery in the chivalric nonsense
of *Tom Sawyer,* or high celestial irony in *The Mysterious
Stranger.* That it satisfied some deep-seated fantasy in the
author's imagination brooks no denial.[17]

Benjamin Lampton, like his father-in-law, the Indian
fighter, and other pioneer ancestors of Mark Twain, was a
farmer with an alert sense of public spirit. He organized and
captained a militia company and supervised road building
in Adair County, meanwhile extending the property he already owned by the purchase of one hundred and forty acres
on Russell's Creek, adjoining the home property of his wife's
parents, the Caseys, four miles west of Columbia.[18] His
daughter Jane was born on June 18, 1803, possibly in the
log house of her grandfather Casey, or more probably in
the near-by log cabin which Benjamin built for his young
wife, beside a straggling path still called Lampton Lane.
Their second daughter, Martha Ann, nicknamed "Patsy,"
was born in 1807.[19] After this cabin caught fire and burned
the Lamptons moved to Columbia, the county seat, which
was growing fast.

For a while the fortunes of Benjamin Lampton grew with
it. In 1811 he obtained a contract to build an office for the
clerk of the County Court, and soon finished a thick-walled

structure that still stands.[20]   At about this time Lewis Lampton, Benjamin's brother, also moved to Columbia, with his wife, Jane Morrison, and secured a license to keep a tavern in his house. It became the popular hostelry in Columbia, famous for its social gaiety, where the publican joined his guests in the conviviality and the quarrels which "tangle foot," "red up," and "blue ruin" stimulated.[21] Between July 1812 and August 1815, Benjamin Lampton was enlisted as lieutenant-colonel in the 52d and 93d regiments of the Kentucky militia, but it is doubtful that he saw active duty. Undoubtedly this commission explains the fact that on October 4, 1814, he took oath before a justice of the peace for Adair County, swearing that he had had no part in any duel since April 1, 1812, and would so continue to abstain "during his continuance in office." [22] In 1814 he bought a half-acre homesite on Main Street near Courthouse Square, and built upon it. [23] In partnership with his brother-in-law, John Montgomery, husband of Peggy's sister Ann, Benjamin Lampton ran a store in the center of town, under the name Lampton & Montgomery.

Late in 1816 Jane's grandfather Colonel Casey died, and after one of the notable funerals in the annals of Adair County, was buried in a chair, sitting bolt upright as he had died after long suffering from arthritis. His tomb was lined with bricks intended for his handsome new house then building on a sloping rise of his Russell's Creek property.[24] Jane, a girl of thirteen, who all her life was a connoisseur of funerals, most likely was there.

From the Casey estate, probated on January 6, 1817, Jane's mother shared with her three sisters the proceeds of a public sale of Colonel Casey's stock of horses, cattle, and sheep, and received a quarter-share of six Negroes and four hundred acres of land. And in April her father was deeded a thirty-six acre farm "for $1, in compliance with a bond executed by . . . William Casey deceased." [25] Probably, at the date of this deed, Jane's mother was no longer living. The Casey inheritance was unfortunately of little consequence in aiding the Lamptons to resist the tide of depression which was moving upon the nation.

In the summer of 1817 Benjamin Lampton journeyed into Pennsylvania to buy merchandise for the store. At Pittsburgh, in late August, in order to raise $2190 in cash he mortgaged his home property to a certain Richard Brown, and then journeyed on to Philadelphia, where on September 7 in payments for goods received from Augustus Cushing he executed a note, under the firm name of Lampton & Montgomery, for $1180.50. These debts proved to be the ruin of Ben Lampton's business career.

Apparently the storekeeping went to smash, and John Montgomery, after deeding to Lampton a lot and large frame house, withdrew from the entangling debts. Benjamin Lampton's brother Lewis came to his help, only to flounder in the quagmire himself. A judgment against the brothers was rendered in September 1819 in the Federal Circuit Court; a few weeks later they sold the Montgomery house to satisfy creditors, and in the following spring Benjamin sold his old farm on Butler's Fork of Russell's Creek to raise $1500 more. In June 1820 he sacrificed two slaves, two horses, a wagon, four bedsteads with featherbeds, a cupboard, a dozen Windsor chairs, and other possessions. In April 1821 his brother Lewis threw more possessions to the wolves of debt, mortgaging six acres of land near Columbia and four brick buildings in town, although he continued to operate Lampton's Tavern in his house on Courthouse Square.

Lewis' election as treasurer of the Town Board of Trustees, during this bankrupt period, has its ironic aspect. The chain reaction of debts can be traced through legal documents during the next two years — with the brothers Lampton declaring themselves "bound to save said John Montgomery from liability" by continued sale of a few more slaves and the mortgage of "Lampton's tavern house."

John Marshall Clemens' early contact with the Lampton clan is shown by these early records. The name of Jane's uncle Lewis Lampton heads the volunteer fire company organized in Columbia on February 4, 1822, with Clemens' name on the same roster. And on April 15, 1823, Benjamin and Lewis Lampton gave power of attorney to John M. Clemens to sell a lot which they owned, also heavily mortgaged, in Sparta, Tennessee. These financial disasters, intensified as they were by Jane's disappointment in love and the advent of a stepmother in 1819, may well have played a part in her hasty decision to marry.[26] There seems little doubt that John M. Clemens, with his inheritance from his father's estate was financially better off than the Lamptons, when, on May 6, 1823, he took Jane as his bride. But the pattern of adversity, in this same uncertain business of storekeeping, was one that later overtook him in double measure.

Such were the progenitors of Mark Twain — a mingling of English middle-class and Irish blood on both sides, of Quakers and Indian fighters, independent farmers and small slaveholders. Almost all of them had reached America in the eighteenth century, before the Revolution, and funneling through Virginia, had spread into the frontier counties of south central Kentucky. Though not aristocrats, save in the dim recollections of some dubious Old World ancestor, they were self-respecting folk and rather proud. In *Rough-*

ing It Mark speaks of his father's bequest as consisting mainly of "a sumptuous legacy of pride in his fine Virginian stock" and in the *Autobiography* how his mother "loved to aggrandize [the Clemenses of Virginia] to me." [27] They were not lacking a tradition of leadership and public service as illustrated by Captain Christopher Clark, Justice of the Peace; Stephen Goggin, Jr., officer in the militia; Captain Benjamin Casey of the Continental Army; Colonel William Casey, community planter and state senator; Samuel B. Clemens, organizer of Mason County, West Virginia; and his son whose lifelong career, as will be seen, ran to duties as public-spirited as they were unremunerative. In fact, by and large this stock appeared to lack the golden touch, even in an age when the riches of inland America hung ripe for the plucking. In Virginia, they had contrived to miss the Tidewater and the Shenandoah Valley, to light upon the Blue Ridge uplands of Bedford County, and beyond the Alleghenies to choose the less fertile tracts of western Virginia and Kentucky. This story would be repeated, even more disappointingly, by John Marshall Clemens in Tennessee and Missouri — until the story of "the Tennessee land," with its infinite frustrations joined the regicide judge and the English earldom among the heirlooms of family mythology. A careful student of this clan, himself a distant relative, has suggested that it was prone to cherish the courtesy, dignity, and leisure which it carried — along with its few slaves as a visible talisman — from Virginia into Kentucky. And prone by temperament to the visionary and unsophisticated, it found itself disadvantaged in the Western country, whether vis-à-vis the more affluent Southern stock or the aggressive Yankee, and thus was foredoomed to the disappointment of its great expectations.[28]

CHAPTER THREE

"THE TENNESSEE LAND"

YOUNG MARSHALL CLEMENS and his bride, sprung from about the same economic level of small frontier slave-holders, began their life together with more hope than tangible prosperity — but unluckily were doomed to lose both, before death parted them a quarter-century later. "She brought him two or three negroes, but nothing else, I think," wrote Mark in his *Autobiography*. Elsewhere he declared that the couple "began their young married life in Lexington, Kentucky, with a small property in the land and six inherited slaves." [1] But this assertion of locale, made by Mark long after his mother's death, is not borne out by the facts. If they settled briefly in Lexington, no trace has been left upon the local records or even traditions there. On the other hand, a two-story brick house in Columbia, Kentucky, in Pinkney Alley near Fortune Street, built by a pioneer named John Field, has long been claimed as "the Clemens house," where they spent the first year or two of their married life. This was the same John Field who in old age was fond of telling the story of how Jane Casey, Jane Clemens' grandmother, accompanied by her husband with his rifle, had taken a long trip early one spring through the Kentucky forests to the lonely outposts where Field had kept a winter vigil. There she had patched his pants — Field, owning only the one pair, staying in bed during the mending.[2]

If the Field house in Columbia were indeed the "honeymoon house" of the Clemenses, it doubtless is the handsomest of the dwellings in which they lived, during a quarter-century of steadily waning fortunes. At some date shortly before the birth of their first child in 1825, the Clemenses moved southward from Adair County over the line into Jackson County, Tennessee, settling near Jane's cousin Dr. Nathan Montgomery at the county seat of Gainesboro. Here the mirage of legal business beckoned to Marshall Clemens as it did some sixty-six years later to another struggling young attorney, Cordell Hull, ere its chronic stagnation soon disillusioned both. It has also been stated on family tradition, that Marshall Clemens' poor health — apparently a weak chest — dictated this removal to the highlands of Tennessee along the upper reaches of the Cumberland River. Here, at any rate, on July 17, 1825, Orion was born — the gentle Orion who inherited all of his mother's impulsiveness and his father's knack for profitless schemes and unrewarding labor. Christened "for the constellation under which he was born," doubtless from Jane's lifelong interest in the fringes of occultism, his celestial name was accented upon the first syllable, since the Clemenses seem to have regarded *Ori'on* as a beggarly Irish pronunciation.[3]

Shortly after the Civil War, in March 1867, Orion revisited his birthplace to find "a log and frame village about forty years old . . . generation after generation grows up and dies, with no more than neighborhood traveling, or an occasional visit to Nashville. . . . Gainesborough presents the melancholy spectacle of doors closed with signs over them indicating past business; windows broken; houses faded or guiltless of paint. . . . Here and there a house with an absent owner is melting away, plank by plank and log by log, to appease the appetite of a neighbor's fire. . . . They hate Yankees with intense bitterness." As a Union man, Orion felt lucky to escape from his natal village without violence, and be allowed to hire a horse and proceed to Jamestown.[4] Plainly, Gainesboro had never had a future.

The road Orion traveled was the same over which his father and mother had taken him as a baby forty years before, after deciding to try their luck in a newer community about thirty-eight miles east of Gainesboro across the Cumberland Mountains. Jamestown, literally nothing but a cluster of sandy springs along an old Indian trace, had just been chosen as site for the seat of Fentress County, then being organized in these early months of 1827. Here Marshall foresaw an opportunity for getting in on the ground floor, as a civic leader and land buyer, even as his father before him had done in Virginia's Mason County. Evidently he persuaded his younger brother, Hannibal Clemens, to join the venture.[5] To Marshall's thoughtful yet visionary gaze the land looked good; heavily-forested mountains, a plateau promising well for farming, a waterway in the Obed River that permitted passage for timber rafts and flatboats, and mineral resources of coal and iron.[6]

Whether from his patrimony, or as seems more likely, the sale of a slave or two, Clemens had a limited supply of cash. Soon after arrival he began to build a house in Jamestown — said to be the first substantial structure erected there — with plaster on the walls and many real glass windows, so that it became the talk of his backwoods neighbors. Mark once described the impact of this dwelling on the dazzled citizenry — " 'Common log house ain't good enough for them — no indeedy! — but they've tuck 'n' gaumed the inside of theirn all over with some kind of nasty disgustin' truck which they say is all the go in Kaintuck amongst the upper hunky, and which they calls it plarsterin'!' " [7]

It is also reported that John Clemens dressed the part of a provincial squire, in blue swallow-tail coat with brass buttons. These symbols of gentility so dear to his Virginia heart, joined to his book learning, legal knowledge, and energy, promptly won him community prestige. From the start a county commissioner, he had drafted plans and specifications dated March 20, 1827, still preserved in his fine copperplate script, for the first courthouse and jail. Contracts were let two months later. He was also chosen the first Circuit Court Clerk of Fentress County, and served intermittently as acting Attorney General, combining these duties with the practice of law.[8]

In the late 1820's and early '30's, John Marshall Clemens entered and obtained grants for thousands of acres of Fentress County land, most of it lying south of Jamestown among the Knobs of the Cumberlands. The Deed and Entry Books of the period record his purchases — from "3 acres 20 poles" at a consideration of $14.37½ to his large-scale entries of five thousand acres. The apocryphal figure of seventy thousand acres to which the Clemens family always clung as the total of their Tennessee land holdings was probably unexaggerated, but whether these acres cost his father $100 or $400, Mark Twain never knew.[9] Thought to be a great bargain for the future enrichment of the Clemenses, this land was covered with fine yellow pine, but eventually was found too poor to yield anything save potatoes and wild

grass. For many a year "the Tennessee land" served alternately as the hope and despair of this family. As Mark wrote
in the *Autobiography,* "it influenced our life in one way or
another during more than a generation. Whenever things
grew dark it rose and put out its hopeful Sellers hand and
cheered us up, and said, 'Do not be afraid — trust in me —
await.' It kept us hoping and hoping during forty years, and
forsook us at last." [10] At the height of his Jamestown enterprises, Marshall Clemens was reputed to be worth no less
than $3500 — a solid sum among the Tennessee Mountain
folk.

But these days, unluckily, marked the apogee in prosperity
of Marshall Clemens' entire life. Having spent his cash in
overexpansion, he found himself in the classic Southern
plight of the land-poor. Law practice offered slim pickings,
and his health was far from good, with racking headaches
added to his other miseries. He opened a store with a small
stock of country wares, ranging no doubt from tin cups to
the books of sermons, manners, and medicine which the
general store of necessity carried. Village storekeeping
seemed the way to wealth, but the hazards of an agricultural
clientele were great. Farmers paid accounts only once a
year and then often in beeswax, whisky, bacon, and home-
made cloth. Under the same roof Clemens housed his family,
which now included two small daughters, Pamela born on
September 13, 1827, and Margaret in May 1830. Between
them had come a boy, Pleasants Hannibal — apparently
named after the two younger brothers of Marshall Clemens
— who lived only three months.[11]

From these Jamestown days two stories survive. One relates how Marshall Clemens, angered by a visiting preacher's
neglect to read in church an announcement handed him

concerning a cow Clemens had lost, strode to the pulpit, elbowed the minister aside, and read the notice himself. The other tells how he used to treat good customers of his store to a drink of whisky, and habitually take a sip before passing the glass over the counter. But presently he discovered that he was enjoying these nips of good-fellowship, and alarmed by his weakness, he swore off alcohol for the rest of his life. If the one testifies to a certain stubborn defense of his rights, the other well illustrates the Puritan bedrock of his character.[12]

Probably in 1831, Marshall Clemens gave up his stake in Jamestown and moved nine miles north of the county seat, to the Three Forks of Wolf River, the junction of three small mountain streams. Here he had acquired nearly two hundred acres of bottom land — beautiful country, clothed in spring with violets and anemones, while the slopes of Double Top Mountain and the Knobs rising against the sky were green with laurel, rhododendron, and flowering cucumber. Clemens built his family a house that revealed the decay of their fortunes; a two-story cabin of rough-hewn logs with two small glass windows, each floor comprising a single room with a ladder connecting them. This was a lonely and romantic spot, later invested with an air of melodrama that would have fascinated Mark himself, who relished backwoods horror and violence. Less than a mile away, a "Colonel Logsdon . . . murdered the three Calaway girls, for which he was hung at Jamestown." [13]

Mark Twain's biographer Paine, who makes no mention of the choice farm land which drew Marshall Clemens to the Three Forks of Wolf, assumed that he set up his store there — and then after a few months once more moved his stock and family to Pall Mall, a neighboring village on the north bank of the Wolf, remembered in later days as the birthplace of Sergeant Alvin York. Certainly Clemens kept a crossroads store with a post office — serving as postmaster himself — at Pall Mall from about 1832 until 1835, when the family left Fentress County for good.[14] But the log cabin in which they lived was not at Pall Mall, as Paine thought, but at the Three Forks, as mentioned above — since a pedagogue preacher named Isaac S. Renneau has testified that he was boarding with the Clemenses here in 1835, and teaching school in the neighborhood, just before they pulled out for Missouri.[15]

Neither farming nor storekeeping did much for the crumbling health and fortunes of Marshall Clemens. Corroding pride, anxiety, and poverty beset the family, to whom another son, Benjamin, had been born in June 1832. Children in this region, as an itinerant dentist remarked, in those days were "rocked in gum logs and educated in thunderstorms, compelled to scratch for a living among wildcats, raccoons and rattlesnakes." Less poetically, Pamela Clemens never forgot the grunting of hogs that rooted under the schoolhouse at her first seat of learning here in Tennessee.[16] But while the Clemens children grew more numerous, the tally of human chattels steadily shrank — until by the time they left Fentress County the Clemenses' six slaves had been reduced to a single house girl, Jennie.

Their decision to try a hazard of new fortunes beyond the Mississippi River is dramatized in *The Gilded Age,* by their son yet unborn. At "Obedstown," with its log cabins, gaunt hounds, and fence of loafers roosting like buzzards, the postmaster and storekeeper, Squire Hawkins — "not more than thirty-five" but with "a worn look that made him seem older" — takes new hope with the arrival of a letter from his optimistic kinsman in Missouri, urging "Come! — rush! — hurry! — don't wait for anything!" In the novel, to the loafers' astonishment, they hurried through their arrangements in four short months, and by wagon and river boat were on their way.[17] Jane Lampton Clemens' adored younger sister Martha Ann, called "Patsy," who had married another Virginian in exile, John Adams Quarles — in Kentucky in June 1825 — and lived for a time in Tennessee, had by this time settled in the tiny Missouri farming hamlet of Florida, in Monroe County.[18]

The wash of migration from Kentucky and Tennessee into the newer territory of Missouri, in the wake of Daniel Boone himself, was now approaching full tide, following the Missouri Compromise. Among the Lamptons and the Clemenses, as with many another middle-class Virginia family, the Pennyrile and the Knobs were but way stations for the tarrying of two or three decades before the westward march swept them across the Great River. America was promises, and mobility burned in the blood. Their scion Mark Twain said he never heard without a nostalgia verging upon tears a scrap of old song that ran:

> John, John, the piper's son
> He married me when I was young.
> We journeyed toward the setting sun,
> Over the hills and far away.

Toward the setting sun Jane Clemens' uncle Joshua Lampton is said to have gone about 1825, settling in Boone County, Missouri. Jane's father, Benjamin, four or five years later seems to have taken a trip to spy out this new land. He came back to tell his son-in-law, John Quarles, that "I have

seen the finest timber in the world" among the forests beyond the Mississippi, "straight grained," unlike the yellow
pine of Tennessee; and he also praised the good spring water
of Missouri. So father and son-in-law, with their families,
eventually packed up and journeyed over the hills and far
away, taking root in Monroe County, near the village of
Florida, which had been laid out in the spring of 1831 on
high ground between the forks of Salt River. They arrived
probably early in 1834. Here, at the northeast corner of the
junction made by the two chief streets, Main and Mill, John
Quarles built a store for general merchandise — an enterprise which old Ben Lampton, a veteran in the mercantile
business, seems at first to have shared.[19]

The hearty self-confidence and jovial humor of John
Quarles as radiated in family letters may well have been
tonic to the dispirited Clemenses among the Knobs of northeastern Tennessee. Of Ben Lampton's persuasions we hear
nothing, but if, as seems likely, he was at John Quarles's
elbow when those letters were dispatched, his presence in
the new land must also have played its part in drawing
thither his eldest daughter and son-in-law. As a final fillip
to their decision, Mark states that his father's "fortunes
were wrecked" in "the great financial crash of '34," although his finances obviously had been shrinking for several
years. Probably Marshall Clemens as a stout Whig never
forgot that Old Hickory's assault upon the Bank of the
United States led that institution in 1833–34 to begin winding up its affairs, refusing long-term loans, collecting its
debts, and in general contracting its operations. This money
famine bore with particular hardship upon the Old Southwest, with the branch banks at Nashville and Natchez the
worst sufferers. The drying up of credit in 1834 may indeed

have affected the precarious fortunes of Marshall Clemens.[20]

At any rate, by early spring of 1835 the Clemenses had sold everything save that touchstone of hope, the great tract of land south of Jamestown, and loaded the three youngest children into a two-horse barouche, relic of grander days, while Orion bestrode the trotting horse and froward wench Jennie the pacing horse.[21] Traveling northward toward Louisville, they stopped briefly at the old home in Adair County, and then reaching the Ohio River took passage on a steamboat for St. Louis, a bustling town of ten thousand, where French fur traders jostled steamboat hands and black slaves bound for the iron and lead mines. Family tradition says they planned to settle in St. Louis, but on arrival were horrified by the recent burning of a Negro at the hands of a mob. Actually this grisly event occurred in the following spring, but certainly it left its indelible scar on the Clemenses' early impressions of Missouri. Over sixty years later, when Mark was projecting a history of lynching in the United States, he told his publisher that among some three thousand incidents, two were imperatives — the mobbing of Lovejoy the abolitionist and a case probably to "be found in the St. Louis Republican of about 1835 — the negro was burned near St. Louis about that time, I think." Mark's project would have disturbed the *Missouri Republican,* which pleaded on April 30, 1836, "Let the veil of oblivion be drawn over the fatal affair!" all the while describing the tragedy — murder "in cold blood" of a constable by a cook off the steamboat *Flora,* and the retributive action by a grim and silent crowd of "several thousand persons." [22]

Very probably it was the cholera then raging in St. Louis that sent the Clemenses on their way. They resumed their journey, almost certainly taking the old Salt Road north-westward from St. Charles on the Missouri, and no doubt choosing the western fork at Bowling Green in Pike County, which would carry them on into "the almost invisible little town of Florida." [23] Somewhere along the way, in the late spring of 1835, Jane Clemens conceived her sixth child, whose genius would lend their journey retrospective luster.

CHAPTER FOUR

FLORIDA, AN ALMOST INVISIBLE TOWN

O N A SUMMER'S EVENING, around the first of June 1835, the Clemenses — still jolting over the meager road through new farm lands, fields of stumps, and forest solitudes in their barouche with Orion and Jennie as outriders — rolled into the village of Florida, to be welcomed by the embraces of Lamptons, the excited outcries of children, and the crushing handshake of John Quarles. Their host in this land of promise was a sanguine Virginian, hearty, strapping, broad-shouldered, with big mouth and nose, twinkling eyes, a leonine head, and hair worn long and flowing in the tradition of the old Southwest frontier. The hospitable, easygoing generosity of the back country belonged to him, no less than its sense of robust fun and ribaldry. His crossroads store — with its small stock of calicoes, New Orleans molasses and sugar, cheeses, kegs of powder, and barrels of native corn whisky — was also the center for the hot-stove league of loafers, dressed in snuff-colored jeans, with their repertoire of horseplay and practical jokes. Quarles himself loved to tell stories in such company — about the cow and the village idiot, or the stuttering Negro, or the greedy Tennessee frog which for amusement he had once fed on a mixed diet of flies and buckshot topped off by a live yellowjacket which caused the frog to regurgitate the ammunition needed by Quarles to proceed on his wild turkey hunt.[1] Friendly and easygoing, Quarles had already grown popular and prosperous in this northeastern Missouri settlement, where he was a prominent Mason and probably the leading citizen; later he became a justice of the peace and county judge. In one important respect he refused to conform, being like his brother-in-law Marshall Clemens, a quiet but courageous freethinker, sometimes calling himself a Universalist. "I have never come across a better man," said Mark Twain over the retrospect of half a century.[2]

The weary travelers, swept into the embrace of their kinfolk, got no doubt the same hospitable treatment that the Hawkinses received in *The Gilded Age*. There was eager and heartening chatter, a mighty meal of fried chicken, bacon, hot corn bread, buttermilk, and coffee — the Quarleses always set a prodigal table. Probably the first few nights were spent in a Quarles or Lampton log cabin already crowded to its garret bedroom. But, within a short time, like the Hawkinses of fiction, the Clemenses were quartered under a shelter all their own — the two-room clapboard house with roof of shakes, on South Mill Street about a hundred feet from John Quarles's store, a humble dwelling which Clemens rented from Major William Nelson Penn, a pioneer settler of the village. This house still stands — despite the vicissitudes of a century which include a removal across the road, use as a printing office, hay barn and stable for a cow, and finally a move to higher ground and conversion into a shrine set in the midst of a state park. Almost surely it is the authentic birthplace of Mark Twain.[3] Upon the original site nothing remains save a grove of cottonwoods and the vestiges of an old well.

The Florida that the Clemenses first saw and their famous son recollected from boyhood has long since vanished: its houses all frame or log chinked with clay, with puncheon floors; its log church with slab benches; its two streets lying ankle-deep in dust or mud, depending on the season, and its lanes mere straggling lines of rail fence with cornfields on either side. The progress of a century and a quarter has brought an asphalt highway through a town ringed by worn-out farms, added a church of glazed brick, substituted a cluster of dejected bungalows for the log cabins — and not quite doubled the one hundred inhabitants it claimed in 1835. "I increased the population by 1 per cent," wrote Mark. "It is more than many of the best men in history could have done for a town. . . . But I did it for Florida, and it shows that I could have done it for any place — even London, I suppose." [4] Long silent and nameless is the booster who predicted in 1831 that Florida, as the projected head of navigation on Salt River, "will in a short time be densely populated . . . [with] an extensive business concentrated at said place." [5] As for Salt River itself, whose banks had already begun to support a few grist and saw mills, the dream of its navigability up those eighty-five miles from the Mississippi has forevermore been abandoned. Still unreclaimed by locks or dredging, its once-clear water, in whose shoals the first settlers speared fish, has long past changed to muddy slate and, with the spoils of land broken by the plow, built alluvial flats and sand bars to its own frustration.[6] The very arrival here in 1835 of John Marshall Clemens — with his fatal facility for getting in upon the ground floor of new enterprises that never rose above the mudsills — to the seer might in itself have seemed an ominous sign.

Nevertheless, with his accustomed energy Clemens fell to

work. For the immediate present he joined John Quarles
in storekeeping, hoping, here as in Jamestown, that better
days would restore him to the dignity of a law practice. And
also retracing the familiar pattern, he looked about for land.
Promptly on June 10, 1835, he entered 120 acres of government land east of Florida, and an 80-acre tract of timber near
the Ralls County line. Little more than a fortnight later
he acquired 40 acres more of government land, half a mile
north of the village. Close to this last tract, on North Mill
Street, he bought on September 3 for $300 a homesite com-
prising two and three quarters acres, from an aged Virginia
veteran of Washington's army named Braxton Pollard.[7]
Here he planned to build the substantial house always linked
with the fruition of his hopes.

In the year 1835 the United States was strangely quiet for
an adolescent nation with so raucous a reputation. It seemed
to pause and ponder before jumping into a new whirl of
events. The light press of foreign affairs was all but ignored
in the heavy push of expansion westward. Even the touchy
French claims controversy stirred up the previous year by
Andy Jackson, the democrat who ruled in Washington,
settled into an undisturbed impasse. Only on the territorial
fringes was there open conflict — in Florida the second Semi-
nole War was beginning and in Texas the Lone Star Repub-
lic was proclaimed, though the Alamo was not to come until
March 1836. This was the mid-year between the Missouri
Compromise and that of 1850 — the watershed of sectional-
ism. The South was withdrawing into its pastoral pod, con-
fident in the strength of its traditions and the rightness of
slavery both morally and socially. The North was throbbing
to the encroachments of steam and an industrial economy,
while the seeds of transcendentalism, already planted, would

flower with the publication of Emerson's essay on *Nature* in 1836. And the West was filling, forming its own distinctive civilization, spreading to the edge of the Great Plain. This was a year of internal activity, a hushed period of introspection, a time of signs and portents for the future. And in the late autumn skies of 1835 the nation — north, south, and west — looked up to see that celestial wanderer, Halley's Comet, notable on this visitation for its large and brilliant head, trailing in its wake a diffuse glory. On November 17 it achieved its perihelion, and began once more slowly to fade, not to return for seventy-four years and five months, again reaching its maximum splendor on April 19, 1910.[8] To Mark Twain, schooled in the omens and clairvoyance of the backwoods, this apparition seemed mystically bound up with his own span from birth to death. "I came in with the Comet," he said, "and I shall go out with the Comet" — this he did. In an unpublished version of *The Mysterious Stranger,* set not in medieval Austria but in Hannibal, he has the Stranger ask: "How do you know, when a comet has swum into your system? Merely by your eye or your telescope — but I, I hear a brilliant far stream of sound come winding through the firmament of majestic sounds and I know the splendid stranger is there without looking." [9]

And as if unconsciously to fulfill the first date of his destiny, he came forth untimely from his mother's womb, a seven-month child, on November 30, 1835. In the little frame house on South Mill Street the feeble baby was delivered by a young country doctor named Thomas Jefferson Chowning. Then just twenty-six, Dr. Chowning did not live past middle age, but left descendants in Florida who still possess a daguerreotype that shows his keen friendly eyes, thin but humorous mouth, gray hair, and stocky shoulders.[10] It is said that the child's premature birth forestalled the readying of a layette, but that Sarah Penn, wife of the Clemenses' landlord, came to the rescue with the outworn clothes of her little daughter.[11] Such are the retrospective ways of fame that no less than seven claimants have been advanced by their kin for the honor of putting the first garment on this child. The likeliest are Polly Ann Buchanan, who seems to have been the daughter of John Quarles's sometime storekeeping partner, R. H. Buchanan, also the village blacksmith, and Mrs. Edmund Damrell, wife of the pioneer who built the first house in Florida. She appears as "old Mrs. Damrell" among the gossips into whose "clack" the luckless Huck Finn blunders in the living room of the Phelps (Quarles) plantation, after the escape of Nigger Jim.[12] The neighborliness of village life, it is certain, rallied round Jane Clemens and the small sickly infant whom they named Samuel, after the father of John Marshall Clemens, and Langhorne, perhaps, as Paine states, for "an old and dear Virginia friend" of his, possibly a cousin.[13]

The infant Samuel barely survived that bleak winter and the next year or two. According to Jane, "When I first saw him I could see no promise in him. But I felt it my duty to do the best I could. To raise him if I could. A lady came in one day and looked at him she turned to me and said you don't expect to raise that babe do you. I said I would try. But he was a poor looking object to raise." Many years later, when his mother was in her eighties, they had a conversation about those times, in which Sam asked, "I suppose that during all that time you were uneasy about me?" "Yes, the whole time." And then, deliberately offering a gambit such as Jane Clemens loved, "Afraid I wouldn't live?" A long pause for reflection — "No, afraid you would." [14]

Jane Clemens was an ardent allopath and hydropath, incessantly dosing and dousing her offspring.[15] Paine says that Benjamin, three years little Sam's senior, undertook to look after him, but in a family of five children it was probably a collective responsibility, with solemn, awkward Orion on the threshold of his teens, Pamela, and rosy-cheeked, black-haired little Margaret, handsomest of the lot, also playing their part. These children, like those of Squire Hawkins, passed part of their time at a backwoods school, "a place where tender young humanity devoted itself for eight or ten hours a day to learning incomprehensible rubbish by heart out of books and reciting it by rote, like parrots," aspiring to "read without stopping to spell the words or take a breath." [16] Mrs. Damrell's daughter Eliza, aged fifteen at the time of Sam's birth, later told her children and grandchildren that she had frequently served in Jane Clemens' absence as baby sitter, that she had often put fresh clothes upon little Sam as a lad of two or three, and that he had always wanted white dresses, insisting that all the rest were "dirty" — a forecast of the famous white serge of later years.[17]

Still more constant was the companionship of slaves, young and old, in this community of cabins and small farms where the "peculiar institution" of black servitude bore less harshly than among the large plantations of the Deep South — not that it was without its punitive incidents. The Clemens children remembered the runaway slave brought to Florida by his six white captors, who tied him up with ropes and left him awhile groaning on the floor of a deserted shack. Nor did they forget the time that the house girl Jennie, scolded for "uppity" behavior by Jane Clemens, had snatched away the whip with which her mistress threatened her — but paid for her insubordination when her white-faced master hurried home, bound her wrists with a bridle rein, and flogged her with a cowhide.[18]

But more typical of daily life was the Negro in his docile, easygoing, cheerful moods — friend and comrade of all children, with much time and boundless inclination to go fishing or hunting wild turkeys or blackberrying over the hills, and even when Sam was too young for such rambles, to entertain him and his brother and sisters with woodlore, African superstitions, song, and stories. These stories, as befitted the credulous and simple-souled who had dwelt always under the shadow of insecurity and intimidation, pivoted upon fear — fear of the night, of evil spells and the dead that walked — stirring the souls of their young listeners with a delicious and unforgettable terror. To analyze the part that terror, sheer animal terror, plays in a book like *Huckleberry Finn,* where death lurks at every bend of road or river, is to glimpse the effect of this early education upon the mind of a child. As for the art of telling a story, Mark Twain's first lessons came not from Artemus Ward or the Gillis brothers, but from the lips of black folk like his father's slave-of-all-work in these Florida days, Uncle Ned, whose story of the Golden Arm ("W-h-a-r-r-s my golden arm?"), with its accusing climax ("*You*'ve got it!"), these children never forgot.

Little Sam also had recollections of his grandfather, old Ben Lampton, from whom Marshall Clemens on May 21, 1836, purchased for $1050 a house on the south side of Main Street, in order to move his family from Major Penn's uncomfortably small cabin.[19] For many years, wrote Mark Twain, "I believed that I remembered helping my grandfather drink his whisky toddy when I was six weeks old," but he was finally driven to admit the fallibility of memory. Yet Mark's cousin the Reverend Eugene Lampton, his senior by three months, whose family had followed the Clemenses from Kentucky to Florida, Missouri, before the end of 1835, maintained on the veracity of a Campbellite minister, that he and little Sam, summoned to kiss old Ben Lampton on his deathbed, had got into a wrestling match with each other upon the coverlet. Since this patriarch of the clan died in Florida on March 18, 1837, this yarn seems inherently as doubtful as that of the whisky toddy.[20]

In Florida, as in Jamestown a decade earlier, Marshall Clemens seemed at first to enjoy a brief bloom of fortune, or rather a hectic flush, before adversity closed in. This year of 1837 marked the high tide of his stay in Florida, although the record speaks more for his characteristic public spirit and energy than for his durable prosperity. In January, by act of the state legislature he was appointed first on a board of sixteen commissioners from three counties to take subscriptions to the capital stock of the Salt River Navigation Company. They hoped to raise enough money to dredge that river and build locks and dams, so that steamboats might ascend from the Mississippi. But funds were never forthcoming, and from an early day the Missouri phrase to "go up Salt River" or be "rowed up Salt River" signified defeat and banishment into the ultimate backwater.[21] Meanwhile to be farsighted it was plain that the future of Florida might depend no less upon the railroad age, then in its infancy, than upon the steamboat era already in its prime. In February 1837 a commission of six members under state incorporation to promote a Florida & Paris Railroad was also headed by J. M. Clemens — another project whose issue is best indicated by the fact that the hamlet of Florida has yet to hear its first whistle of a locomotive. Also in the early months of 1837, foundation of a brave educational effort called the Florida Academy was entrusted to a board of trustees that included both Quarles and Clemens.[22]

About this time, however, Quarles and Clemens dissolved their partnership in merchandising, and the latter set up shop for himself across the street. It is easy to surmise that Clemens' austere dignity and orderliness were bound to clash with the banter and happy-go-lucky ways of his brother-in-law. It can also be guessed that Clemens' sober, industrious, meticulous habits, despite their vindication by all the maxims of business since Poor Richard, were not precisely those most likely to succeed in a small Missouri village where the crossroads store was everyman's club and drinks were on the house. Nor was success guaranteed by the employment of absent-minded Orion as clerk — from youth to age Orion's participation in any commercial venture was the sure kiss of death. Nevertheless at this state, storekeeping promised to be of less importance in the family's support, since Marshall Clemens had begun to make some progress in the practice of law. And on November 6, 1837, we find him taking the oath of office as a judge of the Monroe County Court — the zenith of his professional life, and one that fixed upon him ever after the title of "Judge." [23] It brings to mind the Sunday school scene in *Tom Sawyer,* in which the Sabbatarian dovecotes are fluttered and flattered by the arrival of a middle-aged gentleman with immense dignity and iron-gray hair, who "turned out to be a prodigious personage — no less a one than the county judge — altogether the most august creation these children had ever looked upon." And in *Pudd'nhead Wilson,* Judge Driscoll is "about forty years old, judge of the county court . . . very proud of his Virginian ancestry. . . . To be a gentleman . . . was his only religion. . . . The Judge was a freethinker." [24] In those times county judges in Missouri, elected for a term of four years, concerned themselves mainly with probate jurisdiction, and while sitting drew a salary of two dollars per day.[25] Clearly it was an office of more prestige than profit.

In the meantime Judge Clemens had built a better house for his family on the lot which he had bought before Sam's birth. A one-story frame structure with an ell for the kitchen, known as the double house, it was really two one-room cabins built together with separate walls and roof line, and plainly afforded more room than the family had known since their Jamestown days. Its claim in later years to be Mark Twain's birthplace was rejected by the humorist himself: "No, it is too stylish." Neither was it the second house in Florida which the Clemenses occupied, as Paine asserts, but the third. The second, on East Main, Quarles eventually bought from Clemens, in August 1841, after the latter's removal to Hannibal, for $288.20 — a sum so odd, and so shrunken below the original purchase price, as to suggest a settlement of unpaid debts from the dissolved partnership in the store.[26] Just when the Clemenses left it for their new home is unknown, but probably before the birth of their youngest child, Henry, on June 13, 1838.[27]

But with all his ambitions for Florida and his own future there as its best-educated, most enterprising citizen, Judge Clemens soon came to realize, with a dismay grown all too familiar, that he had made another mistake. Paris as the county seat, with its political activity, its military musters, and its fine race track, was a magnet drawing to itself that civic and legal business which he had hoped to foster in Florida; as for shipping and commerce, Hannibal on the Mississippi was fast proving itself the funnel for the landlocked counties. The chief manufactures of Florida — flour,

whisky, hemp — were of little profit without cheap trans-
portation to a much bigger market. John Quarles, a farmer
at heart, made the best of the situation by shifting to agri-
culture, when in February 1839 he bought seventy acres of
good farm land and a few months later added a hundred and
sixty more.[28] Building himself a rambling farm home, as
friendly and hospitable as himself, Quarles soon settled down
to the life of a country squire, surrounded by his eight
children and ultimately thirty slaves. His cattle throve, and
his Mediterranean wheat yielded thirty to forty bushels per
acre; whatever he did was crowned with affluence, and this
no doubt rankled a little in the heart of his sometime partner.[29] But Clemens, for all his miscellaneous holdings of
real estate in Monroe County was no farmer by knack or
preference. In the world of books, grammar, legalisms, and
urban life he was temperamentally most at home — as is
shown by the few letters surviving from his scholarly pen —
and his ever fragile health recoiled from hard physical labor
or the necessary exposure of an overseer to damp and cold.
Here, in the midst of these honest, kindly, lazy, half-literate
rustics who chewed tobacco, drank hard liquor and loved
to wrestle, but who seldom saw a book or magazine, the
talents of a hard, cold, precise intellect were singularly
wasted. His future in Florida, like Florida itself, presaged
failure.

He is said to have tinkered for a while with a perpetual-
motion machine, that snare for ingenious minds which is
mentioned among the forlorn hopes of the fictional Squire
Hawkins. To earn his family's bread he probably took any
jobs at hand. "Old Judge Clemens was a wagon-maker,"
said a Florida nonagenarian of worthy repute named James
Blue, some years ago. "He made a wagon for my father

before they moved out here to Hannibal, and a good wagon, too." [30] The panic of 1837–40, whose effects lingered for several years in the western country and caused the total collapse of a neighboring promotion scheme, the Marion City which Dickens immortalized as "Eden" in *Martin Chuzzlewit,* undoubtedly took its toll of Florida's expectations and those of J. M. Clemens.

The sharpest blow of ill fortune fell on August 19, 1839, when their lovely little daughter Margaret died of a "bilious fever" and was buried in the lonely cemetery over the westward hill. One night shortly before her death little Sam entered her bedroom fast asleep, and plucked for some time at the coverlet, as the dying are supposed to do — which the family took to be evidence of his second sight. It is certainly the first instance recorded of that sleepwalking which often plagued his boyhood, especially in times of emotional stress.[31] Most important of all, the lad first met the reality of death — in a family that took its losses hard, and, like most folk from the hills of Kentucky and the highlands of Tennessee, tended to clothe these griefs in the grim retrospection of certain dreams, visions, and premonitions, along with heartbreaking farewells and lingering touches of self-reproach. This attitude toward life's last great mystery Mark himself learned early and never lost.

Almost immediately John Marshall Clemens decided to make a fresh start. By mid-autumn his plans were complete. On November 13 he sold to a Hannibal land speculator named Ira Stout the most valuable of his holdings in Monroe County, for $3000. This comprised 160 acres of farm land and the home tract on the north edge of Florida, "including the premises whereon said Clemens lately resided." On that same day he purchased from Stout a quarter of a city block in the heart of Hannibal, for the thumping price of $7000 paid in full. A week later the Clemenses sold Stout 326 acres near the Ralls County line — the cumulative result of their forehandedness in entering government land — for $2000.[32] Beyond question, real estate in Hannibal was more valuable than in a stagnant village like Florida, or along the unimproved fringes of Monroe County, and besides this property included a row of rental buildings and on the corner a small hotel built in 1837 by Ira Stout, called the Virginia House.[33] In 1843, when this property was sold for the benefit of John M. Clemens' creditors, the total price amounted to less than $4000, as will be seen — a difference so striking as to lend color to the Clemenses' later bitter prejudice against Stout as a sharp customer. Concerning the later days of Judge Clemens in Florida, Paine — writing either from Orion's now lost autobiography or Mark's oral authority — with his usual circumspection speaks of a partnership "formed with a man who developed neither capital nor business ability, and proved a disaster in the end." [34] Since, as we shall see, Ira Stout is alleged eventually to have "ruined" Clemens, it is possible that they entered into some joint business venture at this earlier date.[35] At least, it may reasonably be assumed that little cash was involved in this *quid pro quo,* and that these round sums were probably bandied about to impress future buyers of the properties in question.

And so in the autumn of 1839 the Clemenses were once more on the move. Hannibal, some thirty miles overland, appeared to promise all that Florida had denied them. The stiff-necked pride of Clemens the Virginian, no less than his invincible hope, impelled him to quit Florida in the same spirit as that in which he had left Fentress County — being, as his son wrote, "not a person likely to abide among the scenes of his vanished grandeur and be the target for public commiseration." [36] To be the poor relation of the Quarleses was no doubt just as galling.

It was a sensitive family, quick to register slights and affronts — whether those of fortune or of fellowmen. Thus the departure from Florida lingered memorably in the mind of fourteen-year-old Orion because his preoccupied father was about to drive off in the wagon without him — an instance of fancied paternal neglect hoarded through the years like that which Judge Clemens remembered against his own parent. Even Sam imagined years later that this incident had happened to *him,* and so told it in the *North American Review,* with dramatization of the "grisly deep silence" that fell upon the locked house after his family had gone, and the creeping in of night's shadows before he was rescued — all this at the age of "two and a half" rather than near the end of his fourth year when the move to Hannibal occurred, or at the age of seven or eight when he was actually forgotten by his father, for some hours, on a return visit from Hannibal to Florida. [37]

CHAPTER FIVE

THE IDYL BEGINS

I N THE WAKE of the Panic of '37 and the shipwreck of
schemes to make Salt River a minor Mississippi, John M.
Clemens was not alone in his desertion of Florida for Hannibal — "this new and flourishing place [with] sixty families," as Wetmore's *Gazetteer* of Missouri described it in the
year of the panic. A small migration occurred about the
time or soon after the Clemenses uprooted themselves, with
the restlessness so characteristic of Americans along the Western waters. Two bright young Virginians named Will and
Erasmus Moffett — the former destined years later to marry
Pamela Clemens — left jobs in a Florida grocery store to
try their luck in Hannibal, and eventually moved on to
still better opportunities in the St. Louis mercantile and
commission business. Another family of storekeeping Virginians, the Coontzes, also deserted Florida for Hannibal;
their son Benton played with Sam and Henry Clemens, and
like them grew up to take a job on the River. Benton's
son, Admiral Robert Coontz, sometime Commander-in-Chief
of the United States Fleet, became known as "Hannibal's
second most famous son." [1]

The village schoolmistress in Florida, a Virginia spinster
named Mary Ann Newcomb, little Sam's future preceptress,

removed to Hannibal shortly before the Clemenses did. She had come west to teach in Marion College, part of that grandiose development of Marion City, "future metropolis of Missouri" planted by visionary Colonel Muldrow in the muddy bottoms of the Mississippi, the scheme which inspired Dickens' *Martin Chuzzlewit*. But sensible Miss Newcomb had none of Utopia, and settled briefly in Florida, where she struck up a friendship with the Clemenses.

The closest friend of the Clemenses to accompany them to this new community was "that gruff old bass-voiced sailorman, Doctor Meredith, our family physician," as Mark remembered him. A Pennsylvanian who once had shipped before the mast, Hugh Meredith was eight years John M. Clemens' junior but his partner in all those ill-starred plans for Florida's enhancement — the navigation company, the railroad, the academy — which in effect they transplanted along with themselves for Hannibal's benefit. And like John M. Clemens, he was "a known and sterling Whig." In an unpublished scrap of autobiography, Mark observed that Doctor Meredith "probably removed from the hamlet of Florida to the village of Hannibal about the same time that we did, in order to keep my custom." In these early days of young Sam's life — when, as he wrote, "I was sick the first seven years . . . and lived altogether on expensive allopathic medicines" — Doctor Meredith played a major part.[2]

As a child of four or five, Sam is reported to have had "convulsions" which his mother ascribed to worms, telling Doctor Meredith when he arrived that she had found the boy gagging upon worms, and in the emergency administered salt as a vermifuge, which seemed to bring him around. Perhaps Sam, with the experimental turn of mind possessed by many children or the sensation-loving urge to which he so freely admitted in later years, had tricked his mother by putting worms in his mouth. But the doctor was baffled and repeatedly begged Jane Clemens at the next seizure to desist from the salt treatment, and send for him at any hour of the day or night. "Did he think," said the mother in telling the story long afterward, "that I was going to let the child choke?" And so, though the mystery was never solved, the lad survived his "convulsions," and they ceased apparently in early Hannibal days.[3]

Arriving in Hannibal about mid-November 1839, John M. Clemens was promptly drafted for a border war brewing against Iowa over the disputed boundary, but before mid-December the crisis had passed.[4] He settled his family in the Virginia House, the hotel he had acquired along with other frame structures built by Ira Stout in the quarter-block at the northwest corner of Hill and Main — the $7000 purchase which seemingly took most of Clemens' Monroe County holdings and all his cash to achieve.[5] With his careful foresight — doomed, as always, to betray him in the end, despite all his calculated logic — Clemens saw his new holdings as assuring his family a home and an income from rent, as well as a property facing Main Street suitable for opening a general store. On credit he bought probably two thousand dollars' worth of groceries and dry goods from St. Louis merchants and commission houses — Messrs. James Kerr, J. B. Fisher, Woods Christy & Company, Berthold Tesson & Company, and Taylor & Holmes. Late in 1839 and early in 1840 he also borrowed about $250 from James Clemens, Jr., "one of the richest half-dozen citizens of St. Louis," Whig lawyer and merchant of Kentucky origins who accepted the impoverished Clemenses in the northern county as his distant cousins — since he too claimed descent from the regicide

judge.[6] John M. Clemens had also borrowed $747.13 from
James A. H. Lampton, the erratic young half brother of Jane
Clemens, still a minor, who lived near Florida.[7] With these
debts at his back, John M. Clemens opened another in his
endless series of general stores — fronting the muddy thoroughfare of Hannibal, with the great river rolling past the
wharf one block below. And behind the counter as clerk,
"in a new suit of clothes," was Orion, almost fifteen years old,
already bookish, absent-minded, inept. The auguries were
none too good.

The town of Hannibal, bearing the name of a defeated
general — as boosters from the neighboring village of Scipio
delighted to point out — had been founded a quarter-century
before by "earthquake certificate" granted refugees from the
"Big Shakes" of 1811, around New Madrid, Missouri. In its
infancy repeatedly harassed by Indians, the town numbered
only thirty persons in 1830, but within the next decade had
grown to 1034, becoming a miniature porkopolis, cigar
manufactory, whisky distillery, and important river port for
Northern Missouri and transshipment point to St. Joseph,
gateway of the Great West. The rich prairie soil back of
Hannibal, from the time it was broken by the plow, began
to funnel wheat, hemp, and tobacco into its wharves. "The
white town drowsing in the sunshine of a summer morning,"
which Mark Twain remembered, was bound in economic
destiny to "the great Mississippi, the magnificent Mississippi,
rolling its mile-wide tide along." When in 1845 the newly-
incorporated city chose its seal, it found its fitting emblem
in a stern-wheel steamer. The town lies at the mouth of a
valley carved through the hills by Bear Creek — from whose
waters young Sam Clemens, as he later stated, was rescued
six times "in a substantially drown [sic] condition." His

mother's refrain was, " 'People who are born to be hanged
are safe in the water.' " [8] Northward of the town lies Holliday's Hill — Cardiff to readers of *Tom Sawyer* — as the
nearest bluff of an escarpment that flanks the Mississippi for
two miles, cut by a ravine whose "spring branch" supplied
the natural roadbed that ran northwest a dozen miles toward
Palmyra, the county seat. Above Hannibal in this direction
was the old bay mill, with its oak water wheel for grinding
corn and wheat, and blacksmith shop beside it — a communal center much used by Hannibal citizens. South of the
town looms a steeper cliff above the River, called Lover's
Leap, invested with the familiar Indian legend repeated a
hundred times over the face of a romantic nation, a spot
with "many traditions of love and woful tradegy [*sic*]," as
the Hannibal *Gazette* gravely noted in Mark Twain's boyhood.[9]

Past the half-dozen brick houses that Hannibal boasted in
1840 and scores of frame ones with straggling descendants
from the log-cabin era, interspersed with vacant lots fragrant with locust trees in spring and choked with Jimson
weed during the long dry summers, ran streets laid out by
the founder, Abraham Bird. Market Street, later rechristened Broadway, bisected the town in a steep climb up the
hill from the River. Known as "one of the widest streets
in Missouri," it flowed around the market house that stood
athwart its course between Third and Fourth. Circuses,
minstrels, Fourth of July parades, and torchlight processions
— such as the great Log Cabin Campaign rally of July 28 and
29, 1840, which John M. Clemens as a devout Whig surely
attended — all converged upon Market Street. But the spine
of commercial Hannibal has always been Main or Second
Street, intersecting Broadway one block above the riverfront,

and running parallel with the wharves. Two blocks above Broadway, in the direction of Holliday's Hill, Main Street crosses Bird at "Wild-Cat Corner," long famous for its store under the sign of the wildcat; just around the corner on Bird still stands the ramshackle clapboard house where John M. Clemens is said for a time to have had his law office, and where Sam was to see the corpse of the stabbed man lying in a pool of moonlight.

A block beyond, Main crosses Hill Street, at the site of the old Virginia House where the Clemenses first lived, and half a block up the steep grade of Hill they later built the house now familiar to thousands of visitors as the Mark Twain home, across the way from the "Becky Thatcher" place where Laura Hawkins and her family dwelt. Back to back with the old Clemens property but facing upon the less prosperous thoroughfare of North Street stood the big barnlike structure where Tom Blankenship, the original of Huck Finn, lived with his drunken father and slatternly kin, in tempting proximity to young Sam Clemens. These were Hannibal's chief streets, unpaved, deeply rutted by wagon wheels, dusty in summer, cut into ribbons of mud in winter. In late November 1847 the *Gazette* complained that after a week of snow and rain, "the square between Hill & Bird on Main" was so treacherous as not to be attempted unless — in language familiar on the River — the pedestrian was "prepared in making the 'crossings' to wade in 'scant three feet,' or 'march under mud twain.' " [10]

Hog drovers thronged the streets, bringing some ten thousand swine annually to the two "pork houses" in operation by 1840 near the mouth of Bear Creek. A few years later the first city council would find their location a menace to public health, and recommend that all slaughtering of hogs and beeves be done beyond the creek. But the by-products, in that prodigal generation, supplied meat for even the poorest. "Pork-house — free spareribs, livers, hearts, &c.," wrote Mark Twain in an autobiographical jotting.[11] And as another windfall, it will be remembered that Tom Sawyer and his gang in lieu of balloons played with bladders procured from the slaughterhouse.

In addition to its two pork houses, Hannibal by 1844 took pride in four general stores, three sawmills, two planing mills, three blacksmith shops, two hotels, three saloons, two churches, two schools, a tobacco factory, a hemp factory, and a tanyard, as well as a flourishing distillery up at the still-house branch. West of the village lay "Stringtown," so called because its cabins and stock pens were strung out along the road. Here in the forties stood the landmark of Coleman's tavern, where farmers' teams bound to and from market congregated from all over Marion County. Small industry was the life of Hannibal. "Our people have a horrid aversion to the jury box and the witnesses' stand," wrote Orion Clemens in 1851, in words equally true for the previous decade. "They greatly prefer the study of pork and flour barrels, tape, cordwood and the steamboat's whistle." [12]

In a late sketch, Mark recalled the winding country road leading out of his Missouri village, the woods on one side and a rail fence on the other, "with blackberry vines and hazel bushes crowding its angles," a bluebird and a fox squirrel on the topmost rail.[13] Beyond the scraggly town and its smudge of trade beckoned the real, the irresistible charm of that time and place. South of Broadway lay Draper's Meadow, named for the County Judge, "our oldest citizen" who led the list of "Villagers of 1840–3." Here ran a small stream bordered by elder bushes, where the boys used to

fire popguns in their endless Indian games. On higher
ground grew the dim woods with their "solemn twilight"
— the sugar maple and rock maple, scarlet in the autumn
when the sumac flamed crimson, and dogwood and redbud
turned to blood, and the hickory to burnished gold, while
the red oaks deepened into purple and the very shadows
changed from brown to blue, presaging winter. Red haws
and persimmons and hickory nuts and walnuts were the
season's plunder, but for pecans the boys had to cross over
into the Illinois bottoms. Southward winged geese, brant,
ducks, and cranes. Clouds of wild pigeons rose from the
woods by day, and at night could be knocked from the trees
after the lighting of fires to dazzle them. "Game is very
abundant in this vicinity," remarked the local newspaper.
"Every day we hear of some one having killed a deer."
Christmas fare always included venison steaks, ducks, wild
turkey, grouse, and quail.

Mark's cherished memories of winter — beyond the adventure of skating across the black ice of the Mississippi
when it froze — were apt to be those of nights indoors,
whether in Hannibal or sometimes at the Quarles farm, with
the house creaking against the howling wind, the warmth of
blankets, and the snow sifting in around the sashes. Spring
brought new delight to the woods and upland pastures, with
the blue or purple shooting star on the hills, and underfoot as summer advanced a wealth of wild strawberries, blackberries, raspberries, and gooseberries.

In Hannibal young Sam Clemens had reached his predestined great good place. Here during most of each year,
and back on the Quarles's farm during certain summer weeks,
he grew stronger in body and more aware of the world about
him. These streets and the people that walked in them,

each carrying with him some unforgettable mannerism of speech or dress, some vestige of comedy or pathos, the waters, the woods, the hills, the birds and animals, left the boy with a mortal nostalgia all his life. The peaceful clinking of a blacksmith's hammers or the plaintive wail of a spinning wheel, "the most lonesome sound in nature," like old familiar names or the handwriting on an envelope, always had the effect of powerful evocation upon boyhood memories as benign as those of Wordsworth in *The Prelude,* attuned to a sensibility as keen as that of Proust in the remembrance of things past. A quarter-century afterward at Hilo, Hawaii, he spent several tropical nights talking eagerly until dawn with a chance acquaintance named Cony who by coincidence "knew everybody that ever I knew in Hannibal and Palmyra," and on his honeymoon six years later the arrival of a letter from his Hannibal chum Will Bowen caused "the fountains of my great deep" to be broken up, "and I have rained reminiscences for four and twenty hours." [14] In other moods, revolting against Will Bowen's sentimental infatuation with old days in which "there is nothing . . . worth pickling for present or future use," and cruelly rebuking his friend's "mental and moral masturbation [which] belongs eminently to the period usually devoted to *physical* masturbation, and should be left there and outgrown," Sam Clemens was simply turning upon himself and the artist's ultimate inability to escape from this prison house of memory.[15] The prevailing mood reasserted itself when he wrote Will a dozen years later that "I would have liked to bring up every creature we knew in those days — even the dumb animals — it would be bathing in the fabled Fountain of Youth." [16] This fountain of course was the wellspring from which he drew his clearest inspirations — whether for the sketches of Jimmy Finn the town drunkard and the Cadets of Temperance which Mark wrote from New York early in 1867 for the *Alta California; Tom Sawyer,* "simply a hymn, put into prose to give it a worldly air"; the riper masterpiece of *Huckleberry Finn,* and *Life on the Mississippi,* their lifeblood of reminiscence fortified by his return to Hannibal and the River in 1882; or the inescapable background of *Pudd'nhead Wilson* and of *The Mysterious Stranger* with Tom and Huck clothed in medieval dress.

His revisitation of this past was at the beck and call of almost any stimulus: the poems of James Whitcomb Riley — "which make my mouth water for an Elder Time, and a big toe with a rag around it" — or a letter from Jenny Stevens, daughter of the old Hannibal jeweler — "You have spirited me back to a vanished world and the companionship of phantoms . . . in thinking of it, dreaming over it, I have seemed like some banished Adam who is revisiting his half-forgotten Paradise and wondering how the arid outside world could ever have seemed green and fair to him." [17] Even the presence of the serpent in this Eden, as in Mark's story, "The Man That Corrupted Hadleyburg," did not spoil the essential idyl.

After his friend Thomas Bailey Aldrich had sent a volume about his own Boyville — Portsmouth, New Hampshire — to Mark Twain, the latter replied in December 1893, during that grim and lonely winter when Mark was living in "a cheap room at the Players" and nursing his bankrupt finances: "[The book] had worked its spell and Portsmouth was become the town of my boyhood — with all which that implies and compels: the bringing back of one's youth, almost the only time of life worth living over again, the only period whose memories are wholly pathetic — pathetic because we see now that we were in heaven then and there was no one able to make us know it though no doubt many a kindly poor devil tried to." [18]

Whether Americans are a nation stricken with an Oedipus complex, as has often been said in modern times, they are surely sentimentalists about boyhood, as their songs and popular poetry about old oaken buckets, barefoot school days, and invocations to Father Time, bear witness. As an inhabitant of Heaven tells Captain Stormfield, in Mark's *Extract from Captain Stormfield's Visit to Heaven,* neither a man nor a boy ever thinks he is exactly the right age — always straining forward or pining backward, as the case may be. Besides these common considerations, Mark Twain's nostalgia bore a special character. On the one hand, Hannibal was associated in his heart with the pre-industrial, pre-Gold Rush, pre-Civil War tranquillity — the old halcyon small-town America emerging from the rigors of the frontier yet not stripped wholly of its buckskin spirit of adventure, nor of its daily communion with an unspoiled Nature, when to be young was very heaven. And on the personal plane, this Hannibal was linked in his psyche with the age of innocence, before the unrest of puberty or the burdens and perplexities of adulthood settled upon his shoulders. Hannibal forever remained his symbol of security in days when disasters and frustrations were closing in upon him. And yet, as if shielding himself unconsciously from a too trustful reliance upon this symbol, Mark did not dwell so exclusively upon the serenity and beauty of his idyl as to neglect the dangers and terrors it also held for a boy — drownings, corpses, ghosts, African superstitions, mobs, feuds, and manifold shapes of disaster and violent death that seem to lurk at every bend of road and river — even though in the end they are placated and transcended.

Mark Twain's genius always swung like a compass toward his fourteen years' childhood and adolescence in Hannibal. "He was a youth to the end of his days," William Dean Howells said of him.[19] That Mark himself told the story of these days, repeatedly, in fiction, semi-fiction, and purported fact, is clear enough. In 1886, twenty years before dictating the bulk of his *Autobiography,* Mark wrote an English admirer: "Yes, the truth is, my books are simply autobiographies. I do not know that there is an incident in them which sets itself forth as having occurred in my personal experience which did not so occur. If the incidents were dated, they could be strung together in their due order, and the result would be an autobiography." [20] But Mark had a habit that grew with the years of forgetting, or changing, anything he did not like. It was a myth-making process, part of his strange atavistic make-up. All his days he wrote fiction under the cloak of autobiography, and autobiography with the trappings of fiction.

CHAPTER SIX

JUDGE CLEMENS IN HANNIBAL

IN A NOVEL begun in middle life but unfinished and never published, Mark Twain sketches the likeness of a small-town dignitary called Judge Griswold, a gentleman of Virginia stock raised among the buckskin gentry of early Kentucky. He was "very tall, very spare, with a long, thin, smooth-shaven intellectual face, and long black hair that lay close to his head, was kept to the rear by his ears as one keeps curtains back by brackets, and fell straight to his coat collar without a single tolerant kink or relenting curve. He had an eagle's beak and an eagle's eye. Judge Griswold's manner and carriage were of the courtly old-fashioned sort; he had never worked; he was a gentleman." Punctiliously upright, he was not in religious matters a believer, although from decorum he gave some support to the church. An implacable hater, he could be equally strong in devotion — his favorite being his only daughter, aged sixteen — but of emotion he made no demonstration.[1] The image of this parochial Jehovah, the upright judge, the austere lawgiver, the father who dealt sternly with his sons but softly with his daughter, returns insistently in the pages of Mark Twain. And it is significant that Pamela Clemens, deeply devoted to her father, never agreed with her brothers about his glacial temperament.[2]

At the age of thirty-four, doing potboilers for the *Galaxy,* Mark recalled his father as "a stern, unsmiling man" who read poetry aloud "with the same inflectionless judicial frigidity" used in the courtroom. He detested the pert precocity of his son Sam, in the rare intervals when Sam stepped out of his early character as "a backward, cautious, unadventurous boy." "My father and I were always on the most distant terms when I was a boy — a sort of armed neutrality, so to speak." [3] A quarter-century later, in *Following the Equator,* Mark harked back to that "sternly just and upright man" who "laid his hand upon me in punishment only twice in his life, and then not heavily; once for telling him a lie — which surprised me, and showed me how unsuspicious he was, for that was not my maiden effort. He punished me those two times only, and never any other member of the family at all." [4] In the "Villagers of 1840–3" Mark jotted: "Stern, unsmiling, never demonstrated affection for wife or child. . . . Silent, austere, of perfect probity and high principle; ungentle of manner toward his children, but always a gentleman in his phrasing — and never punished them — a look was enough, and more than enough." If he had intimates at all, they were two other Southern gentlemen of the old school: Judge Draper, the South Carolina Whig, and the aged Virginia physician Dr. Peake. Still dressing in knee breeches, buckle shoes, high stock and pigtail, when the Clemenses moved to Hannibal, Peake appears in "The Mysterious Stranger in Hannibal" as Doctor Wheelwright, "the stately old First-Family Virginian and imposing Thinker of the village." [5] Elsewhere among the unpublished papers Mark draws the character of a small-town judge whose way of putting things inclined to the heavy and sententious, the legal rather than the logical. "Mother had cornered him again," writes Mark. "But she was not vain of it, being more or less accustomed to it, always expecting him to be pretty random and to need watching when he wasn't on the Bench." Not infrequently he resorted to irony, but "irony was not his best hold." [6] In still another unprinted sketch, the Judge is given a stinging sense of sarcasm, in ridiculing his inept offspring Oscar (Orion).[7]

More apocryphal is the story told in a newspaper clipping which Mark received in 1882 from an old Hannibal schoolmate, John Robards, who took pains to deny the newspaper reporter's allegation that he, Robards, vouched for its authenticity. The story claimed that John M. Clemens "and a half dozen other old roosters used to meet at his house once a week and over a half-gallon of whiskey and their pipes they would discuss natural history." One day after the Judge had given Sam "a terrible licking," the lad took his revenge by gluing peacock feathers to a dead crow's tail and presenting it to his father as a rare specimen. Not until he had hastily convened the natural history society and displayed this wonder did the Judge find that he had been duped.[8] The conviviality in the story is distinctly out of character, but the strained relations between father and son seem true enough.

Beyond question, however, is the evidence both from Mark Twain's pen and from independent sources that John M. Clemens in Hannibal was soon overtaken by those economic mishaps that always dogged his steps, and this time irrecoverably. Minor disappointments heralded the body blow of bankruptcy. Tenants of the rental properties along Hill and Main in which he had sunk his capital did not always pay, and the Clemens store — between the Judge's heavy debts for stocking it and the dreamy mismanagement of Orion — proved no gold mine. For almost a decade after the Panic of '37, scarcity of cash and the specter of hard times plagued rural and small-town life in the Mississippi Valley, retarding the growth of Hannibal.[9]

"Still a small storekeeper — but progressing," wrote Mark Twain of his father in the sketch called "Villagers." "Then Ira Stout, who got him to go security for a large sum, 'took the benefit of the bankrupt law' and ruined him — in fact made a pauper of him." In the *Autobiography* we read of "the dishonest act of one Ira Stout, to whom my father had lent several thousand dollars," which gave the luckless Judge his *coup de grâce,* condemning him to "several years of grinding poverty and privation" before his death in 1847. How John M. Clemens happened to have several thousand dollars to lend is unexplained, and Mark's memory in these vague but impassioned matters of family history is not to be trusted. But "big Ira Stout," as he is described in a scrap of legal testimony among Marion County records in the handwriting of John M. Clemens, was clearly a dead beat in the early history of Hannibal. In October 1840, for example, he had contracted debts of about a thousand dollars for merchandise bought wholesale from a commission firm, "yet the said defendant . . . intending craftily and subtly to deceive the said plaintiffs have [*sic*] not as yet paid the said sums of money or any part thereof." [10]

Stout was also sued successfully for debts by other Hannibal citizens, including the Hawkinses, the family of "Becky Thatcher." But no record of *Clemens* v. *Stout* occurs within the web of litigation surrounding the latter's business dealings. Nor among the meager bankruptcy records of the

State of Missouri for the 1840's, now preserved in St. Louis and at Jefferson City, is there evidence that Ira Stout "took the benefit of the bankrupt law," either under federal auspices or as an assignment under state law. However, that in some way he was relieved of the heavy debts recalled by Clemens family tradition — leaving in the lurch his surety the Judge — is suggested by tokens of his later prosperity in days when Judge Clemens was still struggling in the quicksand of poverty. Thus in June 1845 Ira Stout is found offering the city of Hannibal $1200 worth of real estate, "to be applied to the purchase of a fire Engine," in return for twenty-five years' tax exemption on all his city property — consisting of about 125 acres.[11] And in the spring of 1847, when Judge Clemens died in extreme penury, Ira Stout in preparing to move to Quincy, Illinois, offered for sale seven hundred lots in Hannibal, "an elegantly finished and commodious cottage," described "as good as any in the city for a residence," besides seven lots on Main Street, and forty acres of timber and bluegrass pasture.[12]

Whether Stout's defaulted debts were in some way enmeshed with Clemens' earlier dealings with him, in their exchange of properties in Florida and Hannibal, cannot be determined today, nor the precise date at which "the dishonest act" occurred. But on October 13, 1841, John and Jane Clemens for the benefit of their creditors transferred the title of their home property, bought from Ira Stout two years earlier, to James Kerr, the St. Louis dry-goods merchant to whom they stood most heavily in debt.[13] A year later, on October 13, 1842, the lot and improvements were offered "for sale, by public auction to the highest bidder, when for want of adequate price offered the same was bid in by the said Trustee for the benefit of the Creditors." Evidently no one present wanted to buy this man's home at public sale. Still later, on October 16, 1843 — apparently after the Clemenses had moved elsewhere — the property was subdivided into seven small parcels and sold for a total of $3920. Though conspicuously less than the $7000 purchase price, it was well over Judge Clemens' indebtedness of some two thousand dollars. What if anything he received after payment of costs incident to the sale is not shown.[14] Among the buyers was William Briggs, father of Sam Clemens' inseparable friend John, the Joe Harper of Tom Sawyer's gang. The only creditor who bought at the sale was James Clemens, Jr., the St. Louis "cousin," who acquired for $330 the meager lot, about midway up Hill Street, twenty and a half feet in width, on which the Clemenses later built the clapboard house still preserved as the Clemens home.

A more striking contrast would be hard to find than that of Ira Stout's and of John M. Clemens' behavior in a tight place. The code of the Virginia gentleman permitted no other course to Mark Twain's father, and the pride which the son took in his father's stripping himself to satisfy all claims — beyond the call of duty, we are told, down to offering the forks and spoons, and every stick of furniture — presaged a similar act in Mark's life half a century later. And Jane Lampton Clemens, whose father had lost everything in Kentucky by shouldering the debts of his partner and brother-in-law, acquiesced in the decision. The Clemenses and Lamptons were not shrewd business folk, but they never forgot that they were gentry.

Judge Clemens tried to make ends meet by the practice of law, at this time probably renting the first-floor room in the little frame building on Bird Street traditionally pointed out as his office. Also the Clemenses parted with their slave girl Jennie, the uppity wench whom the Judge had once whipped, but who had served as "mammy" to Sam and the other young children. Mark's notation in "Villagers" says: "Had but one slave — she wanted to be sold to Beebe, and was. He sold her down the river. Was seen, years later, ch[ambermaid] on a steamboat. Cried and lamented." In another unpublished fragment Mark added that her loss "was a sore trial, for the woman was almost like one of the family; but she pleaded hard — for that man had been beguiling her with all sorts of fine and alluring promises — and my mother yielded, and also persuaded my father." [15] The buyer was William B. Beebe, forwarding and commission merchant of Hannibal, who made a specialty of commerce with New Orleans. From his traffic in human flesh he was called behind his back "the nigger trader," and despised by those who owned slaves themselves but shared the recoil of their own black chattels from the mysterious cruelty of being sold "down the river," where the rigors of the plantation system made slavery more galling. Young Sam Clemens never forgot the sight of a coffle of slaves in Hannibal, lying on the pavement waiting shipment down the river, with "the saddest faces I have ever seen." [16]

In September 1841 John M. Clemens had been one of welve good and lawful men" who sat on a Circuit Court jury at Palmyra and sent to the penitentiary for twelve years three abolitionists — George Thompson, Alanson Work, and James Burr — who had been caught trying to help five Negroes head for "the polar star," each slave "of the value of Five Hundred Dollars." These Negroes had betrayed their would-be rescuers. Testimony of blacks against whites was not legally admissible in court, but since the prosecution needed such testimony to convict the abolitionists, in this case it was allowed. No doubt Judge Clemens and his Carolina friend and fellow juror Judge Draper, with all their schooling in the law, felt that the end justified the means. The chief abolitionist, Thompson, a deeply religious man who later wrote a book about his years in the Missouri penitentiary, in vain tried to justify himself by citing the Golden Rule. Hatred of the abolitionists who had begun to infiltrate northeastern Missouri in the ranks of the new immigrants — "the Eastern run," as it was contemptuously called — agitated for lynch law. But the good stiff sentence meted out by Judge Clemens and his neighbors was received with "considerable applause." [17] Fifty-three years later Mark Twain wrote "A Scrap of Curious History," about the way in which martyrdom nourished the cause of abolition in Missouri in the 1840's, slowly overcoming the fierce prejudice which saw its advocates as devils in human form.

Little Sam Clemens, growing up in a slaveholding community, was prone at first to take for granted the South's "peculiar institution." His mother, schooled in Old Testament texts and sermons that sanctioned slavery, did likewise. But she constantly tempered the operations of the system with a kindly heart, and at least taught her son one lesson in compassion he never forgot. After the sale of Jennie they hired a little black houseboy from "a master back in the country." "He sang the whole day long," Mark recalled many years later, "at the top of his voice; it was intolerable, it was unendurable. At last I went to my mother in a rage about it. But she said —

" 'Think; he is sold away from his mother; she is in Maryland, a thousand miles from here, and he will never see her again, poor thing. When he is singing it is a sign that he is not grieving; the noise of it drives me almost distracted, but I am always listening, and always thankful; it would break my heart if Sandy should stop singing.' " [18]

Doubtless this is the same chore boy whom Mark, with his facility for changing names, both in real life and in fiction, called Lewis, in *Following the Equator* — remembering how the lad's "trifling little blunders and awkwardnesses" provoked John M. Clemens from time to time to "cuff" him. In the original manuscript Judge Clemens had lashed him, but in the margin Mark's wife Livy penciled, "I hate to have your father pictured as lashing a slave boy," and the author cheerfully rejoined, "It's out, and my father is white-washed." [19] Perhaps an earlier act of filial whitewashing led him once to declare in print that his father, though owning a single slave, held that "slavery was a great wrong." [20] No further proof of that conviction survives.

In the winter of 1841–42 Judge Clemens tried to do a little Negro trading himself, in the course of a long and financially unprofitable trip first into the Deep South and then back to the old homestead in Kentucky. "I still have *Charley*," he wrote to "Dear Jane and the Children," aboard a steamboat near Memphis, on January 5, 1842, "the highest price I had affixed for him in New Orleans was $50, and in Vicksburg $40. After performing the journey to Tennessee I expect to sell him for whatever he will bring where I take water again, viz. at Louisville or Nashville." [21] Charley was apparently a slave whom he had picked up in Missouri, with the hope that he would fetch a better price along the lower Mississippi. Coming across this letter in the family papers half a century later, Mark Twain commented wryly upon his father's mention of Charley as if the man had been "an ox — and somebody else's ox. It makes a body homesick for Charley, even after fifty years. Thank God I have no recollection of him as house servant of ours; that is to say, playmate of mine; for I was playmate to all the niggers, preferring their society to that of the elect, I being a person of low-down tastes from the start, notwithstanding my high birth, and ever ready to forsake the communion of high souls if I could strike anything nearer my grade." [22] Charley's fate is unknown, but a promissory note given Judge Clemens by one Abner Phillips "for value received this 24th day of January 1842" suggests that he may have sold the slave for ten barrels of tar to be delivered in Missouri on or before the next Christmas.[23]

In the course of this journey Judge Clemens hoped to collect a note that had long been due from a Mississippian named William Lester. Landing at Vicksburg, Clemens had bought "an old saddle and a new bridle and blanket" and set off riding into the country forty miles through rain and sleet to find his debtor. He wrote to his family:

> My note on Lester and interest for near 20 years amounted to about $470, but it seemed so very hard upon him these hard times to pay such a sum that I could not have the conscience to hold him to it. . . . Upon the whole I consented to take his note payable 1st March next for $250 — and let him off at that — I believe I was quite too lenient and ought to have had at least that amt. down. However he had no money on hand and I could not get it. Every one I enquired of said he was entirely solvent and good for it. . . . My intention is to visit Lexington and Kentucky and try to effect a sale of my Tennessee lands, and then return to see Lester about the time the note falls due.

A later letter, from Clemens in Hannibal to a commission firm in Vicksburg on November 2, 1844, shows him nearly three years later still anxiously trying to collect this debt, entrusting his note to a steamboat captain who then mislaid it.[24] That other debtors were less scrupulous than Judge Clemens seems clear enough. Pondering his father's reluctance to bear hard upon this obscure Mississippian, after all the rigors of his winter journey, Mark added a comment that tempers his customary recollection of Clemens' austerity: "Is not this a humane, a soft-hearted man? If even the gentlest of us had been plowing through ice and snow, horseback and per steamboat for six weeks to collect that little antiquity, wouldn't we have collected it, and the man's scalp along with it? I trust so." [25] The paradox of this humanity toward a white man yet callousness toward a slave struck John Clemens' son forcibly, as he held in his hand these yellowed pages filled with his father's fine precise script.

This letter reveals other characteristic things about the Judge, including concern with his own health — finding that steamboat travel does not agree with him, while horseback riding seems beneficial — and the eternal nursing of hope from the Tennessee land. Judge Clemens also discloses that he is bound for Columbia, Kentucky, undoubtedly to visit his aged mother. Two years later she died, after murmuring on her deathbed "if I could only see Marshal . . . one time more how glad I would be." [26]

This journey, "an expensive trip," as Clemens admitted in his letter home, consumed much time in its futile attempt to raise money. "My present impression is that I may reach home about the middle of March," he wrote. "I do not know yet what I can commence at for a business in the spring. My brain is constantly on the rack with the study, and I can't relieve myself of it. The future taking its complexion from the state of my health, or mind, is alternately beaming in the sunshine, or overshadowed with clouds; but mostly cloudy, as you will readily suppose. I want bodily exercise, some constant and active employment, in the first place; and in the next place I want to be paid for it, if possible." Orion remembered how, after his father's return home empty-handed, Jane Clemens could not help reproaching him for the two hundred dollars he had spent to accomplish nothing; how he had tried mildly to justify himself, and then with a "hopeless expression" on his face, added, "I am not able to dig in the streets." [27]

Whether Orion was at home on a visit from St. Louis at this time, or had not yet begun his employment in the printing shop there, is not clear. He was also in Hannibal in early May 1842, when a further disaster befell this hard-pressed family. Benjamin, nearly ten years old, sickened and after a few days' illness died on May 12. Sam, not yet seven, never forgot this clearest of early exposures taken by his mental camera — namely, that of holding his mother's hand to kneel beside her at the bed on which the little corpse lay, while she wept with moans of "dumb" anguish such as he had never heard before. "The mother made the children feel the cheek of the dead boy," he recalled at another time, "and tried to make them understand the calamity that had befallen." [28] Orion remembered that John and Jane Clemens in their grief kissed each other, a sight equally new in his longer experience.

The Clemenses were a reserved and formal family, their tone set by John Clemens, and while they always shook hands at night before going to bed, warmer gestures of affection played no part in their daily life. But, for that matter, Hannibal was "not a kissing community," said Mark Twain. "The kissing and caressing ended with courtship." [29] The

ice of inhibition early formed upon the surface of his own
emotional nature, not to be melted until the late day of his
own courtship and marriage, when Livy "poured out her
prodigal affections and in a vocabulary of endearments whose
profusion was always an astonishment to me. I was born
reserved as to endearments of speech, and caresses, and hers
broke upon me as the *summer waves* break upon Gibral-
tar."[30]

The painful Puritan shyness of the time and place and
family in which he grew up was never forgotten. Revealing
are a few touches in the unpublished "Huck Finn and Tom
Sawyer Among the Indians," written about 1889. Huck and
Tom fall in with an emigrant family on the Oregon Trail,
whose pride and joy is a lovely girl of seventeen. She is
petted and kissed by her parents and her brothers. Huck, a
true scion of Hannibal, confesses his embarrassment at their
calling her "Peggy dear . . . and it took me two or three days
to get so I could keep from blushing. I was so ashamed for
them, though I knowed it warn't the least harm, because they
was right out of the woods and didn't know no better."[31]

It was under the deepening shadow of poverty, "about
1842," that Orion as a hobbledehoy of seventeen, having
served an apprenticeship in the office of the Hannibal
Journal — that trusty Whig newspaper which Judge Clemens dreamed of buying to give Orion a chance — was sent
to St. Louis to learn the printer's trade in Ustick's job office.[32]
Probably the rich "cousin" James Clemens, who later is
found advising Orion about Sam's career as a printer, made
the arrangements. As the son of a Virginia gentleman, Orion
felt keenly at first the humiliation of manual labor. So
we learn from the biographer Paine, who had read the now
lost autobiography in which Orion had laid bare his soul.[33]

In one of the bits of unpublished Twainiana already mentioned, the wife of the Virginia-born magistrate reproaches
her husband for mishandling the sensibilities of poor
"Oscar," whom she would like to see reading law: "You are
county judge — the position of highest dignity in the gift
of the ballot — and yet you would see your son become a
mechanic." [34] But it was not Orion's nature long to nurse a
slight. With his abiding eagerness and hunger for approval,
he soon threw himself into his new work with fitful industry.
Inspired by Franklin's *Autobiography,* he tried to follow
those rules for diet and self-improvement, soon writing his
mother "that in his boarding house he was confining himself
to bread and water." [35] Shortly he fell under the influence
of Edward Bates, a St. Louis lawyer whose rising star was to
shine on the destinies of both Orion and Mark. In later
years, as Attorney-General in Lincoln's cabinet, Bates maneuvered the appointment of Orion as Secretary of the Territory
of Nevada — Mark in turn became the Secretary's secretary.[36]
Thus, in St. Louis was begun the chain of associations which
pulled Mark westward toward his fulfillment. The encouragement which Bates gave Orion, to begin the study of law
in his spare time and to practice oratory, early served to
revive his self-esteem. But decisively, Judge Clemens had
chosen the printer's path for him — a cul-de-sac as his later
publishing of the *Western Union* and *Journal* was to prove
— and whatever smattering of the law Orion could get had
to be salvaged from the pursuit of this livelihood.

CHAPTER SEVEN

READING, WRITING, AND RELIGION

ONE QUARTER of the children born, die before they are one year old; one half die before they are twenty-one, and not one quarter reach the age of forty." So reported the Hannibal *Gazette* on June 3, 1847. Sam Clemens came close to death in both the first and the second round. A sickly infancy was succeeded by a puny childhood, up through his seventh year. He always spoke of having come "so near going to heaven" at the age of seven that only a hairsbreadth saved him. The malady he did not remember; in the long sequence of fevers, bilious spells, and convulsions such particularities were forgotten. "I had begun to die; the family were grouped for the function; they were familiar with it; so was I." So familiar, through habit, he adds, that "they often went to sleep when I was dying." [1] But he did recall what it was that interfered with the apparent purpose of Providence. "It was half a teacupful of castor oil — straight. That is, without molasses or other ameliorations. . . . I had drunk barrels of castor oil in my time. No, not barrels, kegs; let us postpone exaggeration to a properer time and subject." Along with calomel, rhubarb, and jalap, it was Doctor Meredith's pet specific. Among the purchases made by Judge Clemens at Beebe's store during the last five months of 1842 —

ham, sugar, coffee, bacon, eggs, tobacco, salt, pork, and a pair of shoes and stockings — appears on the ledger the confirmatory entry for a bottle of castor oil on October 11.[2] No doubt it was one of a somber procession. Sometimes it was administered with blandishments. "Castor Oil and molasses," scribbled Mark Twain in a sheaf of notes many years later, when he was weighing his multitude of "auditory" and "visual" memories beside his fewer "tactual" and "gustatory" ones; "65 years ago, but fetch it here and I can tell you if proportions are right."[3]

Jane Clemens' enthusiasm for home remedies, devastating purges, blue-mass pills, poultices, socks full of hot ashes, and "the water treatment — douche, sitz, wet-sheet and shower-bath," was such that Sam, like the suffering hero Billy Rogers under similar circumstances, "felt that what was left of me was dying."[4]

Sam's first cousin Tabitha Quarles, whom he called "Puss" in summer days when they played together at the Quarles farm — a regimen that helped improve his health — remembered him as "a pale, sickly boy who did a great deal more thinking than was good for him, teased girls with green garter snakes he'd caught, loved cats and always had three or more of them for pets."[5] He was plagued by nightmares, and walked in his sleep, "a terror to his whole family." Dreaming that robbers were trying to steal his bedclothes, he would get up, strip off the sheets and blankets, hide them carefully, and returning to bed lie there shivering in his sleep until the cold woke him up. Then he would cry and call for his mother. Once when the family was still in the sitting room, Sam appeared in a trance and to their amusement tried repeatedly to sit on one of Orion's high boots.[6] One night, during a visit to the farm, his Uncle John found

Sam "out in the stable in his night gown. He was astride the old gray horse. He was yelling like a wild Indian and thought he was running a race, while old Gray just pricked up his ears and paid no more attention to Sam's tricks than the rest of us."

Jane Clemens, with her worries of keeping house and home together, and the bursts of temper that tension sometimes wrought upon her kindly nature, found Sam her problem child, with his illnesses, vivid imaginings, habits of wandering toward the nearest creek or river, and didos that seemed to multiply as improving health increased his power for mischief. He was unlike sober, earnest Orion; or Pamela, whose "amiable deportment and faithful application to her various studies" at Mrs. Horr's school in Hannibal won a certificate of commendation in 1840 that is still preserved; or Henry, who even in his tender years began to show those model qualities which marked him as the original of Sid Sawyer, and made him the family favorite through all of his brief life.[7] But Sam was fitful, idle, erratic, unpredictable. With relief his mother looked to school days to take him off her hands.

He once insisted that these days began when he was four and a half, about the spring of 1840, in a small log schoolhouse at the southern end of Main Street.[8] Elizabeth Horr, wife of the village cooper, taught a dame school for many years; their only daughter, Miss Lizzie, began in the mid-1840's to help her mother by teaching the upper grades. In addition to piety and diligence, Mrs. Horr insisted upon good manners, and in the custom of those days always made the boys take off their hats and bow to her when entering the schoolroom. Orion's sole remembered breach of discipline occurred one day when, having forgotten his hat, he pulled his forelock instead — a gesture of servile rusticity which for some reason affronted her.[9]

Sam's breaches of the rules were more frequent and more calculated. On his first day in school he broke a rule twice, he remembered, and on the second round was ordered to go out and find a switch. Obligingly he came back with a cooper's shaving. With less self-interest Jim Dunlap was then sent out, and brought Mrs. Horr a specimen better suited to the purpose. But at another time, six months later, he had in some fashion so impressed her that she exclaimed in the child's own hearing, as he always claimed, that one day he would be "President of the United States, and would stand in the presence of kings unabashed." Another recollection was the time he tested Mrs. Horr's recommendation of the efficacy of prayer. At his desk Sam prayed for gingerbread. And lo, in front of him where sat the German baker's daughter, Margaret Koeneman, a slab of her father's gingerbread lay within easy reach. But when the miracle failed to repeat itself, after many trials, his faith was shaken.[10] For the first time, in many, in the course of a long life, he was disappointed in the pragmatic tests of religion.

Mrs. Horr's associate in this enterprise, who really served as principal of the little school, was Miss Mary Ann Newcomb, the "old maid and thin" who had moved from Florida to Hannibal in 1839.[11] A good friend of the Clemenses, she took some of her meals as their paying guest, and at their table had often seen little Sam steal sugar from the bowl and get his knuckles rapped, in the Tom Sawyer manner. Judge Clemens she recalled as "never a practical man, but an energetic dreamer . . . courteous, well-educated . . . a good conversationalist," and Jane as witty and good-humored. As for Sam Clemens in school, she remembered most vividly that he was slow of speech, but "certainly not slow about thinking up ways of getting out of studying." Flat-bosomed, prim, and angular, Miss Newcomb was a perfect desiccated specimen of "the village schoolmarm type" who appears unfailingly in Mark's retrospect of Hannibal. As a boy he is said often to have grumbled to his mother that he "couldn't see any sense in staying indoors and listening to an 'old maid and a widow all day,' " when spring meadows and autumn woods beckoned through the open window. But with an old pupil's loyalty, on his last visit to Hannibal in 1902 he said, "I owe a great deal to Mary Newcomb, she compelled me to learn to read." [12]

Still another teacher under this roof, apparently kindlier and more easygoing, was Miss Torrey. In one of his torrential bursts of recollection to Will Bowen after almost thirty years, Sam wrote about the time "we got up a rebellion against Miss Newcomb, under Ed. Stevens' leadership, (to force her to let us all go over to Miss Torry's side of the schoolroom,) and gallantly 'sassed' Laura Hawkins when she came out the third time to call us in, and then afterward marched in in threatening and bloodthirsty array, — and meekly yielded, and took each his little thrashing, and resumed his old seat entirely 'reconstructed.' " [13]

Unlike his later experience at Dawson's and Cross's, this tutelage under Miss Newcomb's ferule was wholly a feminine dominion. Prayers, Bible readings, deportment, the ABC's, Webster's speller and McGuffey's reader, and the deafening recitation of the old "blab school" — this was its essence. The most celebrated event of the school year at "Miss Newcomb's select school" fell on May Day — frequently postponed until June on account of the late spring rains in Hannibal — when all the pupils, resplendent in clean shirts and starched pinafores, preceded by the municipal brass band, led by the May Queen, and shepherded by their teachers, marched in solemn gaiety to a grove north of the old graveyard. They gathered round a May pole, these children with their convoy of spinsters — a ceremony of innocence quite unaware of phallic meanings behind such ancient vegetation rites — singing songs in praise of spring, their God, and their country. After one or two declamations, a local citizen orated and the band played "Old Uncle Ned," a great favorite with the children. As the climax, came the crowning of the Queen with a chaplet of flowers, before a throne dressed with roses and pinks, and she responded,

> Oh! strew with fragrant flowers still,
> Our path up Zion's towering hill.

Then followed the picnic dinner. Despite grousing by some local democrats about "the servile bowing of the knee to Royalty . . . by American children," the May Day party of Miss Newcomb's school was transcended in pomp only by the Glorious Fourth.[14] It may well be supposed that Mark Twain's lifelong savoring of the sentimental poetaster's art — from gift books and annuals to the Sweet Singer of Michigan — was laid in those days of beribboned declamation.

Book learning and piety, day school and Sunday school, went hand in hand through the weeks. A parochial faun like wild, curly-haired Sam Clemens soon saw that the seventh day was good for little save church-going. The Puritan Sabbath held Hannibal tightly in its grip. Promptly upon its incorporation in the spring of 1845, the city fathers codified its already ripe traditions of Sunday observance into an ordinance banning the sale of liquor on that day, and making it a misdemeanor to "play at any game of billiard, ten pins or other games of amusement." [15] The first Sunday school which Sam attended, "for two or three years," was in a shabby little brick Methodist church on the public square called the Old Ship of Zion. The class was taught by a kindly stonemason named Richmond. More vividly than his moral precepts Sam always remembered the shape of his thumb, whose nail after injury from a hammer remained twisted and curved like a parrot's beak — to the boy, a possession of great envy.[16] His pupils recited Bible verses from memory, to win the modest right of borrowing "pretty dreary books" from the Sunday school library. Sam took a prize week after week by repeating the same verses about the five foolish virgins.

About 1843 Jane Clemens, always an espouser of almost any religion, joined the Presbyterian church. Its steeple, with a bell from the wrecked steamboat *Chester,* towered over North Fourth Street. Pamela followed her mother's lead on the same day, and soon all the Clemenses became "abandoned Presbyterians," in Mark's phrase, with the exception of Judge Clemens, who as always stood aloof from their "pious joys" and "went to church — once; never again." Their new pastor, the Reverend Joshua Tucker, long afterward recalled Sister Clemens as "a woman of the sunniest temperament, lively, affable, a general favorite. . . . The father was a grave, taciturn man, a foremost citizen in intelligence and wholesome influence." [17] In the basement of this edifice Sam attended his second Sunday school.

As he grew a little older, at about ten or eleven, Sam was also constrained to stay for the sermon — such Calvinist exhortations as Tom Sawyer sweated out, which "dealt in limitless fire and brimstone, and thinned the predestined elect down to a company so small as to be hardly worth the saving." Long afterward, dropping in on a Sunday morning in 1871 at a village church in Illinois, Mark found the whole boyhood experience suddenly reconstructed before his eyes:

There was the high pulpit, with the red plush pillow for the Bible; the hair sofa behind it, and the distinguished minister from the great town a hundred miles away — gray hair pushed up and back in the stern intellectual Jacksonian way — spectacles on forehead — ponderous reflection going on behind them, such as the village would expect to see indexed there. . . . There were the stiff pews; the black velvet contribution-purses attached to long poles, flanking the pulpit; the tall windows and Venetian blinds; the wonderfully scattering congregation; the gallery with ascending seats, opposite the pulpit; six boys scattered through it, with secret spit-ball designs on the bald-headed man dozing below; the wheezy melodeon in the gallery-front; the old maid behind it in severe simplicity of dress; the gay young soprano beside her in ribbons and curls and feathers; the quiet alto; the grim middle-aged bass; the smirking, ineffable tenor (tenors are always conceited).[18]

Then as the voluntary began, the melodeon snored forth its harmonies, the voices joined in with triumphant anguish, "Oh praise the L-o-r-d!" The local preacher lined out a hymn or two, which the choir, abetted by the congregation, murdered zealously. And then came the sermon, and the offertory accompanied by the chink of small silver. All the while Mark's sympathy went out to the captive audience — especially the boy who was catching imaginary flies, and another who "got out a peanut and contemplated it, as if he had an idea of cracking it under cover of some consumptive's cough the first time he got a chance. . . ."[18] In Mark's

breast still lived the Tom Sawyer whose most exalted moment in church had come when the stray poodle sat down
on a pinchbug, and went sailing up the aisle "with his tail
shut down like a hasp." And Tom, the prankster, lived on
in the Mark who in Hartford days tormented a clergyman
by remarking that every word of the sermon just delivered
was in a book he happened to have at home. The preacher
was appalled, aghast at his unconscious plagiarism, until
Mark sent around the book — a dictionary.[19]

Presbyterianism and the Moral Sense it fostered — with
its morbid preoccupations about sin, the last judgment, and
eternal punishment — entered early into the boy's soul, leaving their traces of fascination and repulsion, their afterglow
of hell-fire and terror, through all the years of his adult
"emancipation." He did not believe in Hell, but he was
afraid of it. Even as a sensitive boy, harrowed by the stern
sermons of those times, frightened by near escapes from
drowning, cowed by thunderstorms at night and the lightning that seemed to flash like the terrible swift sword of an
avenging Deity, Sam Clemens appears to have been a silent
rebel withal — like the Tom Sawyer whose illness in bed
left him unregenerate while all his playmates were swept up
in the tide of a village revival. Among some autobiographical notes we find the entry: "Campbellite revival. All converted but me. All sinners again in a week." [20]

The Campbellites were strong in Hannibal, and one of the
noted apostles of that sect, the Reverend Barton W. Stone,
grandfather of Sam's closest boyhood friend, Will Bowen,
often preached in that community, and in 1844 died under
the Bowen roof in Hannibal. Mark Twain used to tell
under various names and guises an incident that had really
happened to him and Will Bowen: how they had almost
been surprised playing euchre and had hidden the deck in

the sleeves of a preacher's "baptising robe" hanging in the closet, and how a few days later when its owner was immersing converts in the river, the cards began to float out upon the water, "the first cards being a couple of bowers and three aces — and how one of the culprits, even through the tears and the flogging, had stoutly remarked of the minister, "I don't see how he could help going out on a hand like that." [21]

Protracted revivals and camp meetings belonged to the intermittent fever of Hannibal's spiritual cycle under whose pentecostal fervor many surrendered and were washed in the blood of the Lamb. Sometimes they were held at Camp Creek, five miles southwest of the village, and sometimes in a clearing of the woods between Hannibal and Palmyra. "There is something about a scenery entirely natural," said Orion Clemens' newspaper in 1851, apropos of the latest revival, "which tends to induce serious contemplation." [22] But such experience, so typical of the Western country since frontier days, undoubtedly helped to build Mark Twain's enduring prejudice against the cult of excitement and fear.

Still clearer manifestations of "wildcat religion" swept over or past Hannibal during Sam's boyhood. On October 22, 1844, local believers in the apocalyptic visions of William Miller donned their ascension robes and took their stations on Lover's Leap, ready for the stars to fall and the firmament to crack before their eyes. On his last visit to these scenes in 1902, Mark Twain rambled Holliday's Hill with his old crony John Briggs, and pointing out across the valley mused, "There is where the Millerites put on their robes one night to go up to heaven. None of them went that night John but no doubt many of them have gone since." [23] And in the same year, at the time of the Nauvoo troubles, the disfavor with which Hannibal regarded its Mormon neighbors — as polygamists and alleged chicken stealers — reached such a pitch that when a boatload of the harried Saints was reported ascending the River, some local citizens rigged up a shotted cannon to salute them with a hot reception; but having been warned, the boat took the channel east of Glasscock's (Jackson's) Island, hugging the Illinois shore. Mark's later interest in the Mormons, strengthened by his tarrying in Salt Lake City in 1861 and his Washoe days, probably stemmed from still earlier times.

Similarly the spiritualism whose phenomena he scoffed at in some of his first writing for Orion's paper in 1853, reported derisively for the San Francisco press, and rejected in *Life on the Mississippi,* had convulsed the Hannibal of his later boyhood. Starting in 1849 it spread until by 1852 it was reported that "nearly every family has two or three mediums in it . . . a source of amusement . . . in this quiet, monotonous city." [24] In an unfinished draft of *The Mysterious Stranger,* Mark wrote a long satiric description of a séance around the parlor table of one gullible villager.[25] The family of his playfellow Bill League patronized these "rappings," while Betty Ruffner, one of their schoolmates, became a locally famous medium, and in 1851 a Hannibal townsman named E. W. Southworth went as far as Cincinnati to consult the celebrated Fox sisters, as reported by Orion Clemens' newspaper.[26] Among the cruelest of adolescent hoaxes, Sam never forgot how another classmate, Roberta Jones, had clothed herself in a sheet one midnight, and creeping into an old maid's parlor "scared [her] into the insane asylum with a skull and a dough-face." [27] Fear, violence, and tragedy always remained curiously inwoven with Sam Clemens' Hannibal.

CHAPTER EIGHT

SUMMERS AT THE FARM

THE HAPPIEST if not the most adventurous intervals in Sam Clemens' boyhood were the golden summer weeks spent each year at the Quarles farm, about three and a half miles northwest of the old home in Florida. These long visits, he said, began in the fourth year after their removal to Hannibal, and continued until Sam was eleven or twelve, that is, till 1847 or 1848.[1] On the first visit, when Sam was seven, the whole family went along. At this time seems to have happened the incident of his accidental abandonment, which Sam never forgot, but which his recollection tricked him into placing at the earlier date of 1839, as if to heighten the pathos. Jane and the other children had set out for the farm in their wagon on a Saturday, leaving Judge Clemens to bring Sam early the next morning; but the absent-minded father saddled his horse and rode off without remembering his charge, who was still asleep. Not until his arrival at the farm was the loss discovered, and Jane's young uncle Wharton Lampton hastily took to the road and fetched the boy — whom he found crying in the twilight, after having spent the lonely day indoors amusing himself by coaxing the grain in a meal sack to run out through a hole.[2] The effect of this "desertion" upon Sam's relations with his father and later feelings about his father's inadequacy, through the years that the son nurtured its memory, can be surmised.

And then as always, when he reached the farm, Sam could not help contrasting Judge Clemens' cold formal reserve and the pinched little household in Hannibal with Uncle John Quarles's warm, hearty, country hospitality — his jolly jokes, his banter with the children, his hunting trips through the woods, and the wonderful table over which he and Aunt Patsy presided, surrounded by their eight happy children and a flock of enchanting slaves. This was the good life.

One of these lucky children, Sam's cousin Puss Quarles, his own age and also his favorite playmate, in recalling his perennial devotion to cats, said: "When he arrived at the farm father would lift his big carpet bag out of the wagon and then would come Sam with a basket in his hand. The basket he would allow no one except himself to carry. In the basket would be his pet cat. This he had trained to sit beside himself at the table. He would play contentedly with a cat for hours, and his cats were very fond of him and very patient when he tried to teach them tricks." In their house at Hannibal, as Mark Twain remembered, in 1845 they had nineteen cats at one time, thanks to an infatuation which his mother could no more resist than he. Judge Clemens' advice to Pamela when she was growing up — that she must learn to be a good housekeeper and see that her husband was comfortable and not have too many cats in the house — was the implied criticism of an orderly mind against a wife whose catholic sympathies vexed him no less than her cheerfully random ways and dislike of housework with all its tedium.[3] On the rare occasions when Jane Clemens the cat-lover bowed to Malthusian realities, said her famous son, she always warmed the water before drowning the kittens.[4]

Among the boys a cat fight inevitably received grateful attention, and when a favorite cat died of natural causes, its relics were treated to a solemn funeral.

At the Quarles farm there was room enough for all creatures, including the hounds that with joyful frenzy joined the boys and Negroes on coon and possum hunts at night through briers and brambles, and on frosty autumn evenings lay blinking before the roaring fireplace. In the stables were horses that a boy could ride, and beyond the fences herds of cows and droves of pigs, whose bounty filled the cool dairy and savory smokehouse. Flocks of chickens pecked around the granary, and the woods were filled with squirrels and geese and pheasants and wild turkeys. Sam learned the stratagems of the turkey hen, pretending to be wounded to draw off the young hunter with his shotgun until, his prey lost altogether after a tramp of many miles, he had to solace himself with the discovery of a "weed-grown garden . . . full of ripe tomatoes." [5] He loved the distant hammering of woodpeckers, the scurry of prairie chickens, and in the blue vault a huge hawk hanging motionless. Sam's curiosity did not overlook the snakes that loved to sun themselves along the dusty roads, soon learning that puff adders and rattlers deserved no fate but death, that the hoopsnake was a fable of terror, while the house snake or garter snake invited fraternization. Puss Quarles remembered how he would hold up a garter snake and let it dart its forked tongue against his hand, while giving "us a comic lecture on the habits of the snake in his slow, drawling voice." A great tease, he liked to coil a snake in Aunt Patsy's work basket for a surprise, or tell his mother, "There's something in my coat pocket for you," and leave her unsuspecting fingers to discover the silky revulsion of a bat.

Dreaming again of boyhood, in old age when he was writing *The Mysterious Stranger* and imagining himself that celestial-demonic visitant straying into some Missouri village, Mark Twain wrote but discarded some passages recapturing his own early pagan rapport with dumb creatures.

Animals could not let him alone, they were so fascinated with him; and this was mutual, for he felt the same way toward them. He often said he would not give a penny for human company when he could get better. You see they were fond of each other because in a manner they were kin, through their mutual property in the absence of the Moral Sense. And kin in another particular, too — to him, as to them, there were no unpleasant smells. . . . He said that the natural man, the savage, had no prejudices about smells, and no shame for his God-made nakedness. . . . The wild creatures trooped in from everywhere, and climbed all over Satan, and sat on his shoulder and his head, and rummaged his pockets, and made themselves at home — squirrels, rabbits, snakes, birds, butterflies, every creature you could name; and the rest would sit around in a crowd and look at him and admire him and worship him, and chatter and squawk and talk and laugh, and he would answer back in their own language.[6]

And wherever he found them in traps he would free them. The Stranger tells his friends that outside this particular universe, so sadly botched by Adam, "in the other worlds the Adams and the rest live millions of years till burnt out like the moon, then are ferried over to heaven *with their animals.*" For all animals, lacking the Moral Sense, inevitably go to heaven. And as a further and final touch of self-identification, Mark's Stranger "thinks well of the cat because she is the only independent; says there is no such thing as an independent human being — all are slaves; no such thing as freedom of thought, freedom of opinion, freedom in politics and religion." [6] Like the shy, wayward, quietly rebellious boy with his ruck of russet curls, roving the Missouri woods in 1845, like the white-maned old man sixty years later waging his private war against the tyranny of conformity, the Mysterious Stranger, visiting this world with his scorn and his hidden gifts of genius, found in the domestic tiger his special symbol and delight — for he too walked alone.

These summer days on the farm planted in him some of those pioneer instincts, the "hard old Injun" ingredient in Mark Twain which Charles Godfrey Leland once remarked. Besides the ways and tracks of animals he came to know the stars and their names, the herbs and minerals, and the fish that lived in the limpid brook below the tobacco-curing house with its dark swimming pools forbidden and therefore much indulged, "for we were Christian children and had early been taught the value of forbidden fruit." And in the oak openings, in the lush grass spangled with prairie pinks and wet with morning dew, he learned to find wild strawberries, or, turning back toward the homestead, discover blackberries hugging the rail fences or a fat ripe watermelon sunning itself among the pumpkin vines. The taste of wild grapes, of pawpaws and persimmons, and of maple sap running from the trough — these belonged to the farm and its "blessed" memories.

Those implacable institutions of society, the school and the church followed him even here, but their angularity was softened in this heavenly air. Beginning with his first season at the farm, he was sent to a summer school that met once or twice a week in a country schoolhouse three miles from his uncle's place. Some twenty-five boys and girls, including no doubt his cousins, in jeans and calico dresses, walked through the forest paths in the morning dew, carrying in a basket their corn dodger and buttermilk that would be devoured at noon under the shade of trees, not returning home till the cool of the day. "It is the part of my education which I look back upon with the most satisfaction," wrote Mark Twain.[7] As for the church, in the village of Florida, it was built of logs with a puncheon floor and slab benches. And the sermon, though dull, was apt to be enlivened by the hogs that slept under the floor, particularly when the dogs got after them and the preacher had to stop until the racket ceased. In summer there were also "fleas enough for all." [8] This little outpost of Zion served him well when Mark came to write of Huck Finn's embroilment in the Shepherdson–Grangerford feud, when he went on a Sunday afternoon to fetch a note left in a Bible after services and found "there warn't anybody at the church, except maybe a hog or two, for there warn't any lock on the door, and hogs likes a puncheon floor in summertime because it's cool." [9]

The Grangerford home — "a big old-fashioned double log house," and its dinner table, groaning with backwoods hospitality — is no less an affectionate reminiscence of the Quarles farmhouse than is the "big double loghouse" of the Silas Phelpses later described in the same novel. The latter debt Mark himself admitted.[10] The old house, struck by lightning and burned in 1926, stood facing north on a knoll in the midst of a spacious yard. It was a double log affair of four big rooms, two on the ground floor and two above, with an open but roofed-over hallway nine feet high, where the dinner table was spread in summer. The floors were oak and the staircase walnut. In the east and west rooms downstairs were mammoth fireplaces built of limestone rocks and home-made brick, with broad stone hearths to provide some safety from vagrant fire-coals. A kitchen sixteen feet square was built onto the southeast corner of the house, and here slaves cooked those fabulous meals of roast pig, fried chicken, freshly-killed venison, ducks, turkeys, geese, and partridges which made Mark "cry to think of them" — with their prodigal accompaniments of biscuits, batter cakes, buck-wheat cakes, corn pone, boiled corn, succotash, string beans, tomatoes, peas, Irish potatoes, sweet milk, clabber, melons, pies, and cobblers.

A sketch by Mark Twain, hitherto unpublished, describes anew the Quarles furniture and atmosphere:

> In the common sitting room was a mighty fireplace, paved with slabs of stone shaped by nature and worn smooth by use. The oaken floor in front of it was thickly freckled, as far as the middle of the room, with black spots burned in it by coals popped out from the hickory fire-wood. There was no carpeting anywhere; but there was a spinning wheel in one corner, a bed in another, with a white counterpane, a dinner table with leaves in another, a tall eight-day clock in the fourth corner, a dozen splint-bottom chairs scattered around, several guns resting upon deer-horns over the mantel piece, and generally a cat or a hound or two curled up on the hearth-stones asleep. . . . A planked passage-way, twenty feet wide, open at the sides but roofed above, ex-tended from the back sitting room door to the log kitchen; and beyond the kitchen stood the smoke-house and three or four little dismal log cabins, otherwise the "negro quarter." [11]

South of the house was a large apple orchard that yielded a thousand bushels in a good season. And on the edge of the forest were swings — the children's delight and hazard —

forty feet long or more, fashioned from the bark of hickory saplings. To the north and east lay the pasture, and clearings on which corn and tobacco were grown. Between the house and the meadows were two log barns, corncrib, stables, smokehouse with slabs of meat dangling from its rafters, and tobacco-curing shed, with the brook below singing over its gravelly bed. But the greatest fascination that pulled the children toward this point of the compass was the slave quarters, which they visited every day. One of their favorites was an ancient bedridden slave woman, believed to be a thousand years old, whose thin white tufts of wool were tied with thread against the power of witches. The world of charms and incantations in which Tom Sawyer and Huck Finn live — spells to cure warts and recover lost marbles, snake rattles as sovereign preventives of cramps, omens of death-watch beetles and howling dogs, signs of the cross to banish ghosts, fear of devil-fire (will-o'-the-wisp) and the prepotent black magic that exhales from corpses — these mysteries the real Sam Clemens learned from the lips of black folk. And their resources for entertainment were pure delight: ghost stories, like the Golden Arm, the lore of Br'er Rabbit, and the spirituals whose melodies were always echoing in Mark Twain's inner ear. In the unpublished "Huck and Tom Among the Indians" Huck describes a girl's blush by saying "her cheeks turned faint red and beautiful, like a nigger's does when he puts a candle in his mouth to surprise a child."

Missourians of the 1840's liked to think their slave system a mild and benevolent one — the majority, like kindly Jane Clemens, failing utterly to see that the institution itself was "a bald, grotesque, and unwarrantable usurpation." [12] Local papers liked to report instances of runaway slaves who, upon reaching the snows and the grim economic struggles of life in Canada, were "all anxious to return." [13] Their columns, nevertheless, were filled with offers of rewards for fugitives, accompanied by the familiar woodcut of a Negro carrying a bundle. And Sam Clemens vividly remembered how, at the age of ten, he had seen a white overseer "fling a lump of iron-ore at a slave-man in anger, for merely doing something awkwardly. . . . He was dead in an hour . . . it seemed a pitiful thing and somehow wrong . . . Nobody in the village approved of that murder, but of course no one said much about it." [14]

But the tragic irony of these relations between black folks and white masters might never have revealed itself to Sam Clemens' mind without the intimacy bred by his summers at the farm. For, although the Clemenses had grown too poor to own slaves during his adolescent years, the Quarleses had many, and under the easygoing daily familiarity of that life he came to know and love them. The buxom black matron called "Aunt Hanner" — whom he confused in the *Autobiography* with the ancient Negress, but who from earlier notes seems to have been quite a different person — probably inspired him to create, in a still unpublished story, the figure of "Aunty Phyllis." She is "as straight as a grenadier, and has the grit and the stride and the warlike bearing of one. But, being black, she is good-natured, to the bone. It is the born privilege and prerogative of her adorable race. She is cheerful, indestructibly cheerful and lively; and what a refreshment she is! Her laugh — her breezy laugh, her inspiring and uplifting laugh — is always ready, always on tap, and comes pealing out, peal upon peal, right from her heart, let the occasion for it be big or little; and it is so cordial and so catching that derelict after derelict has to forget his troubles and join in. . . ." [15]

And quite possibly another Quarles servant was the "gay

and impudent and satirical and delightful young black man
— a slave — who daily preached sermons from the top of his
master's woodpile, with me for sole audience," on the favorite
text, "You tell me whar a man gits his corn pone, en I'll tell
you what his 'pinions is" — Sam's first lesson in the economic
determinism that underlies one's personal viewpoint.[16]

But the most memorable servant of the Quarleses was
middle-aged Uncle Dan'l, sensible, honest, patient, the children's comrade in adventure, their adviser and ally in time
of trouble. "It was on the farm that I got my strong liking
for his race," wrote Mark, "and my appreciation of certain
of its fine qualities." [17] Mark made a trial sketch of him,
under that name, in *The Gilded Age.* Later he became the
acknowledged original of Huck Finn's friend "Nigger Jim,"
whose unshakable loyalty, generous heart, and unconscious
dignity — even when Huck makes game of his credulity —
raise him to the rank of Mark Twain's noblest creation. He
probably intended Joan of Arc for that niche; in his hands
she turns to plaster saint. But Nigger Jim is as vital and
earth-bound as one of the lofty hickories that towered over
the old farmstead. The later Samuel Clemens — who ex-
coriated King Leopold's brutalities in the Congo, and who
was once advised by his wife, as a mollifying rule, to "consider every man colored until he was proved white" — took
the impress of that attitude from these days of boyish friendship.

The ironies of white Christian supremacy never failed to
strike sardonic overtones from this emancipated Southerner.
Huck Finn's report to Aunt Sally Phelps about a steamboat
explosion in which, luckily, no one was hurt, although it
"killed a nigger," rings true to ante-bellum civilization. And
the admission made to Tom by Huck, the homeless river
rat, of how black Uncle Jake has befriended him is equally

revealing: "Sometime I've set right down and eat *with* him. But you needn't tell that. A body's got to do things when he's awful hungry he wouldn't want to do as a steady thing." And in the unfinished draft, "The Mysterious Stranger in Hannibal," the village lunatic Crazy Meadows — whom the children chase and stone "for the fun they get out of it" — refuses to be party to a spiritualist séance where he is requested by an abolitionist to "sit at a table with niggers" and "take them by the hand." Unhinged and despised though he is, he feels obliged to draw the line somewhere. And the slaves themselves well understand, and yearn to be excused. But the Stranger, beyond the conventions of good and evil, is epitomized in a terse notation: "He is courteous to whores and niggers." [18]

Season after season during these impressionable years Sam Clemens returned to the Quarles farm. After his father's death in 1847, and the boy's apprenticeship to a printer — which followed not long afterward — shades of the prison house began to close upon him. Probably around 1848, as the somewhat uncertain chronology of his memory indicates, these halcyon summers ceased. In July 1850 his aunt Martha Ann Quarles died, at the age of forty-three — practically in childbirth, after naming her tenth child "Jane Clemens." Less than two years later John Quarles sold his farm.

Eventually he remarried, and continued to live in the neighborhood of Florida, though with less prosperity than in his palmy days as a country squire. And apparently his contact with the Clemenses through their later vicissitudes of fortune was slight.[19] In 1876, shortly before *Tom Sawyer* was published — the first of the great books in which his nephew recaptured the idyl of those boyhood days — John Quarles died in his seventy-fifth year.[20]

CHAPTER NINE

"THE PRECIOUS GIFT OF DEATH"

I N HANNIBAL the Clemenses' lean years continued. After losing their early anchorage in the hotel at Hill and Main streets, they moved several times, but exact dates and places have been long forgotten. The pungent remembrance that Sam had of his father, that "in 43 he caught me in a statement not well constructed" — by no means his first lie, but the first to be detected and punished, he added — linked itself to a certain house where they dwelt for only a year.[1] Exactly when the family contrived to build a house on the narrow lot which their "cousin" James Clemens had salvaged from the public sale in October 1843 is unknown. No record of an understanding between them survives earlier than a ground lease, for a twenty-eight-dollar annual rental, which James Clemens gave to Orion Clemens on April 12, 1847.[2] But this was after the death of Judge Clemens, who certainly had built this meager frame house for his family. This is the so-called Mark Twain home at 206 Hill Street, known to many thousands of visitors today — a two-story white frame structure built flush with the sidewalk that slopes steeply toward the River. Its small rooms, low ceilings, and box stairway bear proof of cheap construction. In 1846, a fresh access of poverty compelled them to sell off most of their furniture — save the piano, relic of a fitful interlude of prosperity about 1844 — and move to rent-free quarters across the street.[3] Shortly after Clemens' death, however, the family returned to the old home, with Orion as the chief breadwinner. James Clemens' lease of the site to Orion in the spring of 1847 would therefore appear to be the resumption of an old arrangement made but at length broken off during Judge Clemens' last years.

The adversity of those years led Jane Clemens to take paying guests — not only Miss Newcomb the schoolteacher but a mother and daughter named Sexton whom Mark Twain describes as "boarders in 1844 house." Mrs. Sexton, who "pronounced it *Saxton* to make it finer, the nice kind-hearted, smirky, smily dear Christian creature," talked fondly about their better days in New Orleans; her daughter Margaret was a "pretty child of 14" for whose favor Sam and Henry Clemens were rivals.[4]

As for Judge Clemens himself, "Villagers of 1840–3" relates, he "became justice of the peace and lived on its meager pickings." Paine states that he ran for this office in 1840 and was elected, but newspaper accounts of this election do not bear him out.[5] Probably he won this office in the 1842 election, although the scanty records fail us. One day in 1843 young Sam as a truant from school slipped into his father's deserted office, as evening was drawing in, to postpone the wrath to come, and there on the floor a gradually encroaching pool of moonlight revealed the corpse of a man stabbed in the breast. To readers of *The Innocents Abroad* and many a lecture audience Mark related how, at sight of this apparition, "I went out at the window, and I carried the sash along with me; I did not need the sash, but it was handier to take it than it was to leave it, and so I took it."

The presence of a corpse in the room — unlikely garniture for a lawyer's office — is fair presumptive evidence that Judge Clemens was then a justice of the peace, sharing the responsibility for coroners' inquests.[6]

This incident, the memorable first homicide in Hannibal's history, occurred on September 4, 1843. Two Ralls County farmers, Vincent Hudson and James McFarland, had come to town drinking, and in a hardware store on Hill Street between Main and the levee they fell to quarreling over a plow. Hudson drew a sharp shoe-knife "of the length of eight inches" and buried it almost to the handle in the right side of his neighbor's breast. Within a quarter of an hour McFarland was dead. In November a jury found Hudson guilty of manslaughter, and he was sentenced to four years in the penitentiary.[7]

"My father was a justice of the peace," wrote Mark Twain in *Life on the Mississippi,* "and I supposed he possessed the power of life and death over all men, and could hang anybody that offended him." Beyond question he belonged to that tradition of buckskin jurisprudence which had once impelled Andrew Jackson, as a Tennessee Circuit Judge, to leave the bench, pistol in hand, and hale into court a desperado armed to the teeth whom the sheriff had feared to arrest. An old undated clipping from the St. Louis *Republican,* in a scrapbook inherited by Mark Twain's grandnephew Samuel Webster, describes John M. Clemens, Justice of the Peace, as

a stern, unbending man of splendid common sense . . . the autocrat of the little dingy room on Bird Street where he held his court. . . . Its furniture consisted of a dry-goods box which served the double purpose of a desk for the Judge and table for the lawyers, three or four rude stools and a puncheon bench for the jury. And here on court days when the Judge climbed upon his three-legged stool, rapped on the box with his knuckles and demanded "Silence in the court" it was fully expected that silence would reign supreme.

The narrator tells how, one day in the late autumn of 1843, Judge Clemens quelled a disturbance in his court — after a bellicose plaintiff named McDonald had so provoked a witness named Snyder that the latter discharged an old pepper-pot revolver, "filling the room with smoke and consternation" — and in his confusion, clouted the Scot over the head with a hammer, sending him "senseless and quivering to the floor. The irate court was complete master of the situation." A less explicit version was told by Mark Twain, and his biographer Paine took still further liberties. But all agree that Judge Clemens commanded the peace, and obtained it, by wielding a hammer or mallet with summary effect.[8] Furthermore, since McDonald was the turbulent village carpenter who later came near shooting William Elgin in the back of the head — mistaking him in a rear view, it was said, for Judge Clemens — it seems quite probable that McDonald served as the original for the carpenter with homicidal fantasies who figures in *Life on the Mississippi*.[9]

From August 1844 until July 1845 John M. Clemens served as road districting justice of the peace for this township — which meant that he was charged with the surveying of roads, and the allocation of hands among the overseers of road building.[10] In addition, other county records show him at work holding inquests, aiding the court in criminal prosecutions, issuing subpoenas, and taking depositions, for the meager fees that were so vital a source of his family's income.

On January 24, 1845, Hannibal witnessed its first premeditated murder, which left among its relics twenty-eight depositions set down by the hand of John M. Clemens, J.P., and the recollection which his son recaptured in one of *Huckleberry Finn's* most vivid episodes — the shooting of old Boggs by Colonel Sherburn. The village shoemaker named Boggs may have furnished this name, but the real victim was "Uncle Sam" Smarr, "as honest a man as any in the state" a neighbor testified to Judge Clemens, but "when drinking he was a little turbulent," yet "I did not consider him a dangerous man at all." Curiously enough, one of the "damned rascals" against whom Uncle Sam liked to rail when in his cups was "big Ira Stout," of unhappy association with John M. Clemens' business affairs. Another target was a prosperous merchant named William Owsley, whom old Smarr when drinking liked to describe to all within earshot as "a damned pickpocket . . . a damned son of a bitch . . . if he ever does cross my path I will kill him." He believed that Owsley "had stole" two thousand dollars from a friend at Palmyra named Thompson, and had also swindled old Smarr's drinking crony Tom Davis, "and for that he intended to have Owsley whipped." Two or three weeks before the shooting, "Smarr and Davis had been in town, spreeing around and cutting up smart . . . and shooting off pistols." Probably on this same evening, stated another witness named Caldwell, "when on my way home, when opposite to Judge Clemens' office, I heard Mr. Smarr five times call out at different points in the street 'O yes! O yes, here is Bill Owsley, has got a big stack of goods here, and stole two thousand dollars from Thompson in Palmyra.' . . . I returned and went to Mr. Selms' store — Mr. Davis and Mr. Smarr were in there — Davis then went out and I heard the report of a pistol — Mr. Davis and Jimmy Finn then both came in, Jim remarked, 'that would have made a hole in a man's belly....' " (Jimmy Finn, original of Huck's pappy who slept with the hogs in the tanyard, held the distinction of being the village drunkard.) Other witnesses called Smarr sober, "as kind and good a neighbor as any man amongst us," and doubted that he ever carried a pistol, but agreed that he had walked or ridden up in front of Owsley's store shouting drunken abuse, while Owsley within, hearing these words in the presence of his customers, "had a kind of twitching and turned white around the mouth — and said it was insufferable."

The general forecast that "Smarr would catch hell" was fulfilled at noon a few days later, when Smarr came back to town to sell some beef. At the corner of Hill and Main — a few steps from the Clemens doorway — Owsley came up behind Smarr and a friend named Brown, and as the latter told Judge Clemens, the merchant cried out,

"You Sam Smar" — Mr. Smar turned around, seeing Mr. Owsley in the act of drawing a pistol from his pocket, said Mr. Owsley don't fire, or something to that effect. Mr. Owsley was within about four paces of Mr. Smar when he drew the pistol and fired twice in succession, after the second fire, Mr. Smarr fell, when Mr. Owsley turned on his heel and walked off. After Mr. Smarr fell he raised his head and called, "Brown come take me up I am shot and will soon be a dead man." Dr. Grant then came up and invited us to take him to his store. We did so. The while he was begging us to lay him on his back. He then begged me not to leave him saying he must soon die. In about a half an hour from the time he was shot he expired.

Another witness added the detail that Smarr fell backward when shot, while "the gentleman that I saw shoot" kept his arm extended as he fired a second time. Thus, almost without a hairsbreadth of variation, the description in *Huckleberry Finn* of how the Colonel dispatched old Boggs.

In the depositions taken by Judge Clemens no mention is made of the heavy Bible laid by some pious fool upon the dying man's chest, though this "torture of its leaden weight" haunted young Sam's dreams and figured long afterward in his inspired retelling of the story. But Dr. Orville Grant, over whose drugstore at Hill and Main the Clemenses soon took up their abode, attested that the dying man was carried into this shop — where he and a fellow physician opened the victim's clothing and made hasty examination of the wounds, but "he then shewed signs of fainting and we . . . then stood by to see him die." [11]

Owsley, a proud Kentuckian who smoked "fragrant cigars — regalias" and was regarded as something of a swell, may have repelled the threat of mob violence with the same cold contempt displayed by the fictitious Colonel Sherburn. Of this the court record makes no mention, but clearly the first deliberate murder on Hannibal's streets caused uproar and feverish excitement. Long afterward, in writing about the cowardice of lynch mobs, Mark reflected that in such a group "of a certainty there are never ten men in it who would not prefer to be somewhere else — and would be, if they had but the courage to go. When I was a boy I saw a brave gentleman deride and insult a mob and drive it away." [12] Whatever threats Owsley may have faced down in the heat of the hour, he was not brought to trial until more than a year later. A man of wealth and influence, he had friends who were ready from the start to swear that his provocation had been great. At Palmyra on March 14, 1846, a jury returned a verdict of acquittal. Mark Twain's notes tell the sequel:

"His party brought him huzzaing in from Palmyra at mid-night. But there was a cloud upon him — a social chill — and he presently moved away." [13]

The paltriness of a justice's fees is shown well enough by a note on the docket of papers which John M. Clemens prepared in this case — revealing that his fee for writing these 13,500 words was $13.50, and for administering oaths to twenty-nine witnesses, $1.81. Clerical drudgery, in fact, seems to have become the essence of his life. To his daughter Pamela, now helping to support the family by giving piano and guitar lessons in Florida and Paris, in adjoining Monroe County, he wrote a letter on May 5, 1845: "I have removed my office of Justice to Messrs McCune & Holliday's counting room where I have taken Mr. Dawes' place as clerk — I did not succeed in making such arrangements as would enable me to go into business advantageously on my acct — and thought it best therefore not to attempt it at present." [14] The tradition that John M. Clemens "obtained employment for a time in a commission-house on the levee" doubtless belongs to this stage in his ill fortunes.[15]

But under all the batterings of poverty Judge Clemens clung to his pride, his intellectual fastidiousness, and his sense of civic duty. Every letter that survives from his pen is redolent of an old-fashioned dignity. With the loose grammar and slovenly speech of river towns and backwoods — "the fruit of careless habit, not ignorance," as his famous son described it in *Life on the Mississippi* — the Judge made no truce or concession. In August 1845 he began to attend a course of "twenty oral lectures on Grammar . . . by Professor Hull," and made a careful précis of "Rules for Parsing by Transposition" for the benefit of Orion, the prentice printer in St. Louis.[16]

In the spring of 1846, in his justice's office, now moved back to the frame hotel he once owned at Hill and Main, Judge Clemens was host to a group of businessmen interested in building a railroad from Hannibal to St. Joseph. His old friend Judge Draper presided, but the most vigorous advocate was young R. F. Lakenan, lately arrived in Hannibal but already its leading lawyer, possessed of that golden touch which fortune had denied to Clemens. With neither capital nor political influence, Clemens had little to contribute to the scheme save his capacity for dreaming great dreams. Early in 1847 a bill chartering the Hannibal & St. Jo passed the Missouri legislature, but he did not live to see the beginnings of the road. Completed in 1859, it was the first rail route to join the Mississippi and the Missouri rivers, and promptly became a vital juncture in the Pony Express, profiting also by the discovery of gold in Colorado. Lawyer Lakenan, for whom one of the new stations was named, soon grew to be Hannibal's richest citizen, prospering by the realization of Judge Clemens' vision of a railroad town on the banks of the mighty river. In 1886, declining an invitation from the Honorable J. W. Atterbury to attend a celebration of the railroad's foundation, Mark wrote from Hartford: "I have to thank you very much for your letter's astonishing information. I never knew before that my father was a pioneer railroad man; I knew he interested himself in Salt River navigation, but this railroad matter is entirely new to me." [17]

For the future glory of Hannibal Judge Clemens had further schemes. In November 1846 as chairman of a citizens' committee he published a report advocating construction of a macadamized road from Hannibal to St. Joseph, hopefully regarded as a link in the National Road; by family inheritance his son Orion a few years later went all out for the novelty of planked roads, to radiate from Hannibal.[18] In the winter of 1846–47 John M. Clemens worked busily to get a projected Masonic college for the State of Missouri located at Hannibal.[19] A more successful achievement for raising the level of culture was the Hannibal Library Institute, of which he was president at this time. With his good friends Judge Draper, Dr. Meredith, and schoolmaster Samuel Cross, John M. Clemens had taken a main share in its foundation in 1843. Its modest collection of books, housed in Dr. Meredith's second-floor office at "Wild-Cat Corner," was available to borrowers; the society also heard lectures, and held debates on such formidable topics as "liability of private property for corporate debts." This too was a cause that Orion ultimately inherited — although, under the burden of unpaid dues and mislaid books, it was already crumbling to decay before Sam Clemens left Hannibal in 1853.[20]

Meanwhile, unaware that his ill-starred life was drawing to a close, John M. Clemens kept trying to retrieve his fortunes. On September 10, 1846, he signed an agreement with Messrs. Buffum of New York City — a land agency whose head was the Quaker abolitionist Arnold Buffum — to sell his Tennessee lands at not less than twenty cents an acre. It bore no fruit; four years later Buffum began proposing to Orion that the price be cut to ten cents, but still there were no takers.[21] The autumn of 1846 was also troubled by a long-pending litigation between Judge Clemens and William Beebe, Hannibal merchant and "nigger trader," who it will be recalled had bought the slave girl Jennie several years before. Whether as a result of this sale or some other transaction, Clemens held two notes against

Beebe, dating back to 1842 and 1843, totaling nearly five hundred dollars. Late in 1843 the Circuit Court had awarded him judgment for this sum, plus damages, but since Beebe still refused to pay, the sheriff levied this execution "upon one negro girl aged about 9 yrs," along with various barrels, tin plates, sacks of salt, and a screw press which were sold on March 18, 1844, in partial satisfaction of these debts.

In the meantime John M. Clemens had assigned Beebe's note for $300 to his brother-in-law John A. Quarles, but what success Quarles had in its collection is not clear. In retaliation Beebe acquired an IOU for $290.55 which Judge Clemens early in 1842 had given storekeeper Henry Collins, now endorsed in favor of Beebe. Bringing suit against the Judge, in August 1846 Beebe was awarded judgment plus damages of $126.50, and on December 17 of that year obtained a writ of attachment ordering the sheriff to sell "the goods and chattels and real estate of the said John M. Clemens." On the back of this document the sheriff wrote: "Recd this writ Decr 19th 1846 No property found in Marion County on which to levy the within Execution." Very probably by this time the Clemenses had given up not only their house on Hill Street, built upon the lot which James Clemens, Jr., had salvaged for them from an earlier sheriff's sale, but also their furniture, as noted above. This was the ultimate low-water mark of Judge Clemens' fortunes, when he had almost literally no chair nor bed nor spoon that he could call his own. But the case was not settled. On March 11, 1847, at Palmyra, Judge Ezra Hunt of the Circuit Court accepted John M. Clemens' reasonable plea that his own unpaid claims against Beebe be considered as an offset to Beebe's demands upon him — and with that decision the case fades from the records.[22] But the inexorable memory of Sam Clemens, which never forgot the villainy of Ira Stout, also cherished a grudge against Beebe "the nigger trader," who appears as an odious tyrant in the unpublished "Mysterious Stranger in Hannibal." And his son — whom Sam many years later mentioned to Will Bowen, in recalling the days when "Henry Beebe kept that envied slaughter-house, and Joe Craig sold him cats to kill in it," and who lorded it over the other boys' spool cannons with his fine brass artillery — figures in the same fantasy as the school bully, hated by Tom and Huck. He had a fine painted sled that "came from St. Louis, and was the only store-sled in the village." At school he is known as "the new boy . . . whose papa was a 'nigger' trader and rich; a mean boy, he was, and proud of his clothes, and he had a play-slaughterhouse at home . . . and in it he slaughtered puppies and kittens exactly as beeves were done to death down at the 'Point.'" [23] To Sam Clemens the cat-lover this was indeed a sadist. And the scene in this fantasy, in which Henry the school bully dares the Mysterious Stranger to knock a flake of ice off his shoulder and is beaten to a pulp of humiliation, must have been a satisfying one to write.

In the total collapse of their fortunes the Clemenses moved across Hill Street and accepted the invitation of Dr. Orville Grant, that they live with his family over the drugstore at the southwest corner of Hill and Main. In exchange Jane Clemens undertook to board the Grants. This frame house of two and a half stories, later known as the old Levering building, is still standing. With its Greek-revival pilasters painted white, it achieved a classic dignity beyond the cheaper houses huddled along Main Street. Its timbers had been fashioned up the river, destined for the grandiose metropolis of Marion City, but diverted to Hannibal just at the time when Colonel Muldrow's promotional dream was discovered to be a nightmare of the swampy bottoms. Here on the floor of the drugstore old Smarr had breathed his last, and in an upstairs bedroom John M. Clemens soon would end the tragic journey of his life.

But with no prevision of his fate, and something of the invincible optimism of his generation, Judge Clemens believed that better times lay just ahead. On November 5, 1846, the *Gazette* carried the announcement of his candidacy, "at the next August election," for Clerk of the Circuit Court. Even the two-dollar entry fee must have required a little skimping, along with the cost of weekly advertisement in the papers. The incumbent, Rutter, and five other aspirants filed against him. In the late winter a friend signing himself "Senex" — probably his patriarchal friend and fellow Whig, Judge Draper — urged his merits in the *Journal,* praising a citizen "whose clerical skill, business habits and moral character qualify him in an eminent degree for the performance of [the office's] duties. It is scarcely necessary for me to say that I refer to John M. Clemens. So far as I have heard his candidacy meets with general approbation, and I believe that no doubt is entertained of his election." In the same column, another letter signed "Junius" declares that the Democrats are trying to split the Whig majority, in "a desperate effort to appropriate the office of Clerk of the Circuit Court of Marion County," particularly along lines of the traditional feud between Hannibal and Palmyra.[24]

On the same date, the rival *Gazette* printed a communication from "Many Democrats" asserting that despite party ties they favor Clemens, conceiving "Hannibal to be entitled to her share of the offices of the county"; a week later the same newspaper carried a proposal that the Judge's Whig friends refrain from making his candidacy too partisan, pleading that "a man may defend himself against his enemies, but the Gods alone can protect him from his friends." And, adding its appeal on the same day, the *Journal* urged all fair-minded Democrats not to yield to "prejudice" against Judge Clemens. Apparently then his chances were excellent, five months before election day. He was not actually elected, though Mark always claimed in later years that "his splendid new fortune" at long last assured, death struck him down after his return on horseback "half-frozen" from a wintry trip to Palmyra to take the oath of office.[25] This was but a great storyteller's improvement upon the irony of fate.

Quite possibly John M. Clemens had gone to Palmyra for the hearing of his case against Beebe on March 11, and on the way home was overtaken by the sleet storm which numbed him to the bone. Certainly pleurisy set in, succeeded by pneumonia. Day after day he grew weaker. Orion came up from St. Louis to help Jane and Pamela nurse him. Whether in rational or feverish mind, he urged his family to cling to the Tennessee land, the indestructible talisman of hope. But after this mortal chill, medicine could do nothing for his gaunt body, and in a fortnight he was dead, on March 24, 1847. Mark Twain's jottings in "Villagers" sketch the scene:

First instance of affection: discovering that he was dying, chose his daughter from among the weepers, who were kneeling about the room and crying — and motioned her to come to him. Drew her down to him, with his arms about her neck, kissed her (for the first time, no doubt,) and said. "Let me die" — and sunk back and the death rattle came. Ten minutes before, the Presbyterian preacher had said,

"Do you believe on the Lord Jesus Christ, and that through his blood only you can be saved?" "I do." Then the preacher prayed over him and recommended him. He did not say good-bye to his wife, or to any but his daughter.

And then in the manuscript follow two words: *"The autopsy."* They allude to one of the more carefully guarded, because shocking, memories of Sam Clemens' boyhood. He ventured an oblique reference to it in his notebook on October 10, 1903. The entry runs: *"1847.* Witnessed post mortem of my uncle through the keyhole." Since 1847 marked the date of no uncle's demise, but was the never-to-be-forgotten year of his father's death, the true identification is easily made. Orion's lost autobiography told the story in detail, because in those pages William Dean Howells read it. He wrote Mark on June 14, 1880, after the latter had let him see those pages in which Orion had tried painfully, under Mark's exhortation, to tell the whole truth about his own inglorious life — "the autobiography of a damned fool." Orion's candor had also led him to treat other persons and family incidents in the same spirit. Howells found himself both touched and horrified. "But the writer's soul is laid *too* bare; it is shocking," he wrote. " . . . and if you print it anywhere, I hope you won't let your love of the naked truth prevent you from striking out some of the most intimate pages. *Don't* let any one else even *see* those passages about the autopsy. The light on your father's character is most pathetic." [26]

Undoubtedly the thing that happened to the wasted body of Judge Clemens was a post-mortem, not an autopsy, since his death had come through natural causes. His lifelong suffering from mysterious maladies — the excruciating at-

tacks every spring that he had called "sunpain," his nervous
exhaustion and the weak lungs that had sent him in early
manhood to the Cumberland Mountains, and the later years
of self-dosage when he "bought Cook's pills by the box and
took some daily" [27] — this record might well have whetted
a physician's curiosity in days when dissection of the human
cadaver was still a rare and often clandestine privilege. The
family doctor, Hugh Meredith, may have presumed upon his
long intimacy with John M. Clemens to ask this boon of
the widow. Assuredly, for reasons unknown, Sam in later
days nourished some sort of grudge against him. When in
1864 Sam, in far-off Nevada, got news of the old doctor's
death, he wrote his mother a letter which caused Jane Clemens to deal out a mild rebuke: "Sam poor Dr Meredith dont
owe him any ill will. I hope he is happy now for he never
was here." [28] Whatever macabre glimpses young Sam's gaze
of fascination and horror may have caught as he peered
through the keyhole of that death chamber — later unbur-
dening his secret, no doubt, to his elder brother — their effect
can well be imagined upon this sensitive child, so long intim-
idated by the stern man upon whose corpse this last in-
dignity had fallen.

Apparently on good authority, Paine tells how Sam, in a
burst of "heart-wringing" grief and remorse for past dis-
obedience, stood beside his father's coffin and promised his
mother "to be a better boy," with the understanding in
return that he could quit school and soon begin life as "a
faithful and industrious man." [29] Van Wyck Brooks and
others have seen this solemn deathbedside pledge, to obedience, conventionality, and adult responsibility, as the beginning of that "ordeal of Mark Twain" which clipped the
wings of his free spirit. They profess to find confirmation

in the next recorded incident of his young life, when, in the night after his father's funeral and for several nights following, Sam lapsed into his old habit of somnambulism and groped about the house with a sheet wrapped around him, at first appearance terrifying his mother in a way she never forgot. But no doubt the shock of his father's death and the guilty secret of the post-mortem upon which he had spied, had stirred profounder emotional depths within this lad of eleven years than any promise to be a better boy, and its implicit renunciation of freedom.

On the afternoon after his death, March 25, John M. Clemens was buried, with friends and members of the Library Institute present, wearing "the usual badge of crape on the left arm." Even the Democratic *Gazette* eulogized this stalwart Whig for his "public spirit," his "high sense of justice and moral rectitude," and quoted conventional verses:

> Thus man, the sport of bliss and care,
>   Rises on time's eventful sea;
> And having swelled a moment there,
>   He sinks into eternity.

Another Hannibal Whig, Thomas Thompson, immediately stepped into his place as candidate for clerk of the Circuit Court, and four months later was duly elected.[30]

Judge Clemens was buried in the old Baptist Cemetery on a hill about a mile and a half north of the village. Its location, and other details of verisimilitude — including the crazy board fence surrounding it, the high grass and weeds, the worm-eaten headstones with their painted names peeling off, and the wind that moaned in the elms overhead — are reconstructed in *Tom Sawyer*, for that memorable scene in which "young Doctor Robinson" by midnight seeks to get a cadaver for professional purposes, but pays for it with his life.[31] Judge Clemens' grave was marked by a marble head-stone, carved with dates of birth and death, and a hand pointing upward with the legend "Pass'd On" — and this stone, still preserved, in 1876 was transferred with the coffin and that of Henry Clemens to the newer Mount Olivet Ceme-tery southwest of town. To his old schoolmate John Robards, who had offered to oversee the transfer, Mark Twain wrote: "If Henry and my father feel as I would feel under their circumstances, they want no prominent or expensive lot, or luxurious entertainment in the new cemetery. As for a monument — well, if you remember my father, you are aware that he would rise up and demolish it the first night. He was a modest man and would not be able to sleep under a monument." [32] Ever dominated by personal experience, Mark Twain a few months later published a colloquy between two old Connecticut codgers gossiping about the transfer of bodies to a new burial ground — the light handling of this theme creating a chiaroscuro with the dark mood of Mark's last years when he awaited "the precious gift of death." [33]

CHAPTER TEN

THE LITTLE FAMILY

A wag told us the other day," related the Hannibal
Journal of October 12, 1848, "that half of the lawyers
live without a *cause* and die without *effects*." These words
might have served as the punning epitaph of John M. Clemens. The County Court on April 23, 1847, appointed
Orion Clemens administrator of his father's estate. There
was pitifully little to administer. The records show Orion
scraping together a few unpaid justice's fees due his father,
and hopefully writing letters about the sale of the Tennessee
land.[1] After the long depression that trailed the Panic of
'37, Hannibal at last by 1847 found business looking up —
with drays rattling over the streets of "our young city," huge
produce wagons lumbering in from the country, "the
splendid coaches of Messrs. Frink & Co." thundering up
with their passengers, smoke-belching packets calling twice
a day at the wharf, strangers milling about the shops, and
no less than seventy-five persons sitting down at every meal
served by the City Hotel where Judge Clemens' friend Colonel Elgin presided as publican.[2] But with this prosperity
the Clemens family was out of step. Bankruptcy is like
death, wrote a banker shortly before John Clemens' passing,
"and almost as certain; they fall singly and alone, and are

thus forgotten; but there is no escape from it; and he is a fortunate man who *fails young*."[3] But Clemens unhappily had failed in middle life, and destiny allowed him neither luck nor time to recover.

"After my father's death we reorganized the domestic establishment, but on a temporary basis," wrote Mark Twain, "intending to arrange it permanently after the land was sold." Leaving Dr. Grant's house with the pilasters, they moved first to a dwelling that proved too expensive, and then apparently back to the small frame cottage in Hill Street built on James Clemens' lot.[4] The latter still held the title, but as records show, Orion was supposed to pay all the taxes and assessments. As the mainstay of the family, Orion returned to his printer's job in St. Louis, but seems to have come back intermittently and often to Hannibal, where, for example, in the summer of 1847 he taught a Sunday school class and made a Fourth of July oration in a voice "so low (said the newspaper report) that from where we sat, his remarks were inaudible."[5] On one such visit, as Mark Twain remembered with relish, Orion failed to discover that the Clemens family had moved again, and planning to surprise them was himself surprised, after he had slipped silently upstairs and in the dark crept into bed with Dr. Meredith's old-maid sister. And on this or another sojourn in Hannibal, Orion absent-mindedly read until three o'clock in the morning and then unconscious of the hour sallied forth to call upon a young lady, routing instead her father who grimly invited him "to stop to breakfast." Orion's ineptitude — as proverbial as Judge Clemens' but without the latter's dignity — had already become a local legend, and Sam began early to treasure its catalogue of absurdities, which he was later to expand in the mock life story of Orion, the unpublished "Autobiography of a Damned Fool." [6]

Mark Twain's father and his brother Orion were business failures. And by the standards of the times, the Protestant ethic which the author of *The Gilded Age* could not wholly escape, business failure was a sin. These elders whose authority was imposed upon Sam in boyhood — the parent whom he had been compelled to obey and the older brother whose apprentice Sam soon became — had also failed him personally, as they did his mother. Early poverty and debt entered into the soul of this sensitive boy. Long afterward, facing his own sensational bankruptcy and steeling himself to recoup, following the thirty-odd years in which he had been the financial mainstay of his mother, of Orion, and of Orion's wife, Mark Twain harked back to those Hannibal days. To his niece Annie Webster he wrote that his extreme horror of debt came from boyhood memories of the suffering and humiliation it had caused.[7] This emotion lay deep within the constraint he always felt toward his father's memory, intermingled with admiration for his father's unbending integrity in these matters, and the condescension he never outgrew toward Orion, an equally upright but comic figure.

In the months following Judge Clemens' death, "it was pretty hard sledding" for the family, despite Orion's wages in St. Louis and Pamela's fees from piano pupils. As Sam remembered it, he "was taken from school at once upon my father's death and placed in the office of the *Hannibal Courier*," under its proprietor Joseph Ament. But Ament did not set up his *Courier* in Hannibal until 1848.[8] Clearly Mark's memory was playing another of its frequent tricks upon him. His recollection of getting out extras during the Mexican War, particularly after the Battle of Chapultepec in September 1847, furnished the key to this mystery. "Chapultepec — destroyed Extras," reads one such autobiographical scrap. Very probably Sam worked as delivery boy for the *Gazette,* and through the haze of the past this experience blended with his slightly later apprenticeship in Ament's office after the merging of the two papers.[9]

The Mexican War had its memorable impact upon Missouri, home state of Colonel Doniphan and many a less celebrated volunteer. Hannibal raised a company of infantry under Captain Hickman, whose sword, and gray uniform with a yellow stripe down the leg, dazzled Sam and the other schoolboys who followed elatedly in his wake. An "elderly pupil" in the school, Ruel Gridley, did march off to the wars and Sam did not see him again until he turned up some fifteen years later on the sidewalks of Carson City. But other volunteers began trickling back as early as the summer of '47, reporting to stay-at-homes that they had "seen the elephant, trunk, tusk, and all," and were "more than satisfied."[10] In mid-April of that year, to celebrate "the unparalleled victories" of the war, the city fathers had had the town hall illuminated, while the marshal, Captain Bowen, father of Sam's best friend, led a torchlight procession under a huge transparency showing "Old Zac at Buena Vista," martial music blared, and the streets echoed with cheers for "the Missouri boys."[11] Sam Clemens indubitably was there, with his passion for torchlight parades and his longing to be a soldier. But boys of eleven were not wanted, and, as he wrote, "before I had a chance in another war the desire to kill people to whom I had not been introduced had passed away."[12]

Sam looked no older than his years, but having outgrown its sickly days his body was now tough and wiry, tanned and muscular from sun and swimming with playmates in Bear Creek or up at the stillhouse branch. His head, a size too

large, was covered by "a dense ruck" of sandy curls which he
tried to plaster down when wet. Like Tom Sawyer, he "held
curls to be effeminate, and his own filled his life with bitterness." Blue-gray eyes that sometimes looked green, or
opalescent like a cat's, gazed at the world with an appraisal
already keen. The jaw was firm, but the mouth held con-
tours of an engaging grin; the nose was already inclined to
the aquiline. On the farm he wore jeans hitched up with
galluses, and went barefoot all summer; in town, and particularly on Sundays, he probably dressed in a neat round-
about buttoned to the chin, a vast shirt collar, yellow nan-
keen pants, speckled straw in lieu of the weekday slouch hat,
and shoes that had been coated with tallow instead of black-
ing. In his mid-teens Sam began to sport the "cloak of the
time, flung back, lined with bright plaid. Worn with a
swagger. Most rational garment that ever was." An error in
putting on his cloak wrongside out once led his mother to
unmask his deception that he had been to church, when he
had really been out playing with the gang.[13]

His most striking mannerism was the soft-spoken drawl
borrowed from his mother, which she called "Sammy's long
talk." It lent a whimsical turn to what he said, amusing his
playmates even as it diverted audiences in later years when
spoken from the lecture platform, with adroit timing in its
casual surprises and the accompaniment of a deadpan
obliviousness to the climax. In Missouri and the Deep South
it was understood as belonging to a regional eccentricity, but
elsewhere it excited more notice. In his Nevada days Mark
Twain wrote a yarn about meeting an old miner on the
street who said his wife was infatuated with Mark's pieces in
the *Territorial Enterprise,* "and if it warn't that you talk
too slow to ever make love, dang my cats if I wouldn't be
jealous of you." On the other hand, a woman in Hawaii two

years later "thought I was drunk because I talked so long." [14]
Later years somewhat eroded this speech habit in daily talk,
but for humorous effect and upon public occasion he never
abandoned it.

With the death of Judge Clemens and the prolonged
absences of Orion in St. Louis, the head of the little household on Hill Street was Jane Lampton Clemens. No longer
the gay Kentucky belle who at twenty had married the
studious lawyer "to spite another man," and silently accepted
its consequences, she had not escaped the burden of the years,
the bearing of seven children, and the unending struggle
against poverty. Her slight physique she still held proudly
erect, but beneath the auburn curls now beginning to turn
gray, her humorous eyes and mouth held traces of anxiety,
and the impulsive nature that had once hurried her into
wedlock now often found its vent in moods of sharp-tongued
exasperation, and a crack on the skull with a thimble for
wayward Sam. But always its incandescence cooled quickly,
whether toward her children or others, though she never
hesitated to speak her mind in any company. Believing that
a Lampton could do no wrong, she owned only one set of
manners and she used them all the time. For a while she
smoked a pipe, but at length tired of the habit. Her heart —
"always the heart of a young girl," said her famous son —
remained gentle, warm, and generous. A certain grace of
body and mind never forsook her, and despite all mishaps
Jane Clemens, with her sense of fun and chaff, her Southern
charm, her untidy housekeeping and exquisite embroidery,
and her vagaries of grammar and spelling, contrived to
picnic through life. Red she adored, and yearned some day
to dress all in that color. She liked to play cards, and the
theater she loved — although opportunities in these Hannibal days were few — but cared little for concerts, because

she didn't "like anything that's low and solemn." "She **was** of a sunshiny disposition," wrote son Sam, "and her long life was mainly a holiday to her. She was a dancer, from childhood to the end, and as capable a one as the Presbyterian church could show among its communicants. . . . She was very bright, and was fond of banter and playful duels of wit." In Sam, with his badinage and impudence, early and late, she found the perfect foil among her children. Sometimes her literalness was mistaken for humor, as when she listened to a neighbor's story about a man who had been thrown from his horse and killed because a calf ran in his way, and then with genuine interest she asked, "What became of the calf?" [15]

Parades, processions, and funerals she always enjoyed for gregariousness and pageantry's sake,[16] and was a connoisseur — rather than a convert — of religious cults, ranging from the synagogue to the séance. A St. Louis doctor who had not taken a bath for thirty years because he was afraid of losing his magnetic force was a typical object of her inexhaustible curiosity.[17]

Despite the fact that cheerfulness was always breaking in, Jane Clemens wept easily, and had a measure of the Kentucky hill-woman's fascination with direful dreams and the catalogue of human woes — such a tale of deathbeds, funeral notices, disasters, prodigal sons, and the plight of orphans as makes up a typical letter she wrote her "dear children" a few years after their dispersal, about old Hannibal neighbors. "This is a world of trouble," she concludes. "This is a gloomy evening I have written of the troubles of your old friends." [18] Human beings she loved, and the gossip of their doings she adored — the talk of church sociables and quilting bees. Many years later in a casual note her son described it poetically: "The world of gossip of 75 yrs ago, that lies silent, stitched into quilt by hands that long ago lost their taper and silkiness and eyes and face their beauty, and all gone down to dust and silence; and to indifference to all gossip." [19] He often spoke of his mother's gift of "an unstudied and unconscious pathos," along with the unschooled eloquence and the storyteller's art by which she relived her past — a heritage that passed directly to him.

"There was a subtle something in her voice and her manner that was irresistibly pathetic, and perhaps that was where a great part of the power lay; in that and in her moist eyes and trembling lip. I know now that she was the most eloquent person whom I have met in all my days, but I did not know it then, and I suppose that no one in all the village suspected that she was a marvel, or indeed that she was in any degree above the common," he once reflected. "I had been abroad in the world for twenty years and knew and listened to many of its best talkers before it at last dawned upon me that in the matter of moving and pathetic eloquence none of them was the equal of that untrained and artless talker out there in the western village, that obscure little woman with the beautiful spirit and the great heart and the enchanted tongue." [20]

From her Mark Twain drew many of his characteristic attitudes. Playfully he once wrote, "It is at our mother's knee that we acquire our highest and noblest and purest ideals but there is seldom any money in them." [21] She loved animals, rebuked cartmen who beat their horses, refused to trap rats, or kill flies, and adopted waifs and strays on sight. All outcasts enlisted her instant sympathy. Her son liked to tell how she had once been maneuvered into defending the much-maligned Satan, "a sinner . . . like the rest"; he too found the fallen archangel incomparably the most appealing figure in Christian mythology, though probably out of admiration for an arch-rebel. Mark Twain's passionate humanitarianism, his lifelong indignation against bullies and other shapes of overmastering power, came straight from his mother Jane. He liked to tell how in the Hannibal days he once saw her bar the way, with her own small strength, against "a vicious devil of a Corsican" who, a heavy rope in hand, was pursuing his grown daughter who had taken sanctuary inside the Clemens' doorway — and how at last under her tongue-lashing, his foul language dwindled into an apology to "the bravest woman he ever saw," and ever after he was her good friend. From unpublished notes it seems clear that this domestic tyrant was really not a Corsican, but a Pole named Pavey, "a lazy vile-tempered old hellion" whose "wife and daughters did all the work and were treated atrociously" at the seedy little inn called Pavey's Hotel.[22] Jane Clemens, familiar to readers as the Aunt Polly of *Tom Sawyer*, in another fictional recreation is made to declare that " 'I never did think much of those Poles.' She had probably never had an opinion about Poles before, but she was in the humor to hit somebody a thump and the Poles happened to turn up in her head just in time to be useful" — even though prejudice and lasting rancor found no place in her heart, always warmed by "her sex's native sympathy for creatures in distress." [23] Similarly the real Jane Clemens professed to hate Yankees and, from the eve of the Civil War onward, "black Republicans," but meeting them in the flesh and later living amongst them in Fredonia, New York, failed to recognize them as such.

In Orion's absences during these early days of her widowhood, Jane Clemens' mainstay was the next oldest child, Pamela, who returned home and taught "music scollars" (as her mother spelled it). "I have never found any difficulty as yet in getting scholars," Pamela once wrote Orion.[24]

Pamela at twenty had grown into a shy, serious-minded young woman with gray eyes and the curly auburn hair of the Lamptons. Of delicate health, she stayed indoors and read a great deal. Lacking her mother's vigor and sense of humor, Pamela was rarely teased by Sam; when on rare occasions he yielded to temptation in the later years, he soon found himself obliged to tell her he was only joking.[25] In fiction she appears as the gentle cousin Mary of *Tom Sawyer*. Also as fiction may be taken Jane Clemens' recollection in her sunset years that Pamela at the age of five had been stolen from her by Indians; ancestral memories of the Montgomerys and the Caseys in Jane Clemens' blood had probably mastered her sense of veracity.[26]

Beyond any question the family's favorite was Henry — a handsome curly-headed lad with a bright mind and winning sweetness of disposition. Sam, who shared the same bed in these Hannibal days and was in much closer rapport with him than with Orion, always declared that Henry was the flower of the family. He was obedient, industrious, and studious. Family tradition remembered that when Henry was five, a fire broke out in the Clemens household and everybody scrambled for safety; when it was quenched, the child was discovered outside still attentively scanning the book he had been reading. At the age of eleven, so Pamela wrote Orion, "Henry is anxious to have a microscope if it doesn't cost too much." [27] A Lampton cousin in later years always recalled Orion as the absent-minded one, Sam as "a mortal tease," and Henry — who gave her "little keepsakes" — as the lad whom she "loved best of all." [28] His attentive blue eyes looked to parents and his elder brothers with faith and alert obedience, accepting Orion's injunction at their father's grave "that brothers should be kind to each other," no less than Orion's commands and words of encouragement when some three years later Henry went to work in the family printing shop. "But as the boys grew up," wrote Orion, "Sam a rugged, brave, quick-tempered, generous-hearted fellow — Henry quiet, observing, thoughtful, leaning on Sam for protection, — Sam and I too leaning on him for knowledge picked up from conversation or books, for Henry seemed never to forget anything, and devoted much of his leisure hours to reading." [29] At times, asserted Sam, "the unbroken monotony of his goodness and truthfulness and obedience" was a little vexatious, particularly when Henry's sense of duty led him to report Sam's shortcomings to their mother. "He is Sid in *Tom Sawyer*. But Sid was not Henry. Henry was a very much finer and better boy than ever Sid was," but with the same quiet ways, the same innocence that deflected him from "adventurous, troublesome ways." [30] The inescapable odium of the tattletale gathered around Henry's fair curls. And so Henry invited reprisal by his far from model brother. Sam cunningly dared him to jump over a ragged stump, foreseeing with glee that Henry would rip the seat out of his blue velvet breeches. When Henry called their mother's notice to the telltale colored thread on Sam's collar in place of the stitches she had sewed to keep him from going swimming, the latter privately thrashed the informer. This of course is told of Tom and Sid in *Tom Sawyer*. Once Sam caught Henry on the outside stairs and clodded him vivaciously; biding his time, Henry returned the compliment in the harder medium of stone. Still later from the third-floor window of the printing office Sam crowned Henry, passing down the street, with a lush watermelon rind, and once more in an unguarded moment met a well-aimed cobblestone in return. Such spirited revenge, no less than its good marksmanship, raised Henry in Sam's eyes considerably above the level of Sid Sawyer, and between the brothers left no resentment more lasting than the welts it raised.

Despite Mark Twain's impression very late in life that he had stopped school immediately after his father's death and begun work as Ament's printer's devil, this, as we know, is clearly untrue. Sam's age, eleven years and four months, was below that of the customary apprentice. Besides his work as a delivery boy, however, he very likely tried the odd jobs and part-time employment of which he spoke in *Roughing It,* when his recollection was fresher — grocer's clerk for a day, helper in a blacksmith shop, bookseller's assistant "for awhile," and worker in a drugstore "part of a summer." And probably he returned to the Quarles farm as usual for some weeks in the summer of 1847. As for his alleged desertion of the schoolroom, the 1850 census lists Samuel L. Clemens, aged fourteen, and his brother Henry, twelve, as having "attended school within the year." Indeed, Sam was counted twice in that census: as a member of the family of Jane Clemens, and also in the household of Joseph Ament, printer. There seems little question that he continued his education at least until some time in 1849, while helping to support himself by working after hours or between whiles.

Two or three years before his father's death Sam had left the dame school to enroll in the "good common school for boys and girls" kept by a middle-aged Irishman, William O. Cross, up on the public square facing Center Street. Back of this frame house lay a thicket of hazel brush, plum trees, and grapevines that made fine swings. Past the double front door, the street dropped steeply toward the river, making a coasting-hill," as Mark Twain remembered. On icy mornings the boys and girls struggled up Schoolhouse Hill against the wind, some sure to lose their footing and slip on the glaze, to the delight of their companions; and boys who had sleds always brought them along for the fun of coasting home.

Mark once recreated the scene, in a story he never finished. "Sid Sawyer, the good boy, the model boy," trod cautiously; "Tom Sawyer brought his sled, and he, also, arrived without adventure, for Huck Finn was along to help, although he was not a member of the school in these days." And Becky Thatcher was among the pupils in pantalettes. The schoolmaster, here converted from Irish to Scotch, opened the day with prayer and a hymn. Then began the multiplication class and the arithmetic class, and "next came the grammar class of parsing parrots, who knew everything about grammar except how to utilise its rules in common speech." Then followed the spelling class — in which Sam Clemens, a "born speller," in real life shone brightest — and an exercise in Latin for the handful whose parents fancied their offspring upon the pinnacle of learning. But of all the villagers, the schoolmaster alone knew French.[31] His original inspired Sam Clemens to make the first of his few excursions into verse:

> Cross by name and cross by nature —
> Cross jumped over an Irish potato.

This couplet, which Sam's admirer John Briggs chalked boldly on the blackboard at noon, brought down wrath upon the head of the copyist while the poet modestly kept his anonymity.[32]

But the school par excellence of Sam Clemens' youth, immortalized in the pages of *Tom Sawyer,* was that kept by J. D. Dawson, a veteran of fourteen years' pedagogy, as he announced himself, in offering instruction for young ladies and a few boys "of good morals, and of ages under 12 years."

He opened its doors April 14, 1847 — a date that further proves Sam's continuance in school after his father's death.[33] Grateful for all tuition fees, Dawson also admitted several pupils in their late teens and early twenties. As for lads of exemplary behavior, the conspicuously model boy — "we never had but the one," wrote Mark Twain — was the schoolmaster's own son, pop-eyed and "detestably good . . . I would have drowned him if I had had a chance." While Henry Clemens, like Sid Sawyer, approached perfection merely because he was docile, Theodore Dawson, like Willie Mufferson in the novel, added the fatal ingredient of priggishness. For youth, as Mark Twain once observed, "is the prig-time of life." [34] Perfect in deportment, filial piety, and godliness, he obviously satisfied those prescriptions which the Hannibal *Gazette* of December 24, 1846, had laid down "For the Boys": avoid companions who disobey their parents, profane the Sabbath, use "filthy language," "play truant," "are of a quarrelsome temper," "addicted to lying and stealing," maltreat insects and rob birds' nests. Upon most if not all of these counts Sam Clemens, like Tom Sawyer, stood not blameless. Between him and the model boy there was internecine war.

Besides the familiar picture of Dawson's (or Dobbins') schoolroom in the pages of this novel, an unpublished dramatization of the same adds a few fresh lights and shadows:

Enter a scrambling swarm of hot and panting boys and girls in dresses of 40 years ago, and hang up their things and hustle to their places, and go to whispering, cuffing, punching each other, catching flies, giggling, etc. Enter old Dobbins, the schoolmaster . . . a hush falls upon the school, pupils all stare and wait. . . . After Dobbins says "Get to your lessons," he goes into a brown study, and the boys and

girls get to scuffling, pinching, sticking pins in each other —
a boy sits down on a pin, says "ouch!" cuffs his neighbor.
Spit-balls are thrown, peaguns are used, etc., fly-catching
goes on. Buzz of study from some of the better children.

The grammar class begins, and the most glib of the parsing
parrots, Ben Rogers, responds: "Many is an adjective, pos-
sessive case, comparative degree, second person, singular
number, and agrees with its object in number and person."
Turning to arithmetic, the master admonishes Joe Harper:

D. [Dobbins]: Pay attention, now. If A has a barrel of
apples, and sells an eighth of them to B, and a quarter of
them to C, and half of them to D, and gives an eighth of
them to the poor, what remains?
H. [Harper] (Pause) The *barrel*, sir.
D. [Dobbins] (Reflective pause) Correct. — I didn't think
of that. You may go.[35]

Endless were the distractions. The contents of pockets
were stealthily explored, an inventory taken of fishhooks,
twine, white alleys and other "marvels," Barlow knives,
jew's-harps, hunks of maple sugar, birds' eggs, potato guns, and
perhaps "a picture of Adam and Eve without a rag." [36] By
easy association of ideas, the salvage of a piece of shoemaker's
wax instantly suggested the teacher's seat. And there was the
endearing memory of that day when Sam Clemens shared
the antics of a louse that his seat mate Will Bowen had
bought from Arch Fuqua — each trying to stir him up with
a pin, and keep the creature from crossing a line drawn
down the middle of a slate — until Dawson sneaked up
behind and led both boys by the ear up to his throne, and
thrashed the daylights out of them.[37]

But the greatest distraction came in fine weather, when through the open window drifted the drowsy summer sounds from Holliday's Hill, inviting a boy to play hookey as Sam often did, swayed by the sight of idle boys like the Blankenships, "whose fathers ain't able to send them to school," playing and chasing butterflies on the slopes of "that distant boy-Paradise." [38] Recess brought its temporary reprieve, the girls foregathering by themselves while the boys took to games like fox, three-cornered cat, hide-'n'-whoop, spinning of tops and shooting marbles, and playing catch, as well as the swapping and eating of apples, gingerbread, and molasses candy. At noon most of the scholars went home to "dinner." Sometimes there was scuffling, but serious fights were postponed till after school — when the approved ritual of knocking a chip off the shoulder was followed by wrestling, slugging, bloody noses, and torn muddy clothing. For the coward and the sissy, the skulker and poor loser, the sneak and the bully, the liar and the thief at the expense of his schoolmates, the code of boys' town had no use. Its gang, banding together in a romantic conspiracy against the world of adult supremacy, might themselves employ lying as their protective coloration and filch from cupboard and pantry — and in this respect they were quite unlike those paragons which literature like the Rollo Books had long held up to youth's resentful gaze, and whose tyranny Mark Twain himself did so much to end. But at bottom the boys' code of honor was intolerant of meanness, unfair play, and overreaching; rigidly insistent upon personal bravery, simplicity, and democratic camaraderie.

Under this cult, at home and in school, Sam Clemens grew up. If in later years he had any regrets, they came only from the fact that his family sometimes cramped his style. From

Carson City, Nevada, in 1862 he gave Pamela a few words of advice about the upbringing of her Sammy, his namesake:

> As soon as he is old enough to understand you, just tell him, "Now, my boy, every time that you allow another boy to lam you, I'll lam you myself; and whenever a boy lams you, and you fail to pitch into that boy the very next time you see him and lam *him,* I'll lam you *twice.*" And you'll never be sorry for it. Pa wouldn't allow us to fight . . . I warn you to teach Sammy to fight, with the same care that you teach him to pray. If he don't learn it when he is a boy, he'll never learn it afterwards, and it will gain him more respect than any other accomplishment that he can acquire.[39]

At Dawson's school young Sam also encountered "the first Jews I had ever seen. It took me a good while to get over the awe of it. To my fancy they were clothed invisibly in the damp and cobwebby mold of antiquity," recalling the Old Testament, Egypt, and the Pharaohs. These boys were named Levin, and by a jest that never lost its charm nicknamed "Twenty-two": "Twice Levin — twenty-two." [40] Despite the frequent gibes at Jews, their alleged commercial tricks and rapacity, which appear so often in Hannibal newspapers in the latter 1840's, Sam Clemens seems never to have been indoctrinated with this prejudice. He who once shrewdly observed that Jews are human beings — and worse than that he could not say of them — throughout his days regarded them and their ancient culture with sympathy and undisguised admiration.[41] This avoidance of the cheap and ignorant sneer may have been one of the lessons he unconsciously learned in the democracy of Dawson's schoolroom.

CHAPTER ELEVEN

THE GANG

THE AGES of Tom Sawyer and Huck Finn are vague and inconsistent, Bernard DeVoto has remarked. In their forest outlawry, their mischief in the schoolroom, their sham battle, the cure for warts, and the digging for treasure they seem to be about eight or nine. But the Tom who falls in love with Becky and testifies in court, and the boys who camp on Jackson's Island and wrestle with problems of conscience, are clearly twelve or thirteen if not older. The events of these two great books about Tom and Huck are jammed with no apparent break into one long Missouri summer — summer being the season a boy loved and remembered best, because it gave fullest play to his activities in the woods and on the river. The world of *Tom Sawyer* is such pure make-believe — about pirates, robbers, witches, and devils — as to seem clearly more juvenile than most of *Huckleberry Finn,* with its shrewder realism and knotty problems of casuistry. Huck himself, the focus for the second book, plainly is a little older than Tom, and this circumstance helps insensibly to ripen the viewpoint from which his story is told. That is, of course, until Tom waltzes back into the plot, in the later chapters of *Huckleberry Finn,* and once more spins his adolescent fantasy about Nigger

Jim's escape from jail. Consistency of tone, orderly chronology, and careful plotting were never much honored in the
methods of Mark Twain as artist. He proceeded rather by
the "free association" which, as his critic Howells saw, was
often the strength and sometimes the weakness of his genius,
but always its very essence. And in the reservoir of boyhood
memories, from which admittedly he drew practically all the
material in these books, the incidents and personalities of
about ten years were preserved and fused — from about
1843, when Sam emerged from a sickly childhood into active
youth, down to 1853, when he left Hannibal to make his way
in the world.

To disengage this snarl of recollections and reweave the
true sequence of events is not an easy task for the biographer.
Paine did not attempt it; for example, in the same paragraph he told about little Sam's witnessing of the murder of
old Smarr — in January 1845, as court records show — and
the widow's shooting of the marauder on Holliday's Hill,
which by evidence of newspaper files occurred in May 1850.
In undated and unbroken sequence Paine describes the
shock left upon the boy by the discovery of a fugitive slave's
corpse in the morass (August 1847), and the sight of the
stabbed man in the moonlight (November 1843), and the
burning alive of the drunkard in the calaboose (January
1853). The difference in age of the spectator, at these scenes
of violence and terror, is surely a material fact no more to
be neglected than the various inaccuracies wrought by Mark's
recall. Completely to disentangle fact from fantasy, and at
all points to correct the syncopated calendar of memory, is
impossible. But thanks to legal records and old newspapers,
the salient details can generally be reconstructed. And the
labor is justified, because these ten years are the most im-

portant ones, out of the seventy-five in Sam Clemens' life
span, in the quarrying of his two greatest books — books
which remain, in his own luminous phrase, "a hymn to boyhood."

Mark Twain's "St. Petersburg," like Masters' Spoon River
and Sherwood Anderson's Winesburg, was a whole community embalmed with the preservative of the past — the
old small-town Middle America, complete with its epitaphs
of homely joys and domestic tragedies, hopeful youth and
blighted age. In *Pudd'nhead Wilson*, "The Man That Corrupted Hadleyburg," and *The Mysterious Stranger*, its
darker, more cynical themes appear, written when Mark
himself was drifting toward the Great Dark of pessimism and
personal frustration. But at the top of his creative bent he
remembered chiefly the glorious fun of having been a boy,
and even the passing episodes of violence and terror served
but to enhance the security in which a boy's life is rooted and
which weathers all shocks through the infinite powers of
youth's accommodation.

The best-loved experiences of early teen-age days clustered
about the gang, with which the young male animal "trained"
— as they said in those times, in recognition of its real edu-
cative role. The mission of books and teachers was pallid by
comparison. The civilizing pull of womankind — whether
mothers, schoolmarms, or little girls — just now was a force
to be met with either rebellion or shamefaced compromise.
Often the gang spirit broke out in rival camps, recruited
from warring schools or neighborhoods. On Saturday, that
blessed interval between school and Sunday school, came the
big battle. Under such names as the Bengal Tigers or the
Bloody Avengers, in paper hats and clutching tin or wooden
swords, the officers mounted on broomsticks with "one boy

smoking [a] corncob pipe," the gang deployed under a leader whose sash of red, or blue and yellow, was the oriflamme of their advance. In the public square they met and battled. The winners drove the losers down the hill to the slaughter-house, "and lathered them good, and then they surrendered till next Saturday." [1]

Sam Clemens' best friend, his junior by half a year, was Will Bowen, son of Captain Sam Bowen, fire-insurance agent. Will's brothers, Sam and Hart, were also his play-mates; all grew up to realize that dream of Hannibal youth and became pilots on the River. Just now they were care-free boys; certainly the real Will, romantic, sentimental, and mischievous, was one of the prime ingredients in the composite creation of Tom Sawyer. [2] But Will was always Sam Clemens' "first, and oldest and dearest friend." In the spring of 1844, when a virulent epidemic of the measles had swept through Hannibal, causing as many as seven deaths in one day and a seasonal toll of about forty, Sam crawled into the bed of his half-conscious chum — and thus ended the intolerable suspense of waiting for the measles to catch him. He nearly died in consequence, but claimed that he was goaded back to life when the doctor applied bags of hot ashes to his breast, wrists, and ankles. [3]

Several years later, it was Will Bowen who one Saturday afternoon helped Sam Clemens loosen the great boulder on Holliday's Hill. After much sweat they had their reward, and saw it go crashing down the slope, tearing up bushes, scattering a woodpile, leaping over a dray in the road while the Negro driver gazed up in terror, and abolishing a cooper's shop whose workmen swarmed out like bees, before the boys decided it was time to run. [4] And Sam and Will remembered how they used to undress and play Robin Hood in their shirttails with lath swords, in the summer sunshine on the Hill, go swimming, and sometimes go fishing up at "the Bay" miles north of town. Their fun often took a sadistic turn, as when they delighted to lie in wait for Bill Pitts at the pump and "whale him." [5]

Almost as close a friend was John Briggs, a year and a half Sam's junior, who later worked as a stemmer in the tobacco factory and finally became a farmer; his brother Bill more glamorously joined the gold rush in '50, and was later found running a faro table in California. John, the original of adventurous Joe Harper, had also worked hard to pry loose the famous boulder, and had been partners through many a scrape in which Sam was recalled as the ringleader. "We were like brothers once," said Sam on his last visit to Hannibal, putting John in mind of how they once raided the orchard of old man Price, who grew wonderful peaches and had a "raft of bow-legged negroes." "One of those bow-legged negroes set the dogs on us," but the boys drove off the hounds and then chased the black man. "Do you remember, John, that we intended to catch that negro and drown him? Why of course we did." [6] A curious fragment among the Mark Twain Papers tells about John Briggs's devoted Negro lad who took the blame for some "shameful" act John had committed, and to the white boy's horror and remorse was sold down the river.[7]

Norval Brady, four years younger than Sam, was another mischievous member of the band. His father was a carpenter, and in 1845 was chosen first Mayor of Hannibal. Sam Clemens nicknamed him "Gull," because of that favorite, *Gulliver's Travels*. Gull Brady was one of the half-dozen boys, including Sam, who haunted the limestone cave south of town, and "often sat there and discussed what we would do were we a gang of thieves, with a cave as our head-quarters." These boys were also conspirators in a prank, lovingly remembered, involving wholesale distribution of cats inside boxes with detachable lids through all the bedrooms of the Western Star tavern, and the gratifying results caused by escape of these prisoners after the guests at an infare had gone to sleep. Tom Blankenship, original of Huck Finn, was a ringleader in this plot.[8] Barney Farthing, Sam Honeyman, Ed Pierce, and Jimmy McDaniel were also thick as thieves with young Sam Clemens. Jimmy McDaniel, Sam's own age, was envied because his father kept the candy store. To young Sam, running a sweetshop seemed a calling almost as seductive as being a pirate. Jimmy pretended that he didn't care for the stuff, but his bad teeth gave him away. "He was the first human being to whom I ever told a humorous story," Mark recalled. This was the story of Jim Wolfe, a shy apprentice printer from Shelbyville who boarded a while with the Clemenses. One night while Pamela Clemens was giving a candy pull, Sam, who had been sent upstairs to bed, egged on his roommate Jim Wolfe to venture in his nightshirt out on the slippery roof to quell a couple of noisy tomcats, until Jim lost his footing and cascaded down to earth in the midst of the candy pullers. Next morning when Sam related the story, Jimmy McDaniel's uproarious appreciation was such that "I thought he would laugh his remaining teeth out." [9]

Arch Fuqua, about the same age, fellow pupil at Dawson's and son of a tobacco merchant, was envied for a purely personal gift: in summer, when all went barefoot, he could crack his big toe with a snap audible for "thirty yards." The village jeweler's son, Ed Stevens, was handsome and "neat as a cat" but no sissy. Always ready for fun, he led an insurrection that tore down Dick Hardy's stable, as Sam Clemens remembered, and later joined that "rebel company" that lasted for two weeks at outbreak of the Civil War, with the same boyish zest for a lark. The doctor's lad, John Meredith, just now "a meek and bashful boy," under the transformation of that war would become "the cruelest of bushwhacker leaders." And on the other side, George Butler — fun-loving but never quite belonging because he was a Yankee from Massachusetts and wore smart clothes, like a blue suit with leather belt and brass buckle — was destined to become a war hero in Union blue, which was proper enough since he was nephew to General Ben Butler.[10]

Whatever suggested riches, swank, or social superiority was suspect in the little democracy that was Hannibal, "full of liberty, equality, and the Fourth of July." Huck Finn's conviction on the raft that kings are "a mighty ornery lot" chimed with the democratic prejudices of Hannibal, or for that matter any river town. Wasn't it Mike Fink, greatest of river heroes, who in a barroom brawl had kicked out into the street a stranger — not unlike Huck's brummagem lost Dauphin and Duke of Bilgewater — who had claimed the respect due a scion of the Kings of France? Mike had growled, "What if you are a king? Ain't we all kings over here?" And yet, as Mark said of his Hannibal, "you perceived that the aristocratic taint was there." So another boy who did not belong with the gang was Neil Moss, son of the affluent porkpacker, "the envied rich boy of the Meth[odist]. S[unday]. S[chool]." After schooling at Dawson's he was sent to Yale, "a mighty journey and an incomparable distinction. Came back in swell eastern clothes, and the young men dressed up the warped negro bell ringer in a travesty of him — which made him descend to village fashions." This incident furnished the inspiration in *Pudd'nhead Wilson* for high-toned Tom Driscoll's return home from Yale. Drifting off to Nevada, Neil Moss became a panhandler and at last died a defeated man, while his share of the patrimony went to his sister's husband, shrewd lawyer Lakenan.[11]

The rising curve of the success story was more to Hannibal's taste. A popular schoolmate of Sam's, beginning at Mrs. Horr's, was John Garth, son of the tobacconist who taught the boys at Sunday school in the Presbyterian church. John grew up and married pretty Helen Kercheval, daughter of the village tailor, who in later years did not like her father's "trade to be referred to" — that is, after John had grown rich in the tobacco business and banking, in post bellum days becoming Hannibal's leading citizen and host to Mark Twain when in 1882 he revisited these scenes of boyhood.[12] John L. Roberts or Robards, four years younger than Sam Clemens, was another playmate who prospered in later life, changing the spelling of his name to "RoBards" to make it seem finer and more romantic — a trick ridiculed by Mark in "The Private History of a Campaign That Failed" in his yarn about an ambitious youth who transmogrified plain "Dunlap" into "d' Un Lap."[13] John was the son of a flour miller from Kentucky who grew prosperous in Hannibal. According to Sam Clemens, in the days of their schooling at Dawson's, John always won the medal for "amiability" while Sam as invariably won that for "good spelling"; for variety they sometimes swapped. To the gold of '49 "Captain" Robards took a party of fifteen at his own expense, including his little son. John returned with the party around the Horn a year or so later, to become the cynosure of his playmates — with the story of a narrow escape from attack by twelve hundred Indians on the plains. "Rode in the Plains manner," wrote Mark Twain years later, "his long yellow hair flapping. He said he was appointed to West Point and couldn't pass because of a defect in his eye. Probably a lie. There was always a noticeable defect in his veracity . . . a good natured fellow, but not much *to* him. Became a lawyer . . . Procreated a cloud of children. Superintendent of the Old Ship of Zion Sunday School." [14]

A village tragedy that never ceased to fascinate Sam Clemens, with his perennial interest in fate and its caprices, was the case of Tom Nash, a lad of his own age who was the son of old Abner Nash, storekeeper and postmaster — "the aged and needy postmaster, who had seen better days," mentioned casually in *Tom Sawyer*.[15] One winter's night, no doubt in the memorable winter of 1848–49, Sam Clemens and Tom Nash had gone skating on the frozen Mississippi, but hearing the ice breaking up underfoot they sped back toward shore. Sam made the last lap successfully, but Tom in a heavy sweat broke through and plunged into the icy water. As a consequence of the chill he caught "a procession of diseases," ending with scarlet fever that left him deaf and dumb. Sent to the Illinois state institution at Jacksonville, he again learned to talk in the booming tones of the stone-deaf, and delighted Mark many years later — on the latter's last visit to Hannibal — by gesticulating toward the crowd at the station, and roaring in a supposedly confidential aside, "Same damned fools, Sam." [16] Since the census of 1850 reveals that Tom had a younger sister Ellen who was also deaf and dumb, it seems less likely that the icy plunge was actually the cause of Tom's woes, although a scarlet fever epidemic might have been to blame for both.[17] Nevertheless, with the fascination that predestination held for his Calvinist conscience, Mark dwelt much upon his own narrow escape from Tom's fate. In *The Mysterious Stranger* he presented the drowning of young Nikolaus, in his efforts to save a playmate, as more merciful than the alternative which Fate originally had decreed for him — that he catch cold and then scarlet fever, to be left "a paralytic log, deaf, dumb, blind, and praying night and day for the blessed relief of death." Mark's compassionate heart never grew reconciled to the cruel trick that destiny had played upon his boyhood friend.

Poor whites in Hannibal stirred scant interest or sympathy from their adult neighbors of the middle class. Their squalor and shiftlessness branded them as akin to those chill-racked, tobacco-chewing, yellow-faced squatters found in the malaria and ague bottoms of Missouri, or those dirt eaters, pineywoods people, and tattered migrants who haunted all the river towns of the South — often dwelling in shacks or shanty boats or floating down the current on wood-flats. They were the dispossessed wanted by nobody. The Hannibal *Western Union* for May 8, 1851, with Orion as editor, described such a family, a man and wife with four or five children found living in and about a hogshead near the foundry: "A blanket constituted the bedding, a coffee pot and skillet made up the cooking utensils; and a few stones piled up formed a fire place . . . the dirty-faced little cherubs appeared to be as happy as young princes." Later when Dr. Morton presented the town fathers with a bill for medical attendance upon such a family, the council promptly disallowed it, declaring that the "propensity of the man for loafing" exempted the municipality from any responsibility for his luckless brood; nor was there a poorhouse where indoor relief could be sought.[18] Besides, the down-and-outers, being Americans of that day and generation, were by no means servile or disposed to accept patronizing charity. In *Life on the Mississippi* Mark observes that if, in one of his penitential moods he had dared to carry a basket of victuals to the poor, "I knew we had none so poor but they would smash the basket over my head for my pains."

One such family, whose invincible cheerfulness seemed no less a communal scandal than its indolence, is thus sketched in Mark's reminiscent notes: *"Blankenships.* The parents paupers and drunkards; the girls charged with prostitution — not proven. Tom, a kindly young heathen. Bence, a fisherman. These children were never sent to school or church. Played out and disappeared." They lived in a ramshackle old barn of a house on Hill Street — a distance quickly covered by Sam when summoned with stealthy catcalls from Tom. The site is now cherished by the Chamber of Commerce as that of "Huck Finn's home," although the house no longer stands, following several generations of habitation by Negro families whose petty thefts, cutting scrapes, and the didos of a one-time denizen called Cocaine Nell Smith lent it a repute still more dubious than it enjoyed in the Blankenships' day.[19]

Head of the family was Woodson Blankenship, a ne'er-do-well from South Carolina, who fitfully worked at the old sawmill but drank whenever possessed of cash to jingle in his jeans. In 1845 he appears on the roll of tax delinquents as owing twenty-nine cents. His eldest boy Benson, called Bence, did odd jobs but preferred to angle for catfish and tease the playmates of Sam Clemens by knotting their clothes when they went swimming, or clodding them when they came ashore. But he had a kind streak too — probably furnishing the original for Tom and Huck's friend Muff Potter, who loafed and drank, but shared his catch if they were hungry, and mended their kites. In the summer of 1847 Bence befriended secretly a runaway Negro whom he found hiding among the swampy thickets of Sny Island, a part of Illinois's Pike County that hugged the opposite bank of the river from Hannibal. Ignoring the reward posted for the black man, Bence carried food to him week after week and kept mum about his hiding place — thus inspiring that rare tribute to loyalty in *Huckleberry Finn,* in which the homeless river rat rejects all temptations of gain and even elects to "go to Hell" rather than betray his friend Nigger Jim. But one day woodchoppers flushed the fugitive and chased him into a morass called Bird Slough, where he disappeared. Some days later, Sam Clemens, John Briggs, and the Bowen boys were fishing and roaming about the island as they often did — for the sake of its berries, and a fine grove of Illinois pecans such as the woods behind Hannibal did not bear — and made a discovery thus reported in the Hannibal *Journal* of August 19: "While some of our citizens were fishing a few days since on the Sny Island, they discovered in what is called Bird Slough the body of a negro man. On examination of the body, they found it to answer the description of a negro recently advertised in handbills as a runaway from Neriam Todd, of Howard County. He had on a brown jeans frock coat, home-made linen pants, and a new pair of lined and bound shoes. The body when discovered was much mutilated." One account says that the gruesome thing, released from a snag by their poling about in the drift, rose headfirst like an apparition before their eyes.[20] Endless seem the variations upon terror in the boyhood of Sam Clemens.

Among the Blankenships, whose society was a forbidden pleasure and therefore sought as often as possible, Sam's

special joy was the younger brother Tom.[21] Like Huck
Finn, whose image Mark Twain repeatedly identified with
him, Tom was ill-fed, an outrageous wreck of rags, dirty,
ignorant, cheerful, carefree, and altogether enviable, being
"the only really independent person — boy or man — in the
community." [22] Tom went barefoot all the time, both from
freedom and necessity, whereas boys from "quality" families
were forbidden by parents to "come out barefoot" until
warm weather — meanwhile often mocked as "Miss Nancys"
by the more emancipated.[23] The woods and the waters
around Hannibal were his education. Living by his wits,
suspicious of every attempt to civilize him, "to comb him all
to hell," he had none of the unimportant virtues and all the
essential ones. The school of hard knocks had given him
a tenacious grasp on reality, despite his faith in dreams,
omens, and superstitions. But it had not toughened him
into cynicism or crime, and "he had as good a heart as ever
any boy had." The testimony of another witness is interesting, a lad named Ayres, grandson of a pioneer Hannibal
settler named Richmond. Younger than Sam Clemens, he
knew him slightly and was his fellow member in the Cadets
of Temperance, but Tom he knew well and admiringly:

> My grandmother told us that Tom Blankenship was a
> bad boy and we were forbidden to play with him, but when
> we went on a rabbit chase he joined us. . . . Black John (a
> half-grown negro belonging to my grandmother) and Tom
> Blankenship were naturally leading spirits and they led us
> younger "weaker" ones through all our sports. Both were
> "talented," bold, kind, and just, and we all liked them both
> and were easily led by them. We also played down around
> the old Robards mill and the school house in the city
> park.[24]

Long years after, in 1902, Mark heard that his old crony Tom had become justice of the peace and a respected citizen "in a remote village in Montana."

Objects of equal juvenile interest with the Blankenship boys, but naturally less comradeship, were those ultimate dregs of Hannibal society, the village drunkards. Besides old Blankenship himself, the list began with "General" Gaines — an ancient and disreputable relic of the Indian wars, who when full of rotgut used to fancy himself one of the half-man, half-alligator breed, and roar, "Whoop! bow your neck and spread!" like one of the raftmen whose mixture of cockalorum with cowardice Mark hit off in the third chapter of *Life on the Mississippi*. From him the title of town drunkard, "an exceedingly well-defined and unofficial office of those days," descended to Jimmy Finn, who furnished the name and most of the attributes for Huck's pappy. "He was a monument of rags and dirt; he was the profanest man in town; he had bleary eyes, and a nose like a mildewed cauliflower; he slept with the hogs in an abandoned tanyard." Judge Clemens once tried without success to reform him; the Judge's son merely enjoyed him. To Will Bowen in later years Sam recalled how "we stole his dinner while he slept in the vat and fed it to the hogs in order to keep them still till we could mount them and have a ride." [25] It was probably with Jimmy Finn in mind that a town ordinance passed in the spring of 1845 made it a misdemeanor to be "found drunk or intoxicated in any streat, alley, avinue, market place, or public square . . . or found a sleep in any such place not his own." But Finn was not long destined to plague the good citizens of Hannibal. On November 6 of that year, among the county records we find the sum of $8.25 allowed "for making a coffin, furnishing a shroud and burying James Finn a pauper." Mark insisted that he died a natural death in a tan vat, from delirium tremens combined with spontaneous combustion — "I mean it was a natural death for Jimmy Finn to die." [26]

In a scene that Mark once imagined, about the advent of young Satan to Hannibal, occurs the note: "Smiles 'our property' when he sees Injun Joe and Jimmy Finn." [27] The likeness of Injun Joe, the half-breed in *Tom Sawyer*, drunkard and murderer, is probably touched up a good deal from reality. Elsewhere Mark called him "Injun Aleck," said that he "somehow lost his interest" in his mother and hanged her, and hence sentimentalists had hard work of it in persuading the villagers "to accept him as a saint." [28] Judge Clemens tried to reform him too, but Injun Joe sober proved "a dreary spectacle" and fortunately backslid, meeting a bad end that satisfied the purposes of melodrama.[29] That Injun Joe really perished in the cave is improbable, and Mark may even have been mistaken about the fact of his death, because we know of an Osage called Injun Joe, born about 1833 in Oklahoma, in boyhood scalped by Pawnees and left for dead, who in his teens was brought to Hannibal by cattlemen. He lived in a big hollow sycamore on Bear Creek, did his meager cooking at the foot of the trunk, earned a little cash by toting carpetbags between wharf and tavern, wore a red wig to conceal his horrid scar, in later years claimed to remember Sam Clemens, and died in his nineties a respected citizen.[30] His villainy too may have been largely imaginary, his vindictiveness perhaps a memory from the days of Murrell's Gang, whose bloody acts were the common tradition of all river towns in Sam's boyhood.

The mythical Injun Joe's besottedness in the village's

"temperance tavern" serves as reminder that Hannibal in the latter 1840's was a very wet town. It had three distilleries, consumed much, and shipped still greater quantities of whisky up the river to Illinois, Iowa, and Wisconsin.[31] The stillhouse up on the branch, where Tom and Huck dug for treasure, was one of those rectifying plants belonging to the real Hannibal. To dispense liquor Hannibal had at least six groggeries or doggeries. The "rapid growth of the vice of dram drinking and drunkenness in our city" alarmed the editor of the *Journal,* on March 4, 1847, and his hope of a reform movement bore fruit two months later with the organization of a local chapter of the Sons of Temperance. They quickly captured May Day and transformed it into Temperance Day, featuring "cold-water army" parades, addresses on the nobility of abstinence, and songs like "Away the Bowl!" by school choruses; and similarly converted the Fourth of July into even a more moral than patriotic occasion, glorifying "that most blessed of all beverages, pure and sparkling cold water." On "the birth-day of American Liberty" in 1848 it was reported with satisfaction that only "a few, not members of our community" were seen intoxicated on the streets. Orion, an enthusiast for temperance, was occasionally orator of the day; Sam is not mentioned, though his presence and that of his gang is suspected when we read that addresses directed to "the small fry" encountered the difficulty of keeping the youngsters in order, and from pulling and pushing against each other like young steers unaccustomed to the yoke." [32]

In April 1850 a junior adjunct called the Cadets of Temperance was organized in Hannibal, pledged to uproot the tobacco habit. Sam Clemens joined it. As a boy of seven he had been ridiculed for not chewing tobacco, by a strap-

ping sunbonneted girl in the summer school near the
Quarles farm. A year or two later Sam had begun to smoke
— the cheap cigars known as "long nines" and a still ranker
variety known locally as "Garth's damnedest" — as many as
twelve or fifteen a day, but always clandestinely until after
his father died. For a reward of free cigars the boys often
fetched water from the town pump for a "lonely and melancholy little hunchback" who kept shop in the village. Sam
also learned to chew, a manly accompaniment to his growing
emancipation as chore boy and printer's devil. The custom
was almost universal. The Hannibal *Journal* on December
13, 1849, scolded males who attended church seemingly "for
the express purpose of chewing enormous quantities of filthy
tobacco, and flooding the floor with gallons of nauceus [*sic*]
liquid that would make a brute sick to look at" — a complaint as common as that boys and youths were whittling
the benches to pieces, "in the temple of God." But in the
spring of 1850, aged fourteen, Sam Clemens promised "that
I would not smoke during three months" and about the
same time "some one tricked me into making a pledge that
I would stop chewing during thirty days." Renunciation
of the fleshpots came hard, but according to his story (also
applied to Tom Sawyer) he was enchanted with the red
merino sash in which the Cadets paraded, as well as a rosette
and illustrious title which came to him as a personal acco-
lade. Through the two parades on May Day and the Fourth
of July he remained faithful, although phantom cigars
danced through his dreams and he "hungrily fondled the
peeling form" of a plug in his pocket. The roster of Cadets
is still preserved — showing that in this worthy crusade he
had the moral support of Henry Clemens, Tom Nash, Jimmy
McDaniel, John Meredith, and others — but after the name

of No. 1, Samuel L. Clemens, occurs the significant notation "with[d]," no doubt meaning "withheld," or "withdrew." His recollection was that after the second and last parade of the season he resigned, and having picked up a cigar butt from the street, "was smoking, and utterly happy, before I was thirty steps from the lodge door." He also dug out his worn plug and "devoured it like a captive bird set free." With no remorse, he presently increased his cigar allowance to "two hundred a month" by the time he was twenty, briefly swore off at twenty-one, but was soon back on the steady diet — now fully convinced, as he liked to say in later years, that the only sensible rule of abstinence was never to smoke more than one cigar at a time.[33]

CHAPTER TWELVE

ON THE PROWL

THE TOWN had its rowdies — like the Hyde boys, Dick and Ed, older than Sam Clemens' gang. Tough and dissipated, they went armed with pepper-box revolvers, which they occasionally pulled to make some one beg for his life, "a cheap way to build up a reputation, but it was effective." Once Ed held his uncle down while Dick tried to kill him with a pistol that refused fire. "I happened along just then, of course," added Mark Twain. About once a month they got drunk "and rode the streets firing their revolvers in the air and scaring the people out of their wits. They had become the terror of the town." [1] One of the first ordinances passed by the city council in 1845 made it a misdemeanor to disturb the peace "by blowing horns, trumpets, or other instruments, by the rattling or playing organs, drums, tambourines, kettles, pans, tubs, or other sounding vessels . . . and boisterous laughing, bellowing, hallowing, swearing, profane indecent or obscene language." [2] Plainly this ordinance was often violated, in the rough and tough life of a river town. The *Journal* on May 10, 1849, complained that "a gang of boys, black and white . . . are in the habit of congregating themselves about the crossing of Main and Bird streets after dark, and keeping a constant uproar until a late hour of the night, by making use of the most obscene language, and belching forth the most vulgar oaths and imprecations," and threatened these miscreants with the calaboose. Whether Sam Clemens was occasionally involved in these goings-on cannot be known, but the printing office where he was then employed was less than a block away and undoubtedly they did not escape his interest.

Whatever broke the ennui of the village attracted him. Dog fights were among its most dependable amusements. Hannibal's canine population was large. "If a stranger visits our city," said the *Journal,* "the first living creature that welcomes him is a dog; if he leaves the corporate limits, the last living thing that notices him is a dog." [3] The loafers seen by Huck Finn, roosting on dry-goods boxes in front of the stores, chewing tobacco, and whittling with Barlow knives, "laughed at the fun and looked grateful for the noises" whenever a pack of dogs routed a sow, and woke up in earnest whenever a real dog fight started. In one fragment Mark described a village character by writing, "There wasn't anything serious in life to him, he would interrupt a dog-fight if he took the notion." [4] In watermelon season, dogs were often chained in the most tempting patches to frighten off marauders like young Sam Clemens — who had early learned, among other lessons of experience, to tell the green fruit from the ripe before he "hooked" it. [5]

But for adolescents, the three great promises for endless fun and adventure beckoned from Holliday's Hill north of town, the Cave toward the south, and between them the rolling Mississippi with its tributary creeks. Nature had fashioned the setting of Hannibal with peculiar recognition of boyhood's needs and delights, as Mark Twain gratefully remembered when as an author he made them all the property of millions.

Holliday's Hill in those novels is rechristened Cardiff Hill, because — as Mark told the occupant of the old Holliday house, on one of his later visits to the site — it reminded him of a similar hill in Cardiff, South Wales.[6] In his boyhood days, its height of almost three hundred feet seemed "to pierce the skies," like one of the cloud-capped mountains about which he read in school geographies. It belonged to the old Broadax tract, and while its title long remained in dispute its slopes were occupied by a few squatters and many rabbits. Up its flanks the woods grew thick, matted heavily by grapevines, with patches of ragged grass and knobs of boulders such as the one which Sam and his friends dislodged. The wildness of its timber, the sanctuary it offered to game, and the magnificent sweep that it commanded of cornfields and shore and glinting river with the far-off smoke of the steamboats, made the Hill romantic and compelling.

Near the crest lived the Hollidays, their "hill mansion the only palace in the town, and the most hospitable and much the most lavish in the matter of festivities" that Hannibal could boast, as Mark described it in *Tom Sawyer*. Captain Richard Holliday had seen better days, but fell into bankruptcy in 1844 and was appointed justice of the peace to fill an unexpired term, serving concurrently with Judge Clemens. Later he joined the gold rush to California, but died soon after reaching the promised land. His widow, a Virginian whose Scotch father she alleged had been a British general in the Revolution — and whose ivory miniature she wore proudly around her neck — continued to live alone in the old house, with a certain style of threadbare gentility. As the grand old lady of Hannibal she loved to give parties for the young people, with "deadloads" of ice cream, while eagerly casting about for a new husband among the young merchants in town.[7] "Fair, smart, and forty," with her airs of refinement and altogether a generous, well-meaning soul, she is the original of the Widow Douglas in *Tom Sawyer*. In that novel Injun Joe plans to slit her nostrils and notch her ears as a "revenge job," because her late husband as justice of the peace had once had the half-breed whipped publicly, but of course he is frustrated when Huck gives the alarm. In the unpublished fantasy of Tom and Huck among the Indians, mention is made of the ivory locket "of her old ancestors in Scotland" that the Widow Douglas wears.[8] Thus the strong dominion of remembered facts upon the art of Mark Twain. In later years when Sam Clemens was a pilot, Mrs. Holliday sent him to her favorite fortuneteller in New Orleans, Madame Caprell, who had endeared herself to the widow by promising her the long-expected husband whom she never captured. Still later, the poor old lady grew demented, and became a nuisance by appearing on the Clemenses' doorstep wherever they lived and preparing to camp for interminable visits.[9]

In spinning the *Tom Sawyer* incident about Injun Joe's revenge plot against the Widow, and its defeat when Huck summons "the old Welshman" — elsewhere revealed as the Hannibal bookseller John Davies — and two stalwart sons, to fire upon and rout the villain and his ragged confederate, Mark borrowed another leaf from real life. True, it occurred on Holliday's Hill, but both villain and intended victim were substitutes, and the motive was not mutilation but rape or at least sexual affront — something that Mark never would frankly have introduced in a boys' book.[10] The actual happening Mark related in the *Autobiography,* stating that one dark and threatening night he and a companion — John Briggs, he thought — climbed halfway up the hill to eavesdrop while a drunken "young Californian emigrant" yelled "coarse challenges and obscenities" before the door of the "Welshman's house" where lived a respectable widow and her daughter. Armed with a musket, she stood on the porch, gave him warning, and then fired into the night, riddling his breast "to rags." At that instant the storm broke, and the boys fled while "the waiting town swarmed up the hill in the glare of the lightning like an invasion of ants." [11] Joseph Ament's *Missouri Courier* printed a full account of the episode on May 20, 1850. Since Sam Clemens was then working as printer's devil on this paper, it is possible that some of this circumstantial account — which enabled Ament to scoop his rival the *Journal* — came directly from this eyewitness, whether recorded by Sam himself (antedating by two years his first known appearance in print) or by another hand. The account begins:

Caleb W. Lindley, a stranger from Illinois, was shot in this city on Friday night last, by a woman named Weir, a widow, living in a house on Holliday's Hill. He with several others, went to the house of the woman about 11 o'clock at night and demanded admittance, with permission to stay all night. Being refused, they threatened to do violence to the house, if their demands were not gratified. The woman ordered them away, and threatened to shoot, if they did not cease to molest her. One of them, Lindley, bolder than the rest, approached, and told her to "shoot ahead." She accordingly fired, and he fell pierced with two balls and several buck shot. One of the balls passed through the left breast, another entered near the centre of the breast, and several shot took effect in the side and in the wrist, one in the shoulder, one in the abdomen, and one in the front part of the neck. As the man fell, his comrades fled and left him.

Next day the widow was arrested and examined. Testimony showed that she was poor, with several children, and had often received neighborly charity. Nothing appeared "to sustain the public rumor of her ill-fame." After hearing the testimony, the magistrate released the widow, while the attendant crowd responded with "tumultuous applause." The magistrate incidentally was "Esquire Cross," probably Sam Clemens' old schoolmaster, and it is easy to guess that Sam himself was jostling elbows in that crowd.

Still better as a scene for melodrama, real or imaginary, was the limestone cave two miles south of Hannibal, easily reached by skiff or on horseback. A trail thither ran along the willow banks of the Mississippi, skirting the bluff of Lover's Leap, where Mark once dreamed of staging a witches' Sabbath where "Tom and Huck see myriad devils &c." [12] Turning inland half a mile the path ran through a woody hollow and ended at the main entrance to the cave, where a massive iron door had been hung. Discovered in the winter of 1819 by a hunter named Jack Simms, it was first called Simms Cave or sometimes Saltpeter Cave, after the discovery that saltpeter could be made from its deposits of bat guano. In Sam Clemens' boyhood the cave was owned by Dr. E. D. McDowell, who ran a medical school in St. Louis and was famed as "the originator of ovariotomy." In the mid-1840's the eccentric surgeon had stored cannon in the cave, as well as five hundred stand of small arms "for the invasion of Mexico." He also kept there for several years the cadaver of a little girl — said to be his own four-

teen-year-old daughter — in a copper cylinder filled with
alcohol, as an experiment to see whether the limestone
cavern would "petrify" the body. The top of the cylinder
was removable, and according to Mark Twain "the baser
order of tourists" were said to drag the dead face into view
and comment upon it. Another report says that this was
done not from vulgar curiosity but to be sure that the alcohol had not evaporated.[13] Henceforth the caverns were
known as McDowell's Cave, altered in *Tom Sawyer* to
"McDougal's." In *The Gilded Age,* it will be recalled,
Colonel Sellers (Mark's cousin James Lampton) in pre-
siding over his famous turnip dinner declares that turnips
are sovereign against the plague, as he has been assured by
"old Dr. McDowells" of St. Louis. Whether in Hannibal
or St. Louis young Sam Clemens probably met the noted
doctor, since among the unpublished notes he describes
him thus: "great surgeon — contempt for human race —
rough, but at bottom kind." [14] Incidentally, Dr. McDowell
had a son, John, also a physician, whom his father treated
so harshly as to drive him away from home. The young
man took up with Mark's uncle, Dr. James A. H. Lampton,
who in 1849 had married a "loud and vulgar beauty" named
Ella Hunter, and soon opened a meager practice in St.
Louis. "Young Dr. John McDowell boarded with them,"
wrote Mark Twain long afterward in his private notes, "followed them from house to house; an arrant scandal to everybody with eyes — but Jim hadn't any, and believed in the
loyalty of both of them. God took him at last, the only good
luck he ever had after he met Ella. . . . Doctor John and Ella
continued together." [15] Thus the endless tangle of lives
and tragedies in Spoon River.

McDowell's Cave, its limestone labyrinth "dewy with cold

sweat," its sepulchral echoes and dripping waters and flitting bats, and its threat of disaster beyond the rays of a guttering candle, fascinated young Sam. "I got lost in it myself, along with a lady," he wrote in the *Autobiography,* "and our last candle burned down to almost nothing before we glimpsed the search party's lights winding about in the distance." [16] Projected to the peak of terror and garnished with the melodrama of finding the murderer Injun Joe creeping about in the same dark maze, this incident served him well as the climax of *Tom Sawyer.* The treasure buried in the cave was also fictitious, in fact the realization of a fantasy dear to Sam Clemens' gang who, under inspiration of the gold rush in '49, had spent many Saturdays digging for gold in the hollow below the cave's mouth. The discovery of a cement mine in this vicinity many years later beguiled Sam Clemens with the thought that a fortune lay unrecognized under their very noses.[17]

The local steam ferryboat *Hannibal* offered frequent pleasure trips to Cave Hollow, to "explore this remarkable natural curiosity." But the boys usually "borrowed" any idle skiff for the purpose. Boats and the ways of rivercraft were second nature to these young amphibians. Arks, hay boats, keelboats, flatboats, broadhorns, steamboats were as familiar as the makes of automobiles to small-town boys living a century later on some transcontinental highway. The nation's economic lifeblood then flowed north and south more strongly than east and west, and the mighty river that swept past the wharves of Hannibal was thronged by day and night. When the Clemenses first settled there in 1839, the hamlet had been "but a wood-yard, surrounded by a few huts, belonging to some hardy squatters, and such a thing as a steamboat was considered quite a sight," as Sam himself, aged sixteen, wrote in telling a yarn that seems to be his maiden literary effort.[18] But by 1847, the Hannibal *Gazette* reported proudly, over a thousand steamboat arrivals occurred yearly, carrying off produce from the surrounding territory valued at about one and a quarter million dollars. The next year saw the launching of the first steamboat hull "built out and out" at Hannibal, from native white oak, her engines to be installed in St. Louis. Also in 1848 the Scotch shipping magnate of St. Louis, Samuel Gaty, organized a daily service between that city and Keokuk whose "cheap, gaudy packets" as Mark called them — hulls painted Venetian red, with buff shutters, christened with names out of Sir Walter Scott like the *Jeanie Deans, Lucy Bertram,* and *Di Vernon* — galvanized Hannibal into activity twice every day. John Hannicks, the free Negro drayman who always managed to see the first smudge of smoke beyond the point, would yell, "Steeammm-*boat* a-coming!" and cackle with laughter. And the old saddler always went tearing down the street, putting on his coat as he went, then bustling up the gangplank as if in constant expectation of some priceless cargo that never came. Loafers woke up and boys came tumbling — eager to greet the twin-chimneyed boat with her gilded paddle boxes and furnace doors flung open on fires newly stoked with pitch pine to make a brave show, while bells rang and gauge-cocks screamed.[19] It was the most lyric moment of the village day.

The river washed up a certain flotsam of criminal drifters upon Hannibal's shore, so local citizens thought — as they passed ordinances against "all persons who travel about on steam boats . . . for the purposes of gambling," and the "swarm of gentlemen blacklegs who hang around the Coffee Houses ready to . . . fleece any whom they can lure into their meshes." [20] But the growing volume of steamboat traffic also gave the village a window upon the world; the latest newspapers from downriver and the East, new faces and travelers' tales, Mormons fleeing the Gentile wrath at Nauvoo, gold-seekers transshipping to St. Jo, farmers taken aboard complete with their plows and wagons and ox teams.[21] Still more, it fostered restless feet and the fear of appearing provincial. Merchants who made trips to the metropolis of St. Louis were envied by "all the untraveled town," and minor citizens when at last their dreams were realized, stood gawking at the Planters House, the Catholic Cathedral, and the waterfront with its boats sardined at the wharf — marveling that all was just like the pictures they had seen on engraved letterheads. And the return of the native brought its tone of scornful disparagement: "Call *that* a fire-uniform! You ought to see a turn-out in St. L. — blocks and blocks and block [sic] of red shirts and helmets, and more engines and hosecarts and hook and ladder Co's. — my!" [22]

In time, however, a certain sturdy self-regard fortified the civic sense of Hannibal. "If you send a d——d fool to St. Louis, and you don't tell them he's a d——d fool, *they'll* never find it out . . . it's the noblest market in the world for that kind of property," as an old codger told Sam Clemens on the streets of Hannibal in 1882. He was thinking chiefly of "a perfect chucklehead" named Sam Glover, whom Mark had known well in boyhood. He moved to St. Louis in 1849 and eventually became "the first lawyer in the state of Missouri," but Hannibal always stubbornly insisted that he "was a fool and nothing *to* him." In this judgment Mark acquiesced, not alone as a loyal Hannibalian but from conviction, as he expressed it among some miscellaneous notes, that "lawyers are like other people — fools on the average;

but it is easier for an ass to succeed in that trade than any other." [23] And of course Mark, *incognito,* had asked the old codger about Sam Clemens, and claimed he had received a tart reply about "another case of d——d fool. If they'd sent him to St. Louis, he'd have succeeded sooner."

Certainly as a boy he had yearned to join the gay procession of the packets, to become a cabin boy, deck hand, apprentice engineer, or "striker," and as related in *Life on the Mississippi,* jealously regarded one such schoolmate who ran off to follow the river, and returned at last with cash in his pocket and oil on his hair, "an ignorant silver watch," and knowing talk about "St. Looy." According to a reminiscence in *A Tramp Abroad,* at the age of ten Sam had taken his first steamboat voyage — possibly accompanying his father or Orion on a business trip to St. Louis — and with disasters by flood and fire haunting his sleep, in his little shirt had burst into the ladies' saloon under compulsion of a nightmare that the boat was burning up, to be sent back crestfallen to his berth.[24] Certainly the steamboats took their toll of lives. The Hannibal press was filled with constant news of hulls ripped open on snags, boilers bursting with their live steam and tongues of flame, races that ended in collision or other shapes of sudden death. On September 9, 1852, Orion's *Journal* applauded passage of a bill by Congress designed to reduce casualties, by requiring lifeboats on the inland rivers, a life preserver and float for every passenger, forcing pumps, and a quota of fire buckets and axes according to the vessel's size. But the havoc was little abated. And commonly enough, carelessness and violence on river boats left their mute evidence along Hannibal's shore — some person unknown washed up at the mouth of Bear Creek and given a pauper's burial, a man's corpse tangled in driftwood that swam into view in the big rise of '51 but floated off before the coroner arrived, or in the flood of '52 under the red sunrise the apparition of a woman's body "drowned at least a month" clothed in dark bombazine, around her neck "an amulet" which "led to the opinion that she was a Catholic." Captains rarely turned back at the cry of man or woman overboard, we are told, less from indifference than conviction that the boat's wheel seldom missed its mark.[25] It is easy to see why death by water, as well as the cheapness of human life, play so large a part in the world of Tom Sawyer and Huck Finn.

But of course the great river had also its beneficent aspects. "The little steam ferryboat" in which the searching party looks for the lost boys in *Tom Sawyer* was not only Hannibal's mainstay of communication with the opposite Illinois shore, but also its favorite conveyance for picnicking parties and moonlight excursions. In the latter 1840's it was run by Jameson Hawkins, merchant, farmer, and uncle of Laura (Becky Thatcher) and of Sam's boyhood playmate 'Lige. It was no great shakes for glory — that belonged to craft like the *Big Missouri,* which, it will be remembered, Ben Rogers was impersonating when he hove in sight of Tom Sawyer whitewashing the fence — but for purposes of jolly outings could hardly have been improved. To Will Bowen years later Mark recalled how once "I jumped overboard from the ferry boat in the middle of the river that stormy day to get my hat, and swam two or three miles after it (and *got* it,) while all the town collected on the wharf and for an hour or so looked out across the angry waste of 'white. caps' toward where people said Sam. Clemens was last seen before he went down. . . . " One of his unpublished notes says that after "I escaped from ferry boat" a cannon was fired, even as in *Tom Sawyer* and *Huckleberry Finn,* in hopes of raising the drowned body.[26]

In these rolling waters the boys swam and fished, catching mudcat by the dozen and bringing up mussels by the bushel, sometimes finding a pearl in the shell.[27] On Glasscock's Island across from the mouth of Bear Creek, rechristened Jackson's Island in the boyhood idyls, they dug for turtle eggs on the sandy bar, fished for sun perch and bass, cooked bacon over a campfire, smoked their corncob pipes, and lazed in the long summer afternoons. Here was the perfect haven from adult tyranny. Since Robinson Crusoe, fiction has discovered no more blissful isle than Jackson's, and in the 1840's — before the insatiable river devoured it — the fantasy was true. Sometimes, as in the severe winter of 1848–49, the river froze solid, and with shouts the boys skated from shore to shore or played "shinny" on the ice. In the spring, a villager named Davis made it his occupation to catch the floating cakes and store them in his icehouse. The breakup of the ice after a hard winter was a breath-taking sight, as Sam always remembered, with "a moaning and grinding drift and turmoil of monster ice-cakes, which wandered apart at times, by compulsion of the swirling currents, then crashed thunderously together again, piling one upon another, and rising for a moment into rugged hillocks, then falling to ruin and sagging apart once more." [28]

A Sam Clemens growing up in landlocked Florida or elsewhere in the interior of Missouri would have lacked a vital dimension of experience, given him by this greatest of American rivers that swept past his doorway. The Mississippi made him, even in his minority, a citizen of the world, added to his health and resourcefulness, and fostered that appreciation of natural beauty — sunrise and sunset, noon and starlight, the coloration of sky and water — whose stamp appears not only upon *Life on the Mississippi* but all of his travel books from *The Innocents Abroad* to *Following the Equator*. The Father of Waters, in that heyday of the passion for romantic and picturesque scenery, inspired the painting of no less than six monster panoramas in the latter 1840's. To paint the biggest picture in the world was no inappropriate ambition for that spread-eagle era. The most celebrated effort — John Banvard's three-mile strip of canvas showing the Lower Mississippi — was viewed by "admiring thousands" in Louisville, Boston, and New York, as the Hannibal press reported frequently in 1847. Later he went abroad and exhibited it before Queen Victoria. His best competitor, Henry Lewis, contrived to get the entire length of the Mississippi, from the Indian villages of Minnesota to the spires of New Orleans, into a canvas twelve feet high and 1325 yards long. Among his sketches of the Upper Mississippi, made during the summers between 1846 and 1848, Hannibal appears as a cluster of wharves and peak-roofed houses between the promontories of Lover's Leap and Holliday's Hill, with a sailboat in the foreground.[29] But the man whose pen would make Hannibal the treasured property of millions at home and abroad — the nostalgia of Everyman for his lost youth — was still in his barefoot teens.

The secret of that nostalgia and its power over the imagination of others sprang from the spell which these golden days always wrought upon Mark Twain himself. "I should greatly like to re-live my youth, and then get drowned," he wrote half a century later to Will Bowen's widow. "I should like to call back Will Bowen and John Garth and the others, and live the life, and be as we were, and make holiday until 15, then all drown together." [30]

Whether Mark's claim that as a boy learning to swim, he had been rescued in a substantially drowned condition nine times was proof of his notorious luck, as "a cat in disguise," or cause for holding "a grudge" against those "who interfered with the intentions of a Providence wiser than themselves," depended upon his mood.[31] Among his rescuers Mark remembered Neal Champ, Negro servant at the Pavey Hotel; an unnamed slave girl; Charley Meredith, the doctor's son; and an apprentice to old Kercheval the tailor, who saved him from drowning at the age of nine, and "was cursed for it by S[am] for 50 years." [32] From an old-timer's memories it seems that on another occasion Sam and his playmates found Ruel Gridley — the older boy who later joined the colors to fight Mexico — fishing for bullheads in their favorite pond off Bear Creek. To vex him they hurled rocks and sticks into the water, splashing him with mud. In anger he grabbed at the boys and caught Sam, "only a little boy and not quite so active as the others," and pitched him as far as he could out into the deep water. He would have drowned if some men or larger boys had not pulled him out." [33] In *Life on the Mississippi* Mark describes the drowning of a playmate whose real name was Clint Levering, who fell out of an empty flatboat where he was playing, "on a Sunday" — and hence the particular justice of his punishment, which led all the village boys to lie awake that night "repenting." A newspaper account, however, shows that the accident happened on Friday, August 13, 1847, while the ten-year-old boy, "bathing with a number of his playmates, was carried beyond his depth, and in spite of the exertions of those who were with him, was drowned" — "a warning to those parents who permit their children to spend their hours about the water, rowing boats here and there, fishing and bathing, with no one near them to assist in case of accident." [34]   Unidentified remains the German lad called "Dutchy" — from the considerable German population that Hannibal possessed — whose prodigious memory for reciting scriptural verses is mentioned in both *Tom Sawyer* and *Life on the Mississippi*. As if to shake Boyville's faith in a retributive Jehovah, this pious child drowned a few weeks after Clint Levering, according to Sam Clemens, who in the latter book tells how he dived deep to find the body caught among the hoop poles that coopers had sunk to season at the bottom of the muddy creek.[35]

The favorite swimming hole of the gang was in Bear Creek, that meandering tributary to the Mississippi — now almost lost from sight — which in those days emerged from the deep woods to wander through all the southern section of Hannibal, crooking a sharp elbow at the crossing of Market Street with Main. Despite an ordinance of 1845 making it a misdemeanor to "bathe, wash or swim when naked or insufficiently clothed, in the Missippi [*sic*] River or in any other water course, ponds, lakes, or pools of water, within the limits of the City, between one hour before sunrise and one hour after sunset" — these boys knew nothing but the primal freedom of nakedness, even as did Tom and Huck and their companions. Writing of a fictitious tomboy in Hannibal (really basing the sketch on Lily Hitchcock, whom Mark knew years later in San Francisco) the author declared that she "trained with the boys altogether" and "took her full share in all their sports except those of the swimming-hole . . . because bathing-dresses were not worn." [36] Nudity was strictly a male prerogative, and a discreet one; any intimation of the single standard in these matters was unthinkable. Did not the Palmyra *Whig* report the case of a New Orleans woman so "fastidious that she will not change her dress before a lithographic likeness of Gen. Jackson without turning his face to the wall?" [37] A boy's crimson shame over inadvertent exposure of his person was the essence of two favorite adolescent stories of Mark Twain — that of Jim Wolfe's descent in his flying nightshirt amidst the candy pull, and Sam's own gyrations naked while "playing bear" in the moonlight while two girls watched him with secret amusement from behind a screen.[38] In *Tom Sawyer*, Tom surprises Becky catching a stolen look at "a human figure, stark naked" in the schoolmaster's anatomy textbook; when Becky rebukes him for sneaking up on her, in the original version Tom blurts, "How could *I* know it wasn't a nice book? I didn't know girls ever — ," and goes on to reflect upon this curious shame between boys and girls. But unhappily Howells persuaded Mark to expunge this truthful glimpse into adolescent curiosity, the book's only real intimation of sex.[39]

CHAPTER THIRTEEN

INSTRUMENTS OF CULTURE

INDEED the absence of sexuality from Mark Twain's published work has roused comment ever since the Freudian era began. Sophomoric bits of bawdry like *1601*, written for the delectation of Mark's clerical friend Joe Twichell, the speech to the Stomach Club in Paris on "The Science of Onanism," and the Rabelaisian quatrains now preserved in the Yale College Library, were intended strictly for men only, and his lusty "Letters from the Earth" were never meant for publication.[1] But for the general reader — including the young girl, who, as Mark's friend and censor Howells insisted, was the book consumer par excellence in Victorian America — Mark Twain observed the strictest decorum. Only under the protective shield of miscegenation, in the person of the warm-blooded Negress Roxana in *Pudd'nhead Wilson,* is desire even hinted at as a motive for human actions. Not only in those immortal books about boyhood, *Tom Sawyer* and *Huckleberry Finn,* is the illusion of innocence preserved, but even in *Life on the Mississippi,* written about Sam Clemens' adult years aboard those boats which other observers have described as floating brothels. And the heroine of his inmost heart is Joan of Arc, a virgin of unapproachable purity. The root of the matter no doubt is a mixture of personality with environment. Whether that arch-Puritan John Marshall Clemens put the fear of God and an ironclad moral code into the fiber of his impressionable son, a recoil from sex as from something polluting and degrading seems early to have entered Sam Clemens' make-up. Unquestionably the lad grew up in an age and community that largely had repudiated the old sexual frankness of the frontier, with its bundling courtships, horseplay about the nuptial bed, and "camp-meeting babies." [2]

Some of this candor certainly lingered, in the company of men only. The talk of the jug-guzzling raftsmen that Huck overheard — "about differences betwixt hogs and their different kinds of habits; and next about women and their different ways" — was surely no parlor stuff, but so far as the reader learns it glanced imperviously off the boy's mind, as did the obscene antics, so discreetly suggested, of the Duke and the King in "the Royal Nonesuch" played to an all-male audience of Arkansas loafers.

Under the heading "Chastity" Mark Twain afterward recorded, in his notes called "Villagers": "There was the utmost liberty among young people — but no young girl was ever insulted, or seduced, or even scandalously gossiped about. Such things were not even dreamed of in that society, much less spoken of and referred to as possibilities. Two or three times, in the lapse of years, married women were whispered about, but never an unmarried one." About the same time, in the never-finished story he was writing about that tomboy nicknamed Hellfire Hotchkiss, Mark pictured old Aunt Betsy Davis warning the harum-scarum girl in her mid teens that an ugly rumor was going the rounds. A couple of young ruffians — the Hyde brothers, in real life — whom Hellfire had clouted with her baseball bat to keep them from killing a stranger, had deliberately invented it. Since she was always "training" with the boys, these scoundrels alleged, she must have overstepped other conventions too. Even though nobody in the village believed such tales, as Aunt Betsy assured her, Hellfire blazed up with simple indignation and began to think of horsewhips. "There is one kind of gossip that this town has never dealt in before," Aunt Betsy mused, "in the fifty-two years that I've lived in it — and has never had any occasion to. Not in one single case, if you leave out the town drunkard's girls; and even that turned out to be a lie, and was stopped." These were the sisters of "Huck Finn," the Blankenship girls, as mentioned above, whose repute for prostitution was "not proven." In other notes kept by Mark Twain it appears also that Mary Nash, the postmaster's daughter and elder sister of Sam's deaf-and-dumb playmate Tom Nash, was regarded as "wild" and "bad" before her marriage in 1851 to a suitor from Frytown.[3]

Mark Twain's impulse to idealize Hannibal through the haze of years must never be forgotten. That a curious adolescent with a taste for the "low company" of the Blankenships, and tutelage in several newspaper offices, should be wholly unaware of a small town's seamy side is unthinkable. Whether he chose to remember it or not, the town of his boyhood had its stratum of vice. One of its first ordinances passed in the spring of 1845 made it a misdemeanor to "keep, within the City of Hannibal, a Baudy House, or, houses of ill fame, or a house of assignation," as well as a lesser offense to exhibit "any indecent action" of a "stallion, jack, or bull." Nevertheless the *Gazette* some months later declared that "vice, in its worst forms" was making "fearful inroads" in town, reminding the citizens that this license if unchecked might degrade Hannibal to the rank of other river towns like brothel-ridden Louisville or Natchez-under-the-Hill. Asked the editor, "What is to become of the youth now growing up in the city?" [4] Three years later the *Journal* felt improvement had been achieved, boasting that "there is not a more moral, virtuous, and temperate city in the West than Hannibal," its six fine churches outnumbering its four whisky shops, and adding "we hope in another year, to say that there is not a drinking shop or bawdy house in the city." [5] Mark's hypersensitiveness in print, respecting this blot on the civic scutcheon, is disclosed in an afterthought he obeyed in writing *Huckleberry Finn*. Originally, Colonel Sherburn had derided the mob surging against his gate by taunting, "Because you're brave enough to tar and feather poor friendless cast-out women that come along here, lowering themselves to your level to earn a bite of bitter bread to eat." But on revision Mark dropped the last words of this sentence, seemingly as too explicit of their profession. [6]

In general the folkways of Hannibal were as prudish as even Mark himself could have wished. The same *Journal,* on May 16, 1850, reported that the city authorities had charged a leading citizen with "riding through the streets on horseback, with a lady," but acquitted him. The editor jestingly predicted that the municipal fathers would shortly adopt "the Blue Laws of Yankee Connecticut. . . . We understand there will be an ordinance passed very soon, to prevent gentlemen from *kissing* the ladies. Oh! what a country! If this ain't a progressive age, we don't know what is!" The newspapers of the village were filled with badinage about eager old maids, wary bachelors, ways of popping the question, and the like. The sanctions of this society — not "a kissing community," as Mark himself remembered — ran to

courtship without consummation before marriage, and consummation without courtship afterward. Deeply grounded
was the ideal of woman as a paragon of purity, the Divinely-
appointed civilizer of coarse masculine clay. The lady in her
conventional role — and she was nothing if not conventional
— occupied that niche of reverent adoration from which the
Protestant forebears had expelled the Virgin Mary. "God
enshrined peculiar goodness in the form [of woman] that
her beauty might win, her gentle voice invite, and the desire
of her favor persuade men's sterner souls to leave the paths
of sinful strife for the ways of pleasantness and peace," wrote
one local editor in 1846, a few weeks after he had cautioned
the girls that a lady's clothing is always such "that it will not
excite a thought." [7] Orion's editorial career in Hannibal —
which, as a rival remarked, attracted "a host of benevolent
old ladies" ere his paper expired of "water on the brain" —
endorsed these sentiments to the full. Born to be henpecked,
as indeed he was, Orion loved to publish verses describing
Woman as

> A being born to bow and yield,
> Her weakness is her surest shield.[8]

As for his younger brother, Sam eventually outgrew such
saccharine poetry save for sport, but never did he outgrow
the ideal behind it. The influence of his own mother, and of
decorous "Mother" Fairbanks and semi-invalid Livy Langdon in the later years, powerfully re-enforced his conviction
that woman, in her exquisite purity and gentleness, is the
born mentor of the male.

Of course the voice of mild dissent was heard in the land,
and in mid-Victorian Hannibal. The polite arts and graces,

timid and attenuated, that had transformed the pioneer woman into a hothouse flower, were vulnerable to satire. Even Sam Clemens, creator of *Huckleberry Finn*'s Emmeline Grangerford with her tearful quatrains and crayon sketches, could have subscribed to such a "Hint to Girls" as appeared in the village press in 1847: "Frightening a piano into fits, or murdering the King's French, may be a good bait for certain kinds of fish, but they must be of that kind usually found in very *shallow water*." [9] Over the retrospect of time, in limning "the House Beautiful" of the typical river town in his youth, for *Life on the Mississippi* Mark described the parlor with its purely feminine décor: the neat piles of gift books and annuals, goody-goody novels, the current issue of *Godey's Lady's Book*, the wax fruit, the crewelwork and pious mottoes wrought by dainty fingers, the piano with its rack of sentimental music, the Spanish guitar, the simpering family groups perpetrated on canvas, the faded daguerreotypes, the pyramidal whatnot loaded with the clutter of years and egregious bad taste. In "Villagers" he took an inventory of the books — Byron, Scott, Cooper, Marryat, Boz, with "pirates and knights preferred to other society," suggesting his famous argument that the spurious chivalry of Sir Walter had moulded the Southern mind and caused the Civil War. Of the music of the period Mark jotted,

Songs tended to regrets for bygone days and vanished joys: Oft in the Stilly Night; Last Rose of Summer; The Last Link; Bonny Doon; Old Dog Tray; for the Lady I love will soon be a bride Gaily the Troubadour. Bright Alforatan . . . the serenade was a survival or a result of this literature. Any young person would have been proud of a "strain" of Indian blood. Bright Alforata of the blue Juniata got her strain from "a far distant fount." All that sentimentality and romance among young folk seem puerile, now, but when one examines it and compares it with the ideals of to-day, it was the preferable thing. It was soft, sappy, melancholy; but money had no place in it. To get rich was no one's ambition — it was not in any young person's thoughts. The heroes of these young people — even the pirates — were moved by lofty impulses: they waded in blood, in the distant fields of war and adventure and upon the pirate deck, to rescue the helpless, not to make money; they spent their blood and made their self-sacrifices for "honor's" sake, not to capture a giant fortune; they married for love, not for money and position. It was an intensely sentimental age, but it took no sordid form.

Thus Mark Twain, writing after the Gilded Age and the post bellum robber barons, contemplating the idyl of Hannibal in the decade of the Vanderbilt-Marlborough wedding, the heyday of Jay Gould and Mark Hanna, and the imperialist wars.

As for the girl of the period, in the mid-years of the century, she had begun to don hoop skirts, as Mark recalled in "Villagers." They symbolized both her chaste unapproachableness and the sedentary, vegetable life that she was expected to live. The Kentucky girlhood of Jane Lampton Clemens, bold horsewoman, cross-country party goer, and vivacious dancer, had faded into distance. Perhaps the tomboy of whom Mark admiringly dreamed, who broke wild horses and rode them astraddle, and answered fire alarms — whom he placed curiously out of context in the Hannibal of the forties — owed something to his mother, as well as to the gay Lily Hitchcock whom he knew years later in San Francisco. In Hannibal she was plainly a freak, who might well have set gossips' tongues wagging.[10]

Yet even in those days some felt feminization had gone too

far. "We like to look upon a healthy woman — she is a prodigy to the 19th century," wrote the editor of the Hannibal *Gazette,* on April 22, 1847. "Wherever you go, you see scores of spleeny, feeble girls, who can hardly muster courage to make their beds, wash their faces, and drive an intruding cow from the yard." Granddaughters of women who rose with the first streak of dawn and worked like beavers, these exquisites recoiled at thought of fresh air and exercise. Mid-Victorian America, it seems, had been invaded by the vaporings of such genteel females, who shuddered, wept, swooned, and had to be recalled to life by *sal volatile.* Here and there, as rumors of a more assertive spirit penetrated Hannibal — of Lucretia Mott and Elizabeth Cady Stanton and the bloomer girl of the early fifties — a local misogynist would air his suspicions in the papers that a novel type, of Amazonian design, might be in the making, joining the vigor of the pioneer woman to the self-assertion of the new feminist. One "Indignant Bachelor" wrote to Orion's *Journal* June 3, 1852, forecasting women in Congress demanding "appropriations to supply its members with paregoric, Jayne's carminative, sugar plums, &c." He sketched a scene of the new backwoodsman nursing the baby at home, in nervous fear of "some daring housethief or hideous hobgoblin" until his wife returned with unsteady step, summarily quieted the baby and lighted "a fresh regalia."

In these things young Sam Clemens — future creator of such pasteboard females as the political siren Laura Hawkins in *The Gilded Age,* and the ensky'd and sainted Maid of Orleans — took only a casual interest. The only evidence is a squib in his "Assistant's Column" in Orion's *Daily Journal,* May 25, 1853, suggesting that if Miss Lucy Stone "wants to carry a hod, we say, let her alone." To his adolescent mind, femininity meant either a generation of motherly women like Jane Clemens and his teacher Mrs. Horr and the full-blown Mrs. Holliday, or else the little girls in lacy pantalettes and hair ribbons who surrounded him in school. In his attempt to make *Tom Sawyer* into a play he described two such girls, aged about ten, as they appeared around 1844 in a Missouri river village: "Smart summer dresses of fashion of 40 years ago — that is to say, short, with ruffled pantalettes and slippers; aprons coming high on breast, and with ornamented pockets; hair in two long plaited tails down back, ends tied with ribbon. They are nibbling long striped sticks of candy. Broad Leghorn hats, with long broad ribbons. Spit-curl on forehead or in front of ears." After swearing each other to secrecy (" 'deed and 'deed and double 'deed"), Amy discloses her love for Tom Sawyer, while Gracie avows she is the widow of another boy — not that he is dead, but because "I think mourning's nice." She pretends that a ridge of turnips stored for the winter is his grave, and has stood a long piece of stovepipe over it as a monument. But as soon as mourning is over, she plans to get engaged to Joe Harper. He has given her a brass door-knob to plight their troth. "I mean to keep it and love it as long as ever I live. And when I die I want flowers in my coffin, and I want my hands crossed on my breast — so, like Johnny Patterson's was, that died — and I want to hold this door-knob, just so." [11]

In an early fragment published by DeVoto as "Boy's Manuscript" and in *Tom Sawyer*, both the novel and the stillborn play, Mark Twain vividly recaptures the days of calf love: the agonies of boyhood's shyness and the demure coquetry of girlhood, "showing off" as a technique of courtship, the first innocent kiss and the first maudlin billet doux and the first broken heart soon healed by the therapy of fickleness. Significantly, the girl usually represents sense and the boy sensibility. He yearns and pines, weeps secretly, indulges in moody soliloquy like a ham Shakespearean, oscillates between the high heaven of hope and the depths of despond, while she usually keeps her little feet firmly planted upon the earth that he kisses rapturously after she has passed. All this accords with the romantic mould in which Tom Sawyer, like Sam Clemens, was cast — the Tom who dwells in a world of medieval and piratic make-believe, relishes the village grief over his supposed drowning, and nearly swoons upon learning that even such a villain as Injun Joe has been locked in the cave. One recalls Sam Clemens' own testimony, perhaps a trifle exaggerated, of his pleasure in the deathbed rehearsals of his own sickly childhood, his lifelong delight in the trappings of ancient chivalry, and the periodic accesses of remorse and self-accusation which he never outgrew.

"Do you like romances?" Mark wrote to a little girl from Denver named Margaret Blackmer on October 9, 1908.

Very well, here is one. About next Tuesday or Wednesday a Missouri sweetheart of mine is coming here from Missouri to visit me — the very first sweetheart I ever had. It was 68 years ago. She was 5 years old, and I the same. I had an apple, and fell in love with her and gave her the core. I remember it perfectly well, and exactly the place where it happened, and what kind of a day it was. She figures in "Tom Sawyer" as "Becky Thatcher." Or maybe in "Huck Finn" — anyway it's in one of those books. She is bringing one of her granddaughters with her — a grown-up young lady, I guess.[12]

This was Annie Laurie Hawkins, usually called Laura, who had been born in Georgetown, Kentucky, in 1837, and thus was actually two years Sam's junior. In her early childhood her father Elijah ('Lige) Hawkins had moved to Hannibal. At one time they lived almost directly across the street from the Clemenses, in the neat two-story cottage now called the "Becky Thatcher Home," and another time at the corner of Third and Hill, less than a block away. Like Becky, Laura was "a lovely little blue-eyed creature with yellow hair plaited into two long tails, white summer frock and embroidered pantalettes." They were schoolmates together at Mrs. Horr's, and in Miss Torrey's classes. "I can see him in my mind now as we started to our first school together more than sixty years ago," she told an interviewer on the day in 1910 when she received news of Mark Twain's death, "he barefooted and the fingers stained with mulberries as he divided the berries with me, a little girl in calico dress, sunbonnet and pigtails." Another time she recalled that Sam "trained with a gang of boys, and like all boys, they disliked school and often 'played hookey.' Mark Twain was only a commonplace boy. . . . He used to divide his candy and oranges with me and carry my books to school for me. The Clemenses came from very fine stock, but were very poor. . . . As children we considered Mark Twain humorous, not that what he said or the stories he told were particularly so, but he possessed a drawling, appealing voice." [13] She left Hannibal in her mid-teens to attend the Rensselaer Academy at Rensselaer, Missouri, where her roommate — another Hannibal girl named Sara Fuqua — remembered that Laura, like Sam Clemens, walked in her sleep so often that the key to their room had to be hidden. In 1858, while Sam was still a cub pilot on the river, she married a young physician, Dr. James W. Frazer, who during the war was captured by Union troops and condemned to be shot in the notorious "Palmyra Massacre." But at the last moment a young soldier, unmarried, heroically volunteered to take his place, and did so.[14] Laura Hawkins Frazer survived until the age of ninety-one; among her keepsakes was a photograph of Mark Twain, given her on a visit in 1908 to Stormfield — Mark's home in Connecticut — and inscribed, "To Laura Frazer, with the love of her earliest sweetheart." Her name alone he had borrowed for the ill-starred *femme fatale* of *The Gilded Age,* but her true lineaments are those of Tom's Becky.

The first sweetheart who "furnished me a broken heart," Sam Clemens thought, was Mary Miller; she was twice his age, and ignored his existence. Then, according to his *Autobiography,* Sam transferred his suit to Artimisia Briggs, elder sister of his playmate John. She was a year older than Mary Miller, and gently but firmly informed him that she did not want to be "pestered by children," and soon married Sam's Sunday school teacher, the stonemason named Richmond. Here Mark Twain's memory is nothing if not fallible. The 1850 census reveals that she was sixteen years old, and hence Sam's senior by less than two years; the files of Orion's *Journal* disclose that in 1853, a few months before Sam left Hannibal, Artimisia married a man named William Marsh.[15] That Sam underwent the usual crushes upon girls older than he, is clear enough, and to exaggerate their seniority was natural enough. Speaking of John Briggs, local tradition tells how young Sam once went with him, in their mid-adolescent days, to call upon the Willis girls, Julia and Sally, who led a pretty sheltered life. On the way, at Sam's instigation, the boys cooked up a hair-raising piece of news involving a terrible steamboat explosion, to electrify the girls. By prearrangement, John plunged into the yarn and then turned to Sam for confirmation. "Why, this is the first I've ever heard of it," replied Sam, looking blank.[16]

Jennie Brady, sister of Sam's chum "Gull," Mary Bowen, sister of Will and Sam, Kitty Shoot, whose father ran the livery stable, and others were among the "little-girl friends of my early boyhood" whom he never forgot.[17] That he was a favorite with the girls as he grew up into a beau — with his gay spirits, jokes, love of party games and holiday rambles, and the instinctive gallantry with which he treated women all his life — is clear enough. Some of the names of these friends time overlaid with a patina of tragedy or pathos. There was Lavinia Honeyman, whose valedictory oration at school had spoken of that "voice within, which calls us out into the gay crowd . . . to take a post on the busy stage of life." As Mark recorded, she "captured 'celebrated' circus-rider — envied for the unexampled brilliancy of the match — but he got into the penitentiary at Jefferson City and the romance was spoiled," while her younger sister Letitia married another "showy stranger" who turned out a thief and swindler: "She and her baby waited while he served a long term. At the end of it her youth was gone, and her cheery ways." [18]

And there was Mary Moss, the rich pork packer's daughter, "very sweet and pretty at 16 and 17." She fell in love with George Robards, "the Latin pupil" at Dawson's, a pale, slender youth with long black hair that he could toss back in a way much envied by curly-haired Sam Clemens. But her parents broke up the match, and George wandered off to Lima and other far places in South America, and never returned. "Family apparently not disturbed by his absence. But it was known that Mary Moss was." In 1853 her father persuaded her to accept "lawyer Lakenan the rising stranger, held to be a better match. . . . L. made her study hard a year to fit herself to be his intellectual company; then married her, shut her up, the docile and heart-hurt young beauty, and continued her education rigorously. When he was ready to trot her out in society 2 years later and exhibit her, she had become wedded to her seclusion and her melancholy broodings, and begged to be left alone. He compelled her — that is, commanded. She obeyed. Her first exit was her last. The sleigh was overturned, her thigh was broken; it was badly set. She got well with a terrible limp, and forever after stayed in the house and produced children. Saw no company, not even the mates of her girlhood." But long after, in the Indian summer of her widowhood, Mark talked with her in 1902 on his last visit to Missouri, and found her "still beautiful." [19]

In Sam's youth the social life and diversions of the town were simple, hearty, and homespun. Picnics of boys and girls together were gay and innocent, lacking the rigorous chaperonage that a more sophisticated Victorian society might have decreed. "The children were considered safe enough under the wings of a few ladies of eighteen and a few young gentlemen of twenty-three or thereabouts," as Mark wrote in *Tom Sawyer*. The steam ferryboat often carried them downstream to Cave Hollow, with a spread under the oaks and exploration of the Cave to follow. On July Fourth, after the parade of Sunday school classes, Masons, Odd Fellows, Cadets of Temperance, the fire brigade, and "the Fantastics (oh, so funny!)," children and adults ate picnic lunches in the woods or shared a "collation in the cool shade of a tent. Gingerbread in slabs; lemonade; ice cream. Opened with prayer — closed with a blessing." [20] Evening parties were generally candy pullings, sometimes varied with the statelier rites of a cotillion or when the River froze the delirious excitement of spinning from shore to shore behind a sleigh drawn by four horses.[21] On Christmas Day the mayor kept open house and "lots of good cheer" for all comers, and on New Year's the grown-ups and elder youths paid and received calls in "the good old social custom." [22]

Hannibal was much too inconsequential to draw those celebrated troupers on the river circuit who were making Louisville, St. Louis, Memphis, and New Orleans minor capitals of the drama — in drafty playhouse where candles from the boxes dripped upon spectators in the pit, but where Edwin Forrest, Fanny Fitzwilliam, Julia Dean, and Joseph Jefferson were already becoming familiar faces. The hamlets had to satisfy their hunger for the drama as best they could, their appetites whetted as early as the 1830's by William Chapman's rude barge fitted out as a floating theater.

In Palmyra, in the winter of 1836–37 a group of young men calling themselves the Thespian Society began to put on plays over Wise's drugstore, with a drop curtain on which was blazoned in gilt, "Your Smiles, Our Life." Next season a crude theater was built for them. In that time and place no lady could appear on the stage, and feminine roles were taken by men. James Minor, a youth destined for political honors, played Romeo to the Juliet of Presley Lane, dry-goods salesman and future postmaster — a romantic pair probably as convincing as that of Huck Finn's duke and the king mooning over the balcony scene, "soft and sick and languishy." But by 1842, we learn, the Thespians disbanded, discouraged because "the female impersonators had too large beards to perform well." [23] In *Life on the Mississippi* Mark recalls how in his school days a couple of young Englishmen sojourning in Hannibal "one day . . . got themselves up in cheap royal finery and did the Richard III sword-fight with maniac energy and prodigious powwow, in the presence of the village boys" — another favorite in the repertory of Huck's renegades. A cryptic note among further Hannibal memories, "Uncle Tom Cabin '53" may refer to some wandering troupe's offering a year after the appearance of Mrs. Stowe's novel — though its theme could hardly have been popular in slave-owning Hannibal.[24]

In 1845 Hannibal's city fathers penalized anyone daring to "exhibit any indecent or lewd book, picture, statute [*sic*] or other things, or who shall exhibit or perform any immoral or lewd play or other representation." Probably, as one Mark Twain expert has suggested, "The Royal Nonesuch" or "The Burning Shame," as originally called — from which all details are suppressed in *Huckleberry Finn* save that the king came prancing out on all fours as the "cameleopard," naked save for rings and stripes of many-colored paint, and capered to the base instincts of the Arkansas loafers — had to do with a mythical phallic beast known to the old southwest frontier as the "Gyascutus." [25] Although the king and duke "fetched" their loafers by handbills barring ladies and children, the beast was sometimes exhibited a shade more decently. In Palmyra, the *Whig* on October 9, 1845, announced that the Gyascutus is "loose" and the public should be warned. It related that a couple of Yankees roving through the South, finding themselves short of cash and "determined to take advantage of the passion for shows which possessed our people," decided that one should "personate a rare beast, for which they invented the name of 'Gyascutus,' while the other was to be keeper or showman."

At the next village they advertised their find, "captured . . . in the wilds of the Arostook . . . more ferocious and terrible than the gnu, the hyena, or ant-eater of the African desert! Admittance 25 cents, children and servants half price." A great crowd gathered, all agog. Beneath the curtain stretched across a corner of the hall could be seen "four horrible feet, which to less excited fancies would have borne a wonderful resemblance to the feet and hands of a live Yankee, with strips of coonskin sewed round his wrists and ankles." While this monster flapped about and growled, the keeper Jonathan — his pockets heavy with silver — started a lecture on the beast's ferocity, all the while prodding him behind the curtain with a stick. Then came a savage roar, and the warning cry, "Ladies and gentlemen — *save yourselves — the Gyascutus is loose!*" In the pell-mell flight, Jonathan and the Gyascutus retired through the back door. From the old frontier of Missouri, the legendary beast later traveled to the Far West, as newspaper witticisms show. Out there in January 1865 Mark saw some miners on Jackass Hill enact a ribald skit, and jotted cautiously in his notebook in phonetic shorthand, "The 'Tragedians' and the Burning Shame. No Women admitted." [26]

A similar "sell" in Hannibal is reported by Orion Clemens' *Journal* on March 18, 1852, captioned "The ——— Troupe." Sam Clemens' playful touch may be suspected in this account, rather than the heavy hand of Orion. It relates how a few days earlier the town had suddenly blossomed with posters announcing that wonders were imminent at Benton Hall.

> All the little boys in town gazed on the groups of astonishing pictures which appeared on the above mentioned bills, and were thereby wrought up to an intense pitch of excite-

ment. It was to be a real theatre, and the "troupe" (which nobody had ever heard of before,) was so "celebrated." Well, the momentous evening came. Those who enjoyed the felicity of paying a quarter, to see the show, found a large man on the first story, who received the money, and a small man at the top of the second pair of steps, who received the tickets . . . the very persons who were afterwards transformed into heroes and soldiers by the power of paint. In the hall we found forty or fifty of our citizens, sitting in front of a striped curtain, behind which was all the mysterious paraphernalia of the theatre.

When the curtain was pulled to one side, the first appearance on the stage was the large man. . . . He was evidently a novice, and acted his part about as you have seen boys, in a thespian society. He was intended to be a lover of the distinguished danseuse, who played the part of a miss in short dresses, though her apparent age would have justified her in wearing them longer, and we have seen spectacles on younger people. Then the small man, who came in first as a corporal in the army, and then pretended to be drunk, for the amusement of the audience, made up the third character in this burlesque of a farce, the dullness of which was not relieved even by the disgusting blackguardisms with which it was profusely interlarded.

Beyond much doubt, the antics of the king and the duke in *Huckleberry Finn* owe something to the experiences of that night in Benton Hall.

More satisfying glory was brought to Hannibal by an occasional showboat that hove into sight — its band, in brave uniforms, playing on the texas deck, while the sun picked out the brasses, and the calliope throatily piped "Nellie Gray" or "Oh! Susanna" to the echoing woods and hillsides. Hailing the return of Spalding & Rogers' "Floating Palace," fitted up "like a theatre," Orion's *Journal* in the spring of 1853 averred that "no circus company has ever come here with one-half the attractions. Naturally enough everybody is tired of the wandering Arabs who always bring the same old tents, with nothing new under them." Here were mirth, music, pageantry, drama, and "a superior company of actors." [27]

Tom Sawyer and Joe Harper, it will be recalled, happily imitate the routines of the first blackface minstrel to hit their town. Similarly felt the real Sam Clemens: "I remember the first negro-minstrel show I ever saw. It must have been in the early forties. It was a new institution. In our village of Hannibal, on the banks of the Mississippi, we had not heard of it before, and it burst upon us as a glad and stunning surprise." [28] All was captivating: the colloquies of Banjo and Bones with their patter of nonsense ("Now, den, Misto' Johnsing, how does yo' corporosity seem to segashuate?") and their deadly quarrels, the cakewalk, the long dog scratch, the songs comic and gay like "Buffalo Gals," "Camptown Races," and "Old Dan Tucker," or poignant like "Massa's in de Cold Ground," "Swanee River," and "My Old Kentucky Home," whose lines, "De day goes by like a shadow o'er the heart, Wid sorrow where all was delight," haunted Mark Twain. His love for Stephen Foster, Mark never lost. And as for the Negro spiritual, learned still earlier in the Quarleses' slave cabins, his appreciation needed no post bellum discovery by the highbrows that these were works of high art. And in his last days, after disaster and heartbreak had come thick upon him, Mark at Stormfield used to sing, with moving pathos in his fine tenor voice, "Nobody knows de trouble I'se seen," and "Swing low, sweet chariot." His daughter has said his rendering of spirituals was "An emotional outcry, rather than a song." In one of his late unpublished stories Mark pictures his disconsolate hero, in medieval times, visited supernaturally by a Negro banjo player who says, "I gwineter to sing to you, honey, de way de po' slave-niggers sings when dey's sol' away fum dey home en is homesick en down in de mouf." And so he begins, "Way down upon the Swanee River," while the listener miraculously sees "a cabin of logs nestling under spreading trees, a soft vision steeped in a mellow summer twilight." [29]

"Church ain' shucks to a circus," says Tom Sawyer feelingly to Becky, divulging his ambition to grow up and be a clown; after such a treat has come to the village and gone, the gang plays circus continuously for three days "in tents made of rag carpeting." And Huck's delight is equally keen in discovering "a real bully circus" where a supposed drunk lurched into the ring, clung to a horse, and before Huck's incredulous eyes shed his garments one by one to balance giddily as the best equestrian of them all. Sam Clemens had shared all these experiences. After the "shore-nuff circus" had left, he and the gang had set up in business for "six pins admittance," thriving mightily. And in the disenchanted twilight of age he mused upon the vanity of the villagers, wondering "at their interest in life — not worth the trouble; and at their childish ambitions to be circus clowns or kings or constables or Congressmen." It was all one motley make-believe.[30] But in his youth the circus had seemed a passport to paradise. All the river towns had their barns plastered with the bills of yesterday's and tomorrow's troupe. The taprooms of every tavern were covered with the garish chromos, often running up the walls and continued above, with "horses and elephants and musicians all with their heads down like flies from the ceiling," damsels swinging on trapezes and trainers thrusting arms and heads into the lion's mouth, always with a "gaping crowd . . . around one of these mammoth lies." [31]

Mabie's circus arrived in Hannibal in midsummer 1847, with a brass band, "150 men and horses," and the "Great Scotch Giant & Giantess." In October followed Rockwell's with its slack-rope artists, "Tyrolese Vocalists," a clown guaranteed "a perfect gentleman," and as grand finale "the magnificent and gorgeous Gothic spectacle of the Bull Fight." On the Fourth of July 1849, patriotic excitement was compounded by the advent of Raymond's menagerie of lions, tigers, leopards, and cougars, and the next summer saw two visits from Stoke's Mammoth Circus. Dan Rice, impresario of both blackface and circus, was a perennial favorite in Hannibal — although his parodies as "the great Shakesperean clown," in the manner of the travesty on Hamlet's soliloquy that Huck Finn learned from the duke, led one sour "Looker On" in 1848 to describe him as "the great Shakesperean blackguard" whose "dram-shop slang" and "sacrilegious tongue" besmirch "the immortal 'Bard' " with "moral filth and uncleanliness." Nevertheless in May 1853, in the last item that Sam Clemens wrote for his brother's paper before leaving Hannibal, he inserted a plug for Dan Rice.[32] But by the time P. T. Barnum's circus played Hannibal, in September 1853, bringing General Tom Thumb, an armless sharpshooter, wax statuary, ten elephants, and eight beautiful lions — as Orion's paper announced — Sam had already left on his travels, and thus missed crossing the path of enterprise of a master showman who later tried to enlist Mark's wit in advertising the Greatest Show on Earth.[33]

Other blandishments offered by early Hannibal were less apt to quicken an adolescent's blood. In "Villagers" Mark

mentions the Swiss Bell-Ringers. The press reports that in
the early summer of 1850 they gave two of their "chaste,
novel, and select musical entertainments" at the Second
Presbyterian Church. The musical life of the village was
earnest but provincial, revealing no acquaintance with names
like Bach, Mozart, or Beethoven. Mark's derision of grand
opera in *A Tramp Abroad* is pretty clearly the philistinism
of ignorance — which he later modified under occasional
concert-going in the East and abroad, until in his last years
the recorded classical music of the costly orchestrelle at
Stormfield became his daily solace. In the Hannibal days,
however, music meant Coinsky's fiddle — a staple of dances
and charity teas — and "Professor" Holtzermann's brass
band, whose rendition of "Zaff's Gallopade" was much ad-
mired. Amateur concerts, "thinly attended," were sometimes held at the Presbyterian church, featuring favorites
like "There's Many a Rose," "I Wandered by the Brook-
side," the "Cuckoo Solo" on the violin, and as the peak of
aspiration, selections from Rossini on three flutes. "A musical corps of young gents are getting up a string band," announced the *Tri-Weekly Messenger* in December 1852, "with
which to serenade the sleeping demoiselles of our city, these
dull winter nights . . . and occasionally to honor the 'silver
moon.'" The plaintive rendition of *"Ro*-holl on, silver
moo-hoon, guide the *trav*-el-err on his *way"* returned to
mind when Mark wrote the thirty-eighth chapter of *Life
on the Mississippi*. The great artists on tour in mid-century
America heard naught of Hannibal. Jenny Lind's concert
in St. Louis, in March 1851, was excitedly discussed in the
Hannibal press. Sam's fellow printer Urban Hicks "saw
Jenny Lind" and probably talked of it for days; he may
have been the nameless Hannibalian whose letter Orion

published, relating that he had paid ten dollars for his ticket, but felt it was worth every cent: "I am a Jenny Lind man. . . . No mortal, but an angel sings!" [34] Such were the reports from a far country. Young Sam Clemens, in a column briefly undertaken for Orion's *Daily Journal* in May 1853, ungraciously aired the report that the Swedish nightingale's reputation for charity was undeserved, and she "is not near so liberal as she 'used to was.' "

The Innocent who also burlesqued the Old Masters had grown up with the art of lithographs, steel engravings of Leutze and Inman, and local crayon sketches "conceived and committed on the premises by the young ladies." Shortly before Sam left Hannibal, a peripatetic Englishman, George Hare, claiming to be a member of "the Royal Academy of Fine Arts," visited Hannibal. He produced "large and elegant portraits" of lawyer Lakenan and Selmes of the Wild-Cat Store, in probably such depictions of persons "all fresh, raw, and red — apparently skinned," as Mark learned rightly to appraise before writing *Life on the Mississippi*.[35]

This was the age of Manifest Destiny and magniloquent speech, when it was said orators kept the American Eagle so constantly in flight from coast to coast that his shadow wore a trail across the Mississippi Valley. Hannibal too loved the resonant period. Funerary tributes to Old Hickory in the summer of 1845 by loyal Democrats, orations over Old Glory in the halls of Montezuma a couple of years later, a great jubilee rally and illumination of the town in November 1848 to celebrate the triumph of Old Rough and Ready, offered extra dividends to the spellbinders of Independence Day and Washington's Birthday. Thomas Hart Benton, "Old Bullion," was Missouri's favorite statesman and occasional visitor to town, as well as patron of the Hannibal Library Institute. On October 26, 1849, for example, he addressed a large rally of Hannibalians in fiery vein. Obviously Sam Clemens shared Tom Sawyer's emotions when "the greatest man in the world . . . Mr. Benton, an actual United States Senator, proved an overwhelming disappointment — for he was not twenty-five feet high." [36] When Orion entered the sphere of Hannibal journalism, he brought the piety of an ardent Whig to his obituaries of Clay and Webster in 1852, and the loyalties of a protégé to booming Edward Bates of St. Louis for vice-presidential choice on the ticket with Fillmore. But Bates's candidacy blew up — as his namesake the steamboat had done, not long before — and Orion had to wait until Lincoln's election to see Bates come into his own, and gather to himself that modest plum of preferment that sent both Orion and Sam to the Far West in 1861. Politics, however, was an inescapable reality for a newspaper editor's younger brother and assistant growing up in ante bellum Hannibal.

Other sorts of public speaking were plentiful enough. In the autumn of 1851 Orion's paper announced the arrival of Colonel Edward Z. C. Judson, the original "Ned Buntline" and an ardent Filibuster, to lecture on "Cuba and Her Martyrs." At the Christian Church one might hear a disquisition on anatomy, "illustrated by mannekins and plates." And in 1851, a petition signed by Orion Clemens, his rival editor Joseph Ament, postmaster Nash, and others urging the pastors of the Methodist and Christian churches to debate "the points of difference" bore fruit in a series of four doctrinal tussles. Much of the discussion hinged upon a Greek derivation, namely whether "the active transitive verb *bap* is always *dip*" — a naïveté in etymology suggesting the attempt of Huck Finn's king to explain his use of "funeral orgies," "a word that's made up out'n the Greek *orgo,* outside, open, abroad; and the Hebrew *jeesum,* to plant, cover up; hence, in*ter.* So, you see, funeral orgies is an open er public funeral." [37]

Still other types of entertainment, of scientific or pseudo-scientific claims, were better calculated to interest a boy like Sam Clemens. Ventriloquism, phrenology, and the lectures on witchcraft and demonology given by a "Prof. Barton from London" were all popular in his time. During the school vacation, writes the chronicler of *Tom Sawyer,* "a phrenologist and a mesmerizer came — and went again and left the village duller and drearier than ever." On May 6, 1847, reported the Hannibal *Gazette,* at Hawkins' saloon Messrs. Sparhawk & Layton were giving nightly lectures and demonstrations of "human magnetism," admission ten cents. "The subject, (who resides in this city) seemed fully under the magnetic influence." Early in 1849 a Doctor Wood put up at the Brady House, offering to cure diseases by "animal magnetism." Among local citizens, Colonel Elgin fancied he had a great gift for mesmerizing and used it as a parlor trick. Hypnosis, in fact, was all the rage in the latter forties, and local papers loved the joke about some yokel — "a flat-boat Hoosier," according to the superior meridian of Hannibal — who misunderstood the query, "Were you ever in the Mesmeric State?" At one such public exhibition, which he thought was around 1850, and knew was in the month of May, Sam Clemens offered himself as a subject, from envy of the celebrity achieved by Urban Hicks, "our journey-man," who had really fallen into hypnotic trances. Sam pretended to be mesmerized, according to his story, and outdid Hicks. With a rusty old revolver he chased the school bully, who had lately worsted him — incidental evidence that schooldays and printing-shop days overlapped in the youth of Sam Clemens. And by dredging up details from a conversation overheard long ago about Dr. Humphrey Peake's old Southern home, he startled that arch-skeptic into credulity. Despite his denials in later years, Sam's mother refused to believe that he had been faking — remembering Sam's dread encounters with the hypnotist on the street and even the boy's nervous alarm at table if Orion pointed a finger at him, crying, "Make Orion stop! Make Orion stop!" [38]

The family also recalled Sam's neighborhood repute as a "mind reader" and dreamer of premonitory visions. A strain of primitive folk belief in dreams and second sight — gained perhaps from the Quarleses' slaves, perhaps from the backwoods mysticism that entered into the soul of an even greater son of the old frontier, Abraham Lincoln — ran deep in Sam Clemens' nature. Alleged proofs of telepathy and clairvoyance, whether from his own experience or others', never lost their charm. An unpublished sketch called "Clairvoyant" is probably a blend of memory and invention. "When I was a boy there came to our village of Hannibal, on the Mississippi, a young Englishman named John H. Day, and went to work in the shop of old Mr. Stevens the jeweler in Main Street," it begins, referring to the father of Sam's chum Ed Stevens, although of Day himself no independent record can be found. The youth, with eyes like "smouldering fires," kept largely to himself but made a careful study of the villagers. "By and by," continues Mark Twain, "I was apprenticed to the jeweler, and was placed under the tuition of his journeyman . . . I . . . slept in the same room with him every night." Day often sat late and solitary. One summer midnight he sprang from his chair in horror, and snatched his roommate from the bed, crying, "Run! don't stop to dress! Young Ratcliff, the crazy one, is going to murder his mother. Don't tell anybody I said it." So the narrator tore up the deserted street in his nightshirt and "covered the two hundred yards that lay between our shop and the Ratcliff homestead, and was thundering at the ancient knocker of the side door with all my might. Then I came to myself, and felt foolish enough; I turned and looked toward the hut in a corner of the yard [where] young Ratcliff was kept in confinement; and sure enough, here came young Ratcliff flying across the yard in the moonlight, as naked as I was, and I saw the flash of a butcher knife which he was flourishing in his hand. I shouted 'Help!' and 'Murder!' and then fled away. . . ." Soon after he returned to his room, Day came in to report that a crowd had captured the lunatic "after he was inside the house and climbing the stairs toward his mother's room." [39]

That this lurid incident actually happened to Sam Clemens, yet fails to appear in his *Autobiography* and other published writings where a master raconteur could hardly have resisted its inclusion, is doubtful. Yet it must have had some roots, now undiscoverable, in village lore. Dr. James Ratcliff, a Marylander, was a pioneer Hannibal physician in Sam's boyhood. He sat on the first municipal board of health, owned one of the best houses in town, and with his partner, Dr. David Morton, had an affluent practice. The census of 1840 shows that he had one small son and two other boys in their late teens, but that of 1850 indicates that none was living with him. The key to this mystery, with further elucidation of the story above, may lie in Mark Twain's somber account in "Villagers" — written probably in the late nineties — the bleakest tragedy in the Spoon River that was Hannibal:

> *Ratcliffes.* One son lived in a bark hut up at the still house branch and at intervals came home at night and emptied the larder. Back door left open purposely; if notice was taken of him he would not come.
>
> *Another son* had to be locked into a small house in corner of the yard — and chained. Fed through a hole. Would not wear clothes, winter or summer. Could not have fire. Religious mania. Believed his left hand committed a mortal sin and must be sacrificed. Got hold of a hatchet, nobody knows how, and chopped it off. Escaped and chased his stepmother all over the house with a carving knife. The father arrived and rescued her. He seemed to be afraid of his father, and could be cowed by him, but by no one else. He died in that small house.
>
> *One son* became a fine physician and in California ventured to marry; but went mad and finished his days in the asylum. The old Dr., dying, said, "Don't cry; rejoice — shout. This is the only valuable day I have known in my 65 years." His grandfather's generation had been madmen — then the disease skipped to his. He said Nature laid a trap for him: slyly allowed all his children to be born before exposing the taint.[40]

To Mark Twain, child of predestination, and in his later years embittered by the "trap" of circumstance that had mortally stricken his favorite daughter Susy with meningitis and disclosed the taint of epilepsy in her sister Jean, the tragedy of the Ratcliffs held overtones that were inescapably personal.

CHAPTER FOURTEEN

THE PRINTER'S DEVIL

FROM THE TIME that my father died, March 24, 1847, when I was past eleven years old, until the end of 1856, or the first days of 1857, I worked — not diligently, not willingly, but fretfully, lazily, repiningly, complainingly, disgustedly, and always shirking the work when I was not watched. The statistics show that I was a worker about ten years." So wrote Mark Twain in his seventy-second year, remarking that all his later activities — steamboat piloting, mining, reporting, and writing — had been fun rather than labor.[1] The testimony of the 1850 federal census, that Sam Clemens had had some schooling within the year past, as noted above, in addition to many anecdotes of school and of play that belong clearly to the latter 1840's, impeaches the accuracy of his memory that a sharp break between carefree adolescence and workaday drudgery occurred when Judge Clemens died. But part-time employment, as has been suggested, almost certainly entered the daily picture of his life.[2]

In the light of Sam's vivid recollection about helping to get out or deliver the "extras" announcing the victory of Chapultepec in mid-September 1847, it may be significant that on the sixteenth of that month the Hannibal *Gazette* advertised that "An Apprentice to the Printing Business will be taken at this office, if application be made soon. A boy 14 or 15 years old, who can read well; and is from the country would be preferred." A passage near the bottom of the same column, scoffing at the charge of plagiarism made against the Democratic *Gazette* by its Whig rival the *Journal,* seems to evoke the name of the editor's errand boy: "You just cried 'stop thief' in time, neighbor. Here, Sam, take this vest to Minor, and have the buttons sewed on!" Minor Winn was the village tailor — the inference of course being that the *Gazette's* editor had burst his buttons laughing at the absurd accusation. That the jack-of-all-jobs was none other than Sam Clemens is a fair supposition, along with the guess that about this time Sam may have been given the chance to fill an apprentice's shoes, despite his youth and his not hailing "from the country."

The *Gazette* press had lately been moved from "Wild-Cat Corner" to quarters over Brittingham's drugstore, the same office which Joseph Ament acquired along with other assets of the paper in the spring of 1848, and where it is known that Sam Clemens — probably among these assets — did work for that new employer and his *Missouri Courier,* successor to the *Gazette.* The *Gazette* had been launched in November 1846 by Henry La Cossitt, a new arrival in town, who, as was befitting for a Democratic editor, asked his readers to drop the "La" in addressing him. Incidentally, La Cossitt began early to push his circulation in northwest Missouri by securing the services of Sam Clemens' first cousin Ben Quarles and Sam's *accoucheur* Dr. Chowning to be his agents in Florida. The Quarles tie may have been one of the reasons for Sam's employment. But La Cossitt did not prosper, nor strike deep root in Hannibal. In May, 1848, under the plea of ill health, he abandoned the *Gazette* and turned over his equipment to Ament, a young Tennessean who had decided to transfer his *Missouri Courier* from Palmyra to Hannibal.[3]

At the end of May or beginning of June, 1848, Sam Clemens probably went to work for Ament and the new paper. As an apprentice, Mark recalled, he drew no wages, but was entitled to board and two suits of clothes a year. Somewhat bitterly he reflected in his *Autobiography* that the second suit never materialized, while the first consisted of Ament's hand-me-downs — so outsize that "his shirts gave me the uncomfortable sense of living in a circus tent." Some four years later, from the protective cover of Orion's rival newspaper, Sam took pleasure in describing his former boss as a "diminutive chunk of human meat," suggesting exaggeration in the recollections of his old age.[4] No printer is likely to be a hero to his own apprentice, particularly when the latter has the pride, temper, and satiric gift of young Sam Clemens. As for Ament's reputation among his peers, valedictory praise for "his courtesy, and uniformly manly course" from Orion's paper must be set beside a third editor's opinion of him as "the most fretful, peevish, cross-grained, ill-natured, sour-tempered, scolding, obscure little brat we have met with."[5] In the early days of his employment Sam resented Ament's relegation of his three apprentices to feed in the kitchen with the old Negro cook and her mulatto daughter, no less than the stingy fare that drove the lads to raid the cellar for onions and potatoes, which they cooked privately on the printing-office stove. Later they graduated to the Ament family table, where they watched with fascination Mrs. Ament's parsimony in doling out the brown sugar into their coffee. "Mrs. Ament was a bride," runs the *Autobiography*. "She had attained to that distinction very re-

cently, after waiting a good part of a lifetime for it. . . . " [6]
Here again Mark's memory is surely at fault. Almost a year
after moving to Hannibal, on April 12, 1849, Ament took
a bride from Palmyra, Sarah J. Ruff, whose age is given in
the 1850 census as nineteen, seven years less than her husband's. But the census lists, among Sam Clemens and another inmate of the Ament household (a young woman from
Tennessee named Julia Graham), Judith D. Ament, aged
fifty. Perhaps an aunt or much older spinster sister of the
printer was the dispenser of the sugar whose hard-bitten
lineaments Sam cherished so vindictively through the years.

In two unpublished stories — one written in the late
1870's, the other in the latter 1890's — Mark Twain acidly
sketches the character of a small-town printer's wife, who
"had her share of vinegar." In the first she is a dour Calvinist, "a very thin, tall, Yankee person, who came west when
she was thirty, taught school nine years in our town, and
then married. . . . She had ringlets, and a long sharp nose,
and thin, colorless lips, and you could not tell her breast
from her back if she had her head up a stove-pipe hole
looking for something in the attic. She had the only set of
false teeth that had ever been in town, and simple country
people often came to the house and asked to see them."
"Store teeth," "a costly luxury," were truly a curiosity in
early Hannibal.[7] In the second vignette the tyrant of the
apprentices is miserly and meddlesome, "long and lean and
flat-breasted, [with] an active and vicious tongue and a dili-
gent and devilish spirit, and more religion than was good
for her, considering the quality of it." [8] The rancor of these
unlovely portraits stems certainly from experience, pointing
pretty conclusively to the scourge of the Ament household
mentioned by the *Autobiography*. Mark's recollection of

his early schoolteacher, Mary Ann Newcomb, the sharp-tongued spinster who married late, also contributed details to the portrait.[9]

Beyond question his early days as printer's devil held their unhappy memories for Sam Clemens. He says that he slept on a pallet on the printing-shop floor, going to the Ament house only for his meager fare. More than twenty years later, after Mark and his bride settled in Buffalo for the first stable anchorage of their life together, he wrote: "House-keeping is pleasant. I like it much better than boarding, notwithstanding I have done nothing but board since I was thirteen years old." [10] A sense of insecurity and uprootedness entered early and stayed long in his experience, along with familiar knowledge of the greasy, grubby, and bleak tradi-tions of the cheap boardinghouse later sketched in *The American Claimant*. The nearness of his own family, of course, relieved some of Sam's unhappiness in those first months. The Clemenses, as Pamela's daughter Annie said long afterward, "had a very hard time. Almost nothing to live on. My mother never talked about it but she did men-tion it once or twice. Uncle Sam was very lonely at that printer's. They came home late one night and found him asleep on the floor." [11]

Sam's life under Ament was brightened, however, by the presence of a fellow apprentice named Wales McCormick and a "jour" printer called Pet McMurry.[12] The former, a giant of seventeen or eighteen, swaddled and suffocated by the same sizes of castoff clothes that gave Sam a dropsical look, was "a reckless, hilarious, admirable creature" who made rowdy love to the handsome mulatto girl in the kitchen, and had a gourmet's knack of cooking the stolen potatoes. In an unfinished and unpublished version of *The*

Mysterious Stranger, set in an Austrian printing shop soon after the invention of the art, Mark recreated this "wandering comp" who never had "a regular sit" — printer's cant for situation — under the nickname of "Doangivadam." Under all circumstances he "didn't give a damn, and said so. He was always gay and breezy and cheerful, always kind and good and generous and friendly and careless and wasteful, and couldn't keep a cent, and never tried. But let his fortune be up or down you never could catch him other than handsomely dressed, for he was a dandy from the cradle, and a flirt. He was a beauty, and built like Apollo, and was a born masher and knew it. He was not afraid of anything or anybody, and was a fighter by instinct and partiality." Although his temper was slow to ignite, it was "a reliable burner when well going." His baritone voice was equally fine for singing to his own accompaniment or for swearing "in nine languages." Mark always cherished the tale of McCormick's irreverence in setting up a sermon of the great Alexander Campbell — patriarch of the "Campbellites" — and abbreviating the Saviour's name to "J.C.," then when scolded, impishly expanding it into "Jesus H. Christ." [13]

Pet McMurry, a young journeyman who anointed his rolled auburn locks with grease and smoked "Cuba sixes," fancied himself a dandy and cultivated a red goatee and plug hat tipped far over his nose, and walked with a mincing gait.[14] A jolly good fellow, he stood ready to abet Sam and Wales in their pranks but had his conventional moments. In the autumn of 1848 he and that other young village printer, Urban Hicks, took a main share in boosting the Sons of Temperance, and composed a letter of thanks to the young ladies of Hannibal — for the gift of a Bible to their organization — signed "In Love, Purity & Fidelity." [15] Long afterward, Mark recalled the roving "jour" of his youth, his wallet stuffed with one shirt and a hatful of handbills, "for if he couldn't get any type to set he would do a temperance lecture. His way of life was simple, his needs not complex; all he wanted was plate and bed and money enough to get drunk on, and he was satisfied." [16]

A quarter of a century later Mark received a letter from Pet McMurry, recalling those days when Sam himself, "a little sandy-haired boy . . . mounted upon a little box" at the type-case, set type while smoking a big cigar or tiny pipe — all the while interminably singing his song about a comic drunk, or asking Pet to hold his cigar so that he could go "entirely through" that hulking tease Wales McCormick.[17] Sam had begun as a drudge of all work. At first he was green enough to take the customary hazing — of being set to look for "type lice" or dispatched to the village saddler's for "strap oil." But quickly he caught on. He built fires on winter mornings, brought water from the neighborhood pump, swept out the office after picking up yesterday's scattered type from the floor, and as befitted a good devil, sorted out the good for the pi pile from the broken type which he dumped into the hellbox. On Saturdays he wetted down the paper stock and turned it on Sundays. During week days he turpentined the inking-balls, made paste, started up the lye hopper, oiled the platen-springs, manipulated the rollers, and then washed them in the sink along with the forms. With the weekly sheets printed, he folded them and delivered them around town at dawn Thursday — his chief occupational hazard being the short-tempered dogs that saved their spleen for the carrier. The old printing office itself Sam remembered clearly. Its walls were plastered with horse bills, its boxes of type clogged with tallow because the printers propped candles in them at night, and its roller towel "which was not considered soiled until it could stand alone." [18]

In the recollection of these days it was always Mark's humorous purpose to picture himself as the green, lazy, lubberly cub. "When I took a 'take,'" he wrote, "foremen were in the habit of suggesting that it would be wanted 'some time during the year.'" Yet it was Orion's sober testimony that when Sam came to him, he was "swift and clean as a good journeyman," who turned out as good a proof as Henry set a dirty one — so that Sam sometimes worked till midnight making amends for his younger brother, even shedding tears of fatigue and exasperation.[19] That he learned these habits in Ament's shop is a fair assumption. In the fragmentary "Mysterious Stranger" Mark described, with some heat, the slovenly work often perpetrated in a printing shop — one compositor "justifying like a last week's cub," and another "with a click on his rule, justifying like a rail fence, spacing like an old witch's teeth — hair-spaces and m-quads turn about — just a living allegory of falseness and pretence from his green silk eye-shade down to his lifting and sinking heels, making show and hustle enough for 3,000 an hour, yet never good for 600 on a fat take and double leaded at that. It was inscrutable that God would endure a comp. like that, and lightning so cheap." [20] By and large, the compositors were a shiftless, easygoing, rowdy lot, suspicious of hard work or perfection in craftsmanship. In the same sketch he recalled how they liked to express "sarcastic applause" by mocking laughter accompanied by the noise made in sawing their boxes with their composing-rules: "It is the most capable and eloquent expression of derision that human beings have ever invented.

It is an urgent and strenuous and hideous sound, and when an expert makes it it shrieks out like the braying of a jackass."

In such a school of slackness, that set a ceiling upon effort, Sam Clemens nevertheless learned much. The same bright mind and aptitude for techniques that later mastered the calling of river pilot made him, before long, a kind of subeditor on the *Courier*. When Ament was absent Sam took growing responsibilities, including that of rounding up this unreliable editor when more copy was required in the shadow of an imminent deadline.[21] The smell of printer's ink came to seem a good smell in his nostrils — presaging the day when he would begin to write copy himself, and the still more distant times when his appreciation of printers' drudgery would lead him unluckily to sink his fortune in a mechanical typesetter. Another self-made youth, Abraham Lincoln, liked to call the printing shop "the poor boy's college." The phrase was not original with him. Under that caption the Hannibal *Gazette* on April 1, 1847, had observed: "There is something in the very atmosphere of a printing office, calculated to awake the mind and inspire a thirst for knowledge."

Hannibal's literary resources in Sam Clemens' youth were sparse enough. Besides the modest shelves of the Library Institute, a civic responsibility passed on from Judge Clemens to Orion but slowly collapsing, the town offered few contacts with what the world called literature. Although Judge Clemens had bought an occasional book as he could afford it, the impoverished family left after his death probably had nothing to spare for such luxuries — even though Jeff Jerman's bookshop on Main near Hill was less than a block from their door. Three more booksellers and stationers set up business in town in 1850–51. One of them, F. B. McElroy, at the sign of the Big Book, across Main Street from Ament's shop, bravely advertised "histories, biographies, poems, miscellanies, Latin, Greek, and French books, scientific works, juveniles." If anybody in Hannibal could read Greek, or anyone save the schoolmaster knew much Latin or even a smattering of French, the fact has escaped record. The *Southern Literary Messenger* — far superior to "the wishy-washy concerns that issue from the Eastern cities," as the Hannibal *Journal* asserted with some regional pride in July 1848 — is frequently announced for sale, with notice paid its stories by Edgar Allan Poe. And among the torrent of advertisements of tobacco, whisky, guns, ready-made clothes, saddles, cheese, queensware, and remedies for piles and consumption, one meets an occasional plug for *Godey's, Graham's Magazine,* and Philadelphia's *Saturday Evening Post.* The real Hannibal was neither the total cultural desert imagined by Van Wyck Brooks in *The Ordeal of Mark Twain* nor the seat of the muses patriotically conceived by Minnie Brashear in *Mark Twain, Son of Missouri* on the strength of these casual advertisements. The basic culture of Sam Clemens' Hannibal was literate but not literary.

Mark Twain himself remembered the gift books and annuals, the sentimental romances like *Alonzo and Melissa,* the popular minor classics like Ossian and Scott and *Thaddeus of Warsaw,* and above all the languishing love poetry of the time. Curiously enough, two such poems "To Juliet," signed "Mark," appeared in Ament's *Courier* in the summer of 1849. One of them invites the young lady to "be my

Queen of May" and ramble with him over hill and dale, with dreams "as bright as childhood's prayers," or venture in

> our little canoe
> Upon the moonlit starry tide,
> With nervous arm the oar I'll draw,
> Until we reach Missouri's side, —
> And when arrived within the town,
> Our friends half serious, half in glee,
> Will laugh and say, I'm 'done up brown,'
> And I will own the truth to thee.
>
> MARK

An appended note, dated Hannibal, May 1849, hopes these lines will "be understood by the lady to whom they are addressed. I trust she will accept my invitation, and I will be her obliged humble servant, MARK."

Later in the summer, on August 23, the *Courier* printed another salutation to her bearing the same signature:

> My love for thee bright hopes will bring,
> And teach me still to win a name;
> Thy beauty, like perpetual spring,
> Will lure me on the road to fame.

That Sam the apprentice — who loved to print favorite poems on scraps of cotton or silk for his girl friends — could write such lines in his fourteenth year seems possible enough, but that he had already assumed part of his great pseudonym may tax our credulity. Another trifle, however, addressed not to Juliet but to "Sweet Julia, lovely prairie flower," over the signature "C." appears somewhat later in Orion's *Western Union,* and known poems by the cub printer to his girl friends in the same conventional style will be mentioned in their place.[22]

In later years Mark made much of a turning point in his life which happened within the two years of his apprenticeship to Ament. He was going home from the shop one afternoon when the wind blew across his path a stray leaf from a book about Joan of Arc. It described the Maid's persecution in prison by her English captors, a subject likely to enlist the sympathy of one who always hated bullies and championed womankind. According to Paine, Sam took the leaf to Henry, the family bookworm, and found that Joan was a real person. According to Isabel Lyon, Mark Twain's secretary in the later years, he himself told her that he had consulted his mother and received this answer.[23] At all events, he began to read whatever he could find about Joan and medieval history — unconsciously laying the base not only for his *Personal Recollections of Joan of Arc* but also for those enchantments of the Middle Age that inspired *The Prince and the Pauper, A Connecticut Yankee,* and *The Mysterious Stranger,* with their common delight in antique speech along with the pomp and ornament of chivalry, and their common indignation against the tyranny of Crown and Church and the special horror of the heretic's tragedy, death by fire. Most important of all, Mark believed, this stray leaf opened to him the kingdom of literature and its power over the imagination of man. The plodding lessons of Mrs. Horr and Miss Newcomb, of Dawson and Cross, had struck no such spark in Sam Clemens as this discovery made by himself. Paine says that under this fresh stimulus the young printer began to learn a little German by ear from the village shoemaker, briefly tackled Latin, and about five years later was teaching himself French. Meanwhile, as he once stated, he read the Bible through "before I was 15 years old." [24] Certainly the medium in which he worked every day, the printed word, began to hold for him a more personal import.

The last full year that Sam served under Joseph Ament, that of 1849, brought more than its share of excitements to Hannibal. Chief among them were the cholera epidemic, a grim tragedy in local race relations, and the start of the California gold rush. All are reflected upon the pages that Sam Clemens ran through the press, and the second and third at least left their lasting impress upon his memory.

A standard joke, repeated *ad nauseam* in the Hannibal press, reported that its doctors called the town "distressingly healthy." But something of the unwarranted optimism of the spread-eagle era entered into that jest. With the onset of summer, the press was compelled regularly to warn that "the sickly season is near at hand." Along with the slaughterhouse, the stillhouse, and the hog pens, the "pond down by the big elm tree" was a minor plague spot on the local map — associated both with noxious odors and with the breeding of mosquitoes.[25] Mark Twain recalled Bear Creek as "a famous breeder of chills and fever in its day. I remember one summer when everybody in town had this disease at once." [26] These conditions of course were in no wise peculiar to Hannibal. The itinerant artist Henry Lewis, going along the river towns of Missouri and Illinois in 1848, remarked the white-faced children "shaking away bravely," alternately burning up with fever and racked to the bone with chills.[27] Agues and other malarias were so common as barely to excite notice among this sickly yet somehow hardy generation. And Hannibal editors liked to quote the great Doctor Benjamin Rush, who once declared that every new settlement had to pass through "its Bilious period." But the cholera was a graver matter. Its perennial capital was New

Orleans, and every two or three years a virulent outbreak in the Deep South would spread port by port as warm weather advanced and the steamboat traffic carried infection farther and farther up the great River. Boats often moored long enough to bury their dead in shallow graves on the shore. In the late winter of 1849 the Hannibal papers reported with dread an untimely advance of the plague that had already reached St. Louis. In early April "a woman who came passenger on a steamboat" brought the year's first case to Hannibal, but luckily the natives escaped. A month later the papers denied, with some indignation, a rumor spread among the gold-seekers going west concerning a toll of "six to seven deaths per day, by Cholera and Small Pox in Hannibal" — reporting that only the one cholera victim had appeared, and three cases of smallpox among Negro servants of the Brady House. But on June 21 Ament's *Courier* could not deny three cholera deaths within the week, and as the summer ran its course other fatalities occurred, including Sam Honeyman, father of Sam Clemens' playmates. In all, before cold weather fell the mortality was probably less than the thirty deaths Hannibal had witnessed in the summer of 1846, when "very many people" fled the town. Ament's pages recommended "soap and courage" as the best preventives, while the rival *Journal* advised that "a flannel or woollen belt be worn around the belly." Paine's biography states that "Pain killer" — the famous nostrum that Sam Clemens, like Tom Sawyer, once gave to Peter the cat — was also a preventive against cholera, and that Sam had been dosed with it "liberally" for that purpose. Since Aunt Polly compels Tom to swallow a spoonful, that clearly is the way Mark remembered it. But Hannibal's advertisements of Perry Davis' Pain Killer, even in the plague scare of '49, speak only of "bruises, sores, and burns" and commend it plainly for external use — as Peter the cat, if articulate, doubtless would have agreed.[28]

The visitations of Hannibal were not done. In the following winter, 1849–50, the town was ravaged by the equally dreaded yellow fever. Pamela wrote Orion in St. Louis, on January 29: "I suppose you have not been attacked with the yellow fever, that by the way is raging so here that it is feared it will carry off nearly half the inhabitants, if it does [not] indeed depopulate the town. In consequence of it many of our best citizens intend starting for California so soon as they can make preparations." [29] Then in 1851, with summer creeping up the Valley, cholera struck again at Hannibal, carrying off that distinguished-looking old aristocrat Colonel Elgin and twenty-three other citizens, while Orion's columns related on June 5 that steamboats were "burying their passengers at every wood yard, both from cabin and deck." The somewhat grim levity of Mark Twain's reflections, in *Life on the Mississippi*, about inhumation and cremation in times of plague, probably owes something to these early days.[30]

The most spectacular news story of local origin in 1849 was carried by Ament's *Courier* beginning on November 8 under the headline "ATROCIOUS MURDER AND RAPE." A young Negro known as "Glasscock's Ben," a slave owned by Thomas Glasscock, while hauling rock from a quarry through the woods not far from Hannibal, had stopped to commit a crime that sent "a thrill of horror . . . through our whole county." With a rock he had killed a white lad of ten, then raped the boy's sister, aged twelve, and proceeded to cut her throat with a "common Barlow knife." Quickly detected, he was hustled to jail at Palmyra. On December 6, Ament treated his readers to a long account of the trial, at which the Negro was sentenced to death. On January 11, 1850, he was hanged before a huge crowd — the first legal execution in the history of Marion County. His confession at the foot of the gallows was printed as a pamphlet in February by Sam Clemens' enterprising boss, and sold at twenty-five cents a copy. Upon Sam himself the crime left a lurid impression, and probably he intended some day to write a story about it. In "Villagers," he noted: *"The Hanged Nigger.* He raped and murdered a girl of 13 in the woods. He confessed to forcing three young women in Virginia, and was brought away in a feather bed to save his life — which was a valuable property."

Glasscock's Ben is said to have boasted that since he was worth a thousand dollars, the law would never hang him — a claim which suggests the irony of *Pudd'nhead Wilson* in which the colored Tom Driscoll, though a murderer, goes unpunished because as a slave he involves property interests that would disclaim him had he been a white or freedman. In 1901, when contemplating a book about the history of lynching, Mark Twain wrote his publisher Bliss about wanting data on a case to be found in old newspaper files "about 1849, I should say. It may be that this time the negro was not lynched — I can't remember. . . . He raped a young girl and clubbed her and her young brother to death. It was in Marion County, Missouri, between Hannibal and Palmyra. I remember all about it. It came out that his owner smuggled him out of Virginia because he had raped three white women there and his commercial value was deteriorating." [31] That the slave escaped lynching, considering the crime and the hot passions of rural Missouri, was the most remarkable feature of this case.

The third great news story of the year, "the California Yellow Fever," as the Hannibal *Journal* called it, turned into a serial that ran for a long time. Even before the town was electrified by reports of gold, the magnetic pull of the West had long been felt in Hannibal. A picturesque veteran of Lewis and Clark's expedition, 'Peg-leg' Shannon, after belated study of the law had settled there to practice in 1828; later he moved on to St. Charles, Missouri, but returned to Marion County and died in court at Palmyra in 1836.[32] His presence there may have left romantic deposits from the great frontier for Sam Clemens' generation to absorb. At any rate, a fantasy like the unfinished "Tom and Huck Among the Indians," carrying the boys across the plains where they encounter covered wagons and Indians, is some indication of that spell. In those days all the valves seemed to open one way, westward, and the Oregon Trail drew steady rivulets from Hannibal and other river towns of the midlands, to join the main channel that flowed up the Missouri and through St. Joseph. In 1845, reported the press, "the California mania" was rife in Marion County.[33]

The big news from Sutter's Mill quickened the pace. By the last week of 1848, Hannibal editors reported that the "gold dust of California" is "carrying away crowds of our citizens." Early in the new year the local press was filled with claims that California is "perhaps the richest mineral country on the globe," with fantastic wages drawn by laborers, common clerks, and unskilled Kanakas. Cabin class passengers could reach California by way of the Isthmus for $500 apiece, but sailing vessels around the Horn charged only $100 to $150, if one could wait an additional two months to make his fortune. Benjamin Horr, husband of Sam Clemens' first schoolteacher, set out on New Year's Day, fittingly enough a few days after he had gone bankrupt. Scores planned to go in the spring, "as soon as grass grows and water runs." T. R. Selmes advertised a complete outfitting from his Wild-Cat Store, goods "manufactured expressly for the western and California markets . . . step up and encourage Hannibal manufacture — come and see how far we Western B'hoys can beat the Yankees." Editors — while cautioning subscribers not to leave unpaid bills — urged that the road from Hannibal to Independence or St. Jo "is among the best in the western country, and all the streams it crosses are bridged or have ferries," while emigrants would find the town an ideal way station. By mid-April it was reported that the streets were "thronged with California emigrants and teams on their way to the Missouri river," their wagons bearing such blithe legends as

> Although the road is rough and thorny,
> We're on our way to Californy.

Judge Clemens' friend Dr. Meredith took his son Charles along, John Briggs's father joined the trek, Captain Hickman, veteran of the Mexican War, persuaded the Brittinghams to leave their drugstore, and Captain Robards organized a party of twelve including his young son John whom Sam Clemens so keenly envied, riding off into the sunset. In all, some eighty Hannibalians left for the Far West that spring.[34]

First reports were glowing. As Pamela wrote Orion on January 29, 1850, "Nearly all those who went from here last spring have written back that they are making large fortunes in California."[35] But Ament's *Courier*, reflecting probably the editor's dour opinions rather than the subeditor's envy of his old playmates, early took a dim view of the mirage. On May 31, 1849, he chronicled the deaths of six Marion County argonauts on the trail, relating that "new made graves were found strewed along the whole road." Cholera, as well as Indians, took its toll on the plains. After another spring had drained the community of still more hopefuls, Ament observed the "deplorable" effect upon Missouri, in robbing her of "the *producing classes*," foretelling that the great majority would return empty-handed. "The curse of California — to the western States at least — has just begun." [36] Indeed Marion County's population in 1852 showed a net loss of 311 citizens since the census of 1850, for which the gold rush was blamed.[37] The fever was not yet spent; in the spring of '52 the Averill Panorama of the overland route to the mines was being shown nightly in Hannibal, supplanting that earlier enthusiasm for panoramas of the Mississippi. But the tide unmistakably was turning. The year 1851 brought back Dr. Meredith and Captain Robards with their parties, wiser but not conspicuously richer. Two years later Orion's *Journal* — the newspaper Joe Buchanan had abandoned — printed a California letter from C. C. Brady relating that "many old miners who came out in '48 and '49 are still here, and as poor as ever . . . the mining is gradually working into the hands of capitalists. . . . The best diggings now take capital to work." [38] One such casualty of the drift was Sam Clemens' first cousin, Jim Quarles. A gay young beau, flutist and dancer, he had come from Florida to Hannibal in 1848, set up as a tinsmith with a capital of three thousand dollars from his father old John Quarles, married, and promptly sired two babies. Mark's hasty notes complete the story: "Father highly disapproved the marriage. Dissipation — often drunk. Neglected the business — and the child-wife and babies. Left them and went to California. The little family went to Jim's father. Jim became a drunken loafer in California, and so died." [39]

Sam Clemens, who deferred until 1861 his own fortune-seeking in the West, observed this migration with interest, as revealed by his *Autobiography* as well as three items he ran in his "Assistant's Column" in May 1853 about the floods of emigrants still pouring through Hannibal and St. Joseph "in seach of what a wise man once said is the root of all evil — gold." [40] But his most vivid recollection was "the young California emigrant who was stabbed with a bowie knife by a drunken comrade; I saw the red life gush from his breast." This is probably the tragedy reported by Ament's *Courier* on April 11, 1850, in the high tide of migration, when two Illinoisians, named Davis and Crooks, fell to blows in a "drinking house in this city," and Crooks received a deep stab in the breast from a knife.[41]

To the backward view, Mark Twain thought the gold rush had wrought corruption upon the kindly, neighborly, sentimental life he had first known in Hannibal. In "Villagers" he wrote: "The Californian rush for wealth in '49 introduced the change and begot the lust for money which is the rule of life today, and the hardness and cynicism which is the spirit of today." And of the pristine Hannibal he added: "The three 'rich' men were not worshiped, and not envied. They were neither arrogant, nor assertive, nor tyrannical, nor exigent. It was California that changed the spirit of the people and lowered their ideals to the plane of today." The big three, comfortably well off but certainly not rich in comparison, say, with James Clemens, Jr., of St. Louis, were probably Lakenan, the town's most successful lawyer, Captain Robards the flour miller, and Russell Moss the pork packer — the latter two explicitly called "rich" in "Villagers." The census of 1850 shows that most Hannibal citizens listed their real property as worth $200, $300, or $400, although a few, like the widow Mary Fuqua, mother of Sam's crony Arch, owned real estate worth $10,000 or thereabouts. When Tom and Huck dig up the cache of Murrell's gang, and it counts up to $12,000, says Mark Twain, "it was more than any one present had ever seen at one time before, though several persons were there who were worth considerably more than that in property."

In dictating his *Autobiography* Mark could not help contrasting the unsavory ethics and dollar-worship of Jay Gould's generation with the sturdy democracy of early Hannibal: "In my youth there was nothing resembling a worship of money or of its possessor, in our region. And in our region no well-to-do man was ever charged with having acquired his money by shady methods." [42] This is going a little too far, in the idealistic haze with which Mark so often invested his Hannibal. One thinks for example of Ira Stout, who according to Mark swindled his father into bankruptcy, and perhaps of Beebe the crafty nigger-trader. In comparison with Jay Gould they were of course small operators, but according to their opportunities seem to have done well enough. In a more naïve sphere, Hannibal seems to have had its measure of appreciation for shrewd horse-trading and rustic rascality. John Briggs told Paine a story, that the latter solemnly recorded in his biography, about how Tom Blankenship with the approval of Sam Clemens' gang once sold old Selmes the same coonskin over and over for ten cents a time, only to reach through a back window and retrieve it when the storekeeper was not looking — to Selmes's vast amusement when the trick was finally discovered. The yarn is as old as the Crockett saga, if not older — so that it was Paine, after all, who was sold a bill of shopworn goods.[43] Such tales are as plentiful as June blackberries, and as American as wooden nutmegs, spavined horses, and gold bricks, and in the context of Jay Gould's experience belong to the age of innocence.

But more to the point is a piece published in Orion's *Journal* on April 1, 1852, appealing to farmers to do their trading in Hannibal rather than the neighboring Glasgow. "Hannibal is quite changed from what it once was," avers this booster. "It is a fact, that at one time the majority of her business men were rascals, or at least they acted very rascally with the citizens of the county; but at this time they bear quite a different character." And it must be remembered that "Hadleyburg" was another facet of Hannibal — the town whose honesty was only skin-deep, and whose covert greed was lustful in the extreme. Honeycombed with moral dry rot, penny-pinching, and hypocrisy, it needs only a sardonic practical joke to pull the whole temple of churchly decorum about the ears of its inhabitants. That, and the mocking laughter of the only free spirit, Jack Halliday, "the loafing, good-natured, no-account, irreverent fisherman, hunter, boys' friend, stray-dogs' friend." He sounds somewhat like Bence Blankenship, who spurned a reward to befriend a runaway Negro — save that poor Bence doubtless lacked Jack's wit and Olympian mirth. Jack, who leads a Gilbert and Sullivan parody upon the Incorruptibles of Hadleyburg, is surely the physical frame of Bence the fisherman, gifted with Mark Twain's own ripened irony. And after all, perhaps this is post-Gold Rush Hannibal. For, among its most repulsive characters is "Pinkerton the banker," "the little mean, smirking, oily Pinkerton" — and it is worth noting that Hannibal did not get its first banking house until the winter of 1852–53, when Blatchford & Whitney set up in business at Wild-Cat Corner.[44] Certainly "The Man That Corrupted Hadleyburg," along with *Pudd'nhead Wilson* and its overtones of village stupidity and venality, and *The Mysterious Stranger* in its unpublished draft with a Hannibal locale, report something about the river town of Mark Twain's dreams that the earlier *Tom Sawyer* and *Huckleberry Finn* had omitted or hastily glossed over. Those late tales chime of course with Mark's growing disenchantment, with his darkening skepticism about "the damned human race." For all his continued loyalty to the integrity of boyhood, they suggest that the old dream world — in so far as it involved adults, at any rate, with their greeds and passions — was revealed at last to be illusory and rotten at the heart.

CHAPTER FIFTEEN

ORION AND SAM

On January 30, 1850, in the midst of the latest yellow fever scare, Jane Clemens — always calm through pestilence and war — wrote tranquilly to her son Orion in St. Louis about a matter of more personal concern. This was her hope: that he might enter the newspaper business in Hannibal. "Big Joe" Buchanan, ex-steamboat engineer turned editor, was about to join the California gold stampede with his brother Robert. The *Journal*, which he had run since 1842 as a sound Whig organ, was the chief asset he left behind him. Judge Clemens, it will be recalled, had once wanted to buy into this paper whose political principles he approved, in order to give Orion a chance, but poverty undoubtedly prevented. Oldest of the newspapers still going in Hannibal, its equipment included a double medium Washington Press, "an elegant second hand Imperial Press," and plenty of type.[1]

When the elder Buchanans decided early in 1850 to seek their fortunes in the gold fields, the paper was turned over to "Young Bob" Buchanan, with "Little Joe" as devil, and a partner found in Sam Raymond, a "St. Louis swell" who — as Mark Twain remembered him — "affected fine city language, and always said 'Toosday.' " Jane Clemens was not much impressed with the new combination. "I have not heard much said about it," she commented to Orion. "Sam says little Joe told him his mother said she would rather have Orion than Sam Rayman. I think about the time you come up they will be through and you can get it at your own way." Knowing that Orion lacked capital she advised him to get some prosperous St. Louis printer to put up the cash and leave Orion in charge. "Robert Buchannan [sic] will have the office in his hands and I think will be sick of his bargin by that time if you could have a partner in St. Louis to help you. I could board the hands and you could have Henry. Sam says he can't leave Ament, he intends to make him pay wages and you would want him to wait, he can't credit any." [2] Sam Clemens' two years' apprenticeship under Ament were now drawing to a close, and his services as "sub-editor" probably valuable enough to justify more than the "board and clothes" for which he had been drudging, even to the niggardly eyes of his boss. But even if Sam could not be detached, Jane Clemens felt that with the help of young Henry, still in school, and her own willingness to run an apprentices' boardinghouse, Orion could make a go of it.

In mid-April 1850 the older Buchanans started off for the West, Robert leaving their family piano behind for Pamela to use in teaching her "scholars." A few days later her Uncle James Lampton, the young doctor, and his wife the "loud vulgar beauty" Ella, came over from New London to visit the Clemenses in Hannibal. "You had better come with them, and then we can talk this matter over," wrote Pamela in businesslike fashion to her brother.[3] Whether he came is unknown, but almost certainly these plans were talked over — since, when Orion started his own paper a few months

later, Dr. Lampton became his agent in New London at the
same time that Uncle John Quarles took the agency at
Florida.[4] It was plainly a family affair. During the summer
of 1850 Orion probably wound up his job in St. Louis, and
returned hopefully to Hannibal. To the surprise of humble
and loveless Orion, his mother and sister "greeted him with
kisses and tears." [5] The little clan was once more reunited.

Probably out of savings, or the $50 paid for a fragment of
the Tennessee land sold on May 3, 1850, Orion contrived to
buy a press and some type of his own, in St. Louis or elsewhere, and started a new Whig weekly in Hannibal which
he called the *Western Union*.[6] The first issue, which has not
survived, evidently appeared on September 6. The office, on
Bird Street between First and Main, also undertook job
printing. The earliest issue known, that for October 10,
lists an unclaimed letter held by postmaster Nash for
"Clemens, Sam'l L." [7] Quite probably Sam kept on working
for Ament during the first few months of Orion's venture.
But, as will be seen, he certainly quit that employment long
before Ament sold out in the autumn of 1852.[8]

From about the beginning of 1851 until he left Hannibal
near the end of May 1853, Sam Clemens' life was closely
interwoven with that of his elder brother, whom he served
daily as printer and editorial assistant. These years largely
conditioned the attitude which he kept toward Orion all the
rest of their lives. An individualist, and in many ways con-
stitutionally a rebel, Sam never took kindly to male dominion or authority — a very different thing from the voluntary deference he paid in later years to friends like Howells
and H. H. Rogers, and wholly unlike the chivalrous sweetness and compliance that entered into his relations with
women. Probably the sternness of John Marshall Clemens

had entered so deep and early into his soul, that he bridled unconsciously at every surrogate image of it — whether Orion as elder brother and employer, the overbearing pilot Brown of the steamboat *Pennsylvania,* or the endless succession of publishers with whom he battled during forty years. Toward Orion he soon developed, and kept, an attitude curiously ambivalent, a mixture of affection and contempt, which later days hardened into an amalgam of generosity and sadism.

Orion in turn was the perfect masochist. Nagged by his womenfolk, derided by Sam, buffeted by the world, he remained forever a gentle, kindly, plodding, inept soul of almost saintly humility and patience. Now, at the age of twenty-five, he had grown to be a tall, handsome, serious-faced young man, whose hair and beard soon began to turn prematurely gray. Like his father, he was a bookish sort, his head filled with ambitious dreams and schemes, a hard worker dogged by a fatal habit of failure. But in his son, John Clemens' magisterial austerity was tempered by the heritage of Jane Clemens' tender heart. In a fragmentary sketch of his brother, Mark recalls his "grave mien and big earnest eyes that seemed to be always searching, seeking, weighing, considering," as well as his "voracious appetite for books and study. He had no playmates, of course; he had nothing to offer them, they had nothing to offer him." 9 Orion's life was a tissue of frustrations. He sometimes fancied that his ambition to be an orator — in which his St. Louis patron Edward Bates had briefly encouraged him — might have brought him fame and fortune; but his boardinghouse keeper is said to have objected to the solitary declamations and rantings he practiced in his room. He yearned uncomforted to give his life to the spoken rather than the printed word. Yet his indifferent success in addressing church audiences, temperance societies, or any group that would listen to him, along with his chronic failure as a lawyer, suggests that no Webster was lost in the deflection of Orion Clemens.

After starting the *Western Union* with his usual ardor for any new project, setting an example to his younger brothers and the apprentices by working "like a slave," Orion soon fell into the doldrums and harked back to this ancient grievance. "I grew more despondent," he wrote in his autobiography, that document written years later under Sam's admonition to be brutally frank in stripping his soul.

My prospect was gloomy. It had never been my ambition to become an editor or printer. I embarked in the business with no more partiality for it than for any other occupation. If I could have been so employed that daily practice in the art of speaking would have been part of my duty, my life would have been full of bliss during all my working hours. But that had been forbidden by my father, who had placed me at the toil of printing and editing, because his own preference was in that direction. His pleasure in knowing that I was so engaged, must have been slight, compared with the happiness I might have enjoyed if I had been permitted to pursue a course warmed by the fervor and illumined by the light of my childish dreams. The idea I derived was an additional argument in favor of the theory that the more suffering the greater the reward. I felt as if my business had been forced upon me that my character might receive the elevating and chastening influence of daily and hourly affliction. There being no pleasure in the mechanical part of the business, and no hope of attaining a position where I could work at editing, free from the embarrassments of business, I began to yearn for a chance to get away from the office, and rest and breathe fresh air.[10]

Orion's attempts in his St. Louis printing days with Ustick to persuade fellow workers to forswear beer and to follow the Christlike life apparently inspired the nickname "Parson Snivel." "All of which pleased him," wrote Mark Twain in later years, "and made him a hero to himself: for he was turning the other cheek, as commanded, he was being reviled and persecuted for righteousness' sake, and all that. Privately his little Presbyterian mother was not pleased with this too-literal loyalty to the theoretical Bible-teachings which he had acquired through her agency, for, slender and delicately moulded as she was, she had a dauntless courage and a high spirit, and was not of the cheek-turning sort." Jane Clemens was a Christian, but no willing martyr like her milksop son; when inconsistency between her theory and practice was pointed out, she would reply, "Religion is a jugfull; I hold a dipperfull. . . . I know that a person that can turn his cheek is higher and holier than I am . . . but I despise him, too, and wouldn't have him for a doormat." [11]

His eager enthusiasm and deep desponds resembled those in the character of his brother Sam, but the latter's purposeful rebellions along with his genius were absent from Orion's nature. Save for his basic honesty and truthfulness, his loyalty to persons, and a few stubborn tenets like his beliefs about the wrongs of slavery and alcohol and the menace of Popery, Orion was a weather vane. He was well aware of his own pliability. "I followed all the advice I received," he wrote naïvely. "If two or more persons conflicted with each other, I adopted the views of the last." [12] His "intense lust for approval . . . so girlishly anxious to be approved by anybody and everybody," as Mark once observed, led him a wild-goose chase among the fields of opinion. In "light matters . . . like religion and politics . . . he never acquired a conviction that could survive a disapproving remark from a cat." [13] In one of Mark's many attempts to put his brother into a fictional frame, he wrote: "He changed his principles with the moon, his politics with the weather, and his religion with his shirt." With exaggeration Mark here described him as having been by turns a Mohammedan, Methodist, Buddhist, Baptist, Parsee, Catholic, and Atheist — but his Presbyterian wife, "as steady as an anvil . . . knew there was a patient and compassionate Providence watching over him that would see to it that he died in his Presbyterian period." [14] Into Orion's experience the Presbyterian wife had not yet entered.

But neither now nor later did Orion become a Moslem, as Mark sportively claimed in another sketch about his luckless brother called the "Autobiography of a Damned Fool" — although the story's portrayal of the young printer oscillating between Sunday school orthodoxy and free-thinking, depending upon the last book or human persuader he had met, is not untrue. From Methodism he seems to have followed Jane and the Clemens family into Presbyterianism. In St. Louis, Mark says, his brother shopped around from one sect to another. In his editorial days in Hannibal Orion is found lecturing at the Baptist Church, yet printing an article espousing Universalism.[15] Further mutations were yet to come, including re-conversion to Calvinism in his Nevada phase in 1864 and his being solemnly "excommunicated" for heresy in Keokuk twelve years later.[16] But from youth in Hannibal to old age in Iowa, when he took up with the American Protective Association, Orion stood firm in battling the Scarlet Woman of the Seven Hills. Perhaps he had never met a persuasive Catholic. During his editorial days in Hannibal he assailed Orestes Brownson for believing apparently "that the rusty old Pope in Rome has a right to dictate who shall be our Presidents, Governors, Senators, Representatives, &c." [17] A couple of days later he fired another salvo, beginning "Wherever there is Catholic rule there is blight." This was about the time that Hannibal was discussing the issue of building a Catholic church, which had never before lifted its spire in the village.[18] Its Catholic population was probably quite small, recruited chiefly from the Germans and Irish who had begun to arrive in the later forties. The mystery of this faith, so sinister to the rural Protestant mind, is mirrored in a scene that Mark wrote for the dramatization of *Tom Sawyer,* in which Becky's rival Amy Lawrence in "mooning around" the schoolroom cries:

> Why if the *key* isn't in the teacher's desk! I'd just give the *world* to know what it is he puts in there every day, done up in a rag. *I* believe it's a crucifix — heaps of people think he's a *Catholic,* and *some* talk right out and say so. And many and many's the time he puts his head in this desk and appears to be praying to something — and *I* believe he is. *(Keeps an eye on Tom — gets out the rag, exposes a whisky bottle — puts it to her nose)* pah! *(Bottle falls and breaks. She stands horrified and speechless. Tom rises and gazes. She begins to cry.)* Tom Sawyer, you're just as mean as *you* can be, to sneak up on a person and — and — ." [19]

Thus the substitute for the anatomy textbook and its "human figure, stark naked," in the novel. Curiously enough, on February 3, 1853, Orion's *Journal* printed a letter from a Methodist clergyman, clearing the reputation of Miss Martha Smith, new head of the Hannibal Female Seminary, from imputations of local gossip: "I likewise have been acquainted with the parents of Miss Smith upwards of thirty years . . . and I know they are not Roman Catholics, and never have been, but are true Protestants." Mark Twain, citizen of the world and traveler abroad, freed himself from much of the provincial naïveté in which he and his brothers had been schooled, but a residue of anti-Catholicism lingers for example in *A Connecticut Yankee.*

Both Orion and Sam, it is said, had youthful thoughts of entering the ministry — in Orion's case, probably because its public speaking attracted him, with Sam "because it never occurred to me that a preacher could be damned." [20] One printer's apprentice of these days, a former playmate of Sam named Frank Walden, did become a country preacher without "a cent." "I am glad you are in the ministry," Mark wrote him after a lapse of twenty years. "It is the highest dignity to which a man may aspire in this life." [21] But with neither Orion nor Sam did the aspiration long remain. Each in his own way and time followed the skeptic's road blazed by their free-thinking father. A lonely road, because agnosticism was feared as much as Romanism by the society in which they grew up. In "Villagers" Mark states that the town had but one avowed "unbeliever," whom he calls by the fictitious name Blennerhasset, "the young Kentucky lawyer, a fascinating cuss." Profane and blasphemous, he "was vain of being prayed for in the revivals," and of the young ladies' desire to convert him. The villagers "believed the devil would come for him in person some stormy night." At last he went back to Kentucky to get married, and Mark tells the grisly sequel:

All present at the wedding but himself. Shame and grief of the bride; indignation of the rest. A year later he would be found — bridally clad — shut into the family vault in the graveyard — spring lock and the key on the outside. His mother had but one pet and he was the one — because he was an infidel and the target of bitter public opinion. He always visited her tomb when at home, but the others didn't. So the judgment hit him at last. He was found when they came to bury a sister. There had been a theft of money in the town, and the people managed to suspect him; but it was not found on him.[22]

No such incident is recalled in the folklore of Hannibal today. It may have been Mark's imagination, fed in youth upon tales of premature burial — such as Orion's *Journal* printed in a series in April 1853, gratifying those numerous readers "who delight in a perusal of the horrible." Or else recalled by the story of Mark's friend Thomas Bailey Aldrich called "A Struggle for Life," about a man supposed to have been locked accidentally into the vault of his dead fiancee.[23] But the retribution awaiting the scoffer at least is true to the expectations of God-fearing Hannibal.

In the catalogue of Orion's opinions, some qualification is needed of Mark Twain's assertion that, although "born and reared among slaves and slaveholders, he was yet an aboli-tionist from his boyhood to his death." [24] This praise of Orion's consistency on one score is as exaggerated as Mark's thrust at his political fickleness, "Whig today, Democrat next week." The facts show that Orion was steadily a Whig, and later a Lincoln Republican, during the stormy years when these opinions required some backbone in a Missour-ian, but that his attitude toward solution of the slavery question did undergo change. "We are entirely conserva-tive," he wrote in the *Western Union* on August 28, 1851, "and while our contempt for the Abolitionists of the North knows no bounds, we are loath to claim brotherhood with the 'Fire-eaters' of the South." A few months earlier he had reported the misconduct of a free Negro in cheating a small boy of Hannibal out of a three-dollar bill, adding: "This is one of the Free Soilers you read about, and we think Seward would find it a good speculation to get this colored member of the 'higher law party' to act as his private secretary." As conservative Whig he attacked "Freesoilism," avowing that "we consider any legislation upon the subject of slavery in the territories by Congress as highly inexpedient." [25] On the other hand, to judge by the spate of articles about Liberia appearing in both his *Western Union* and *Journal,* Orion seems to have been sympathetic to the idea of colonization. Clearly one gathers the impression that he was no apologist for slavery, that he probably regarded it throughout as a moral wrong. Yet to call him in the 1850's an abolitionist is as inaccurate as to apply the term to many another idealist with moderate views, say Abraham Lincoln, although Orion probably approached that position on the brink of the Civil War. Obvious caricature inspired a notation Mark made about Orion in the "Autobiography of a Damned Fool": "Thinks it his duty to marry a wench. This is carrying abolitionism too far. Is notified to draw the line or will be tarred." [26] Gleams of liberalism appear much earlier athwart his editorial opinions, as in an editorial written for the *Journal* of July 8, 1852, deprecating a city ordinance requiring a surety bond of $100 plus a tax of $10 a head against every free Negro for the privilege of living in Hannibal. "A negro," says Orion, "capable of honor and gratitude has principle enough under his sooty hide to behave himself without security." [27] Thieving white men, he adds, are a greater menace to Hannibal than free Negroes.

Wiser heads than Orion's, in the middle years of the century, did not know how to bring to an end, peaceably and justly, the South's "peculiar institution"; if he failed to find the answer, or wavered somewhat in his opinions, no discredit need ensue. More consistent than his views about this or any other public issue was the kindliness of Orion's heart. Anger, spite, envy, and malice seem almost wholly absent from his character — as mirrored now in his editorials, and later in the hundreds of private letters from his pen preserved among the family papers. The intermittent rages, the cracklings of satire, the occasional sweeps of misanthropy that flashed from his younger brother Sam never found their counterpart in Orion. Trivially enough, he remembered, it was always Sam who had the resolution needed in those early days whenever the Clemenses' feline population reached plague proportions — even though Sam yielded to none, as boy and man, in his devotion to cats. "We had too many kittens," Orion writes, apparently of the printing-shop years. "Sam was again the only one of the family who could nerve himself to the point of doing a very disagreeable thing. He enclosed them in a bag which he swung over his shoulder and took to the river, where he sunk to the bottom the little creatures, whose only offence was that they lived." On the other hand, he remembered at another time, "if a stray kitten was to be fed and taken care of Henry was expected to attend to it, and he would faithfully do so." [28]

If Orion was the gentlest of men, he was already one of the most wool-gathering. "I know you to be (without exception) one of the most absent persons in existence," began a "private letter" from a lady, calling his attention to the new feminine fashions, which he printed on April 8, 1852, in the *Journal*. He could never remember to mail a letter, even on a special trip to the post office, and was so oblivious to time that he always escaped living under the tyranny of the clock. Keeping books and balancing accounts, whether for his own affairs or the church funds sometimes rashly placed in his hands, were ever his cheerful despair. And yet this was the industrious apprentice who early had taken Franklin for his guide, from vegetarian diet to cold baths, who scattered maxims of the Philadelphia sage through the Hannibal papers he edited in the early fifties, and a little later in Keokuk hopefully named his establishment the Ben Franklin Book & Job Office. In the light of Orion's hero worship, Sam developed an aversion to Franklin's precepts, "full of animosity toward boys." [29] Young Orion's patron saint was the apostle of success. Yet Orion from start to finish was a failure. Like millions of other Americans, by the world's standards he was a failure — but his was the misfortune of having a brilliant brother, whose successes Orion never seemed to envy but rejoiced in, yet one whose luster lit with a cruel light the corner where Orion might have lived and died in decent obscurity.

Of these things he had of course no prevision when, probably around the first of January 1851 he took Sam away from Ament. He promised the boy the generous wage of $3.50 a week but as Mark stated, "never was able to pay me a single penny as long as I was with him." [30] In tangible goods Sam profited nothing by the exchange. Orion could furnish only "poor, shabby clothes," as he himself described them, and board under the Clemens roof, with Jane doing the cooking with groceries bought by Orion — "a regular diet of bacon, butter, bread, and coffee." [31] But at least the enforced poverty that Sam understood so well, from having grown up in it, was better than the miserliness decreed by the Aments. And if he lost the jolly comradeship of Wales McCormick and Pet McMurry, he gained that of his own brother Henry, to whom Sam was deeply devoted, and of that bashful apprentice Jim Wolfe, whose adventure with the cats has been mentioned. Hazing Jim was Sam's delight — sending him out for strap oil or a round square, and all the other knowing tricks Sam had learned by this sophomoric stage. And when Jim used to make the composition rollers in the back yard over a big fire in the kettle, it was Sam's pleasure to get passing girls to the back of the shop and ask Jim to explain the process to them, while Sam watched out the window to observe the flustered behavior of a painfully shy boy. But one day, in response to Sam's pranks, Jim dealt him a bloody nose, and after that the teasing stopped. It was similar to the rock treatment administered by long-suffering Henry Clemens, who notwithstanding was Sam's accomplice in the chivying of Jim Wolfe. With ripening maturity Sam decided that in the main, practical jokes were "cruel" and "barren of wit." [32]

A rough date for Sam's entry into Orion's employment is offered by a fire that broke out one door from the printing office on January 9, 1851, in which Jim figured. Paine incorrectly states that this was the fire which burned Orion out, confusing it with the disaster that happened a year later, whereas this one did no damage to the office. But, he adds, this fire inspired Sam to write a sketch picturing the excitement that had led Jim to carry "the office broom half a mile and had then come back after the wash-pan." [33] On turning to the *Western Union* for January 16, 1851, we find what, in the light of Paine's testimony, is the first known venture of Sam Clemens into print. He tells how fire broke out, about one o'clock in the morning, at Parker's grocery just one door from the printing office. It was in fact discovered by the hands of Orion's papers, when quitting their nightly labors.

Our gallant *devil*, seeing us somewhat excited, concluded he would perform a noble deed, and immediately gathered the broom, an old mallet, the wash-pan and a dirty towel, and in a fit of patriotic exictement, rushed out of the office and deposited his precious burden some ten squares off, out

of danger. Being of a *snailish* disposition, even in his quick-
est moments, the fire had been extinguished during his
absence. He returned in the course of an hour, nearly out
of breath, and thinking he had immortalized himself, threw
his giant frame in a tragic attitude, and exclaimed, with an
eloquent expression: "If that thar fire hadn't bin put out,
thar'd a'bin the greatest *confirmation* of the age!"

In the issue that the boys were printing when the fire
broke out next door, Orion had announced his intention to
launch a tri-weekly paper in mid-January. But a few days
later, on January 23, he had to admit the scheme was impossible. He could get no telegraphic reports from Washington
— "as conducted now, the wire is about as much use as a
woollen string" — and besides he saw that costs would greatly
outweight profits. Sam remembered that his brother was
always making managerial blunders, juggling subscription
and advertising prices up and down according to somebody's
offhand advice, in the hope of gain but actually to the general confusion and loss of business. Cordwood, cabbages,
turnips, clean linen, and cotton rags were taken in lieu of
cash, involving the shop in a dreary morass of barter. Extra
favors, whether a bunch of parsnips, "a thimblefull of strawberries done up in a most enchanting style," a free dinner
at the City Hotel, or a slice of wedding cake sent in tacit
payment for the announcement, were all gratefully acknowledged in print. The product itself must have seemed worth
little more. As Mark recalled it, the classic village newspaper
was "a wretchedly printed little sheet, being very vague and
pale in spots, and in other spots so caked with ink as to be
hardly decipherable," crammed with local advertisements
run again and again as fillers long after their paid lifetime
had expired, cheek by jowl with laudations of "glorified
quack-poisons," sappy fiction and poetry, and alleged "Wit

& Humor." [34] Orion himself wrote that he took up half a page publishing schoolgirls' compositions, "to please them and their friends," but "the idea of publishing local news to interest the general reader never occurred to me, and local matters usually received very slight attention." [35] Yet Hannibal, now claiming a population of 2500, must have pined to read about its own doings.

Among homegrown efforts at wit and humor now appearing in the *Western Union* one suspects the prentice hand of Sam Clemens — if for no other reasons than Orion's own lack of journalistic playfulness and Sam's early itch for scribbling. In late May 1851 a municipal ordinance compelling farmers to sell their eggs through the city market inspired a letter to the editor sarcastically praising this "most eggs-cellent, eggs-plicit, eggs-travagant and eggs-traordinary ordinance." And a few days later, on June 5, when the highest water ever known on the Upper Mississippi brought the river almost up to Main Street, a waggish paragraph congratulated the city that the Father of Waters is "safe enough in the calaboose." On the other hand, it is not hard to suspect Orion's easygoing ways in the editor's remarks on June 26 that "idle boys" have been breaking into the office, striking off cuts, spoiling some fine cards, and "battering a lot of type till it was useless. We do not like to put a curb on aspiring youth" who "probably meant no harm." But since Orion, as a female correspondent had complained, never knew "one article of dress from another," probably it was Sam who fathered a piece on July 10 about the first bloomer costume seen in Hannibal. Its fair devotee, appearing on a Sunday afternoon, caused such consternation that the pilot of the *Bon Accord* "became so abstracted as to run the bow of his boat on a raft . . . the pilot of the *Wyoming* . . . actually attempted to steer his boat up the hill," while one-legged

Higgins the Negro and the drayman John Hannicks — both favorites with Mark Twain — appeared greatly embarrassed.[36] Plainly enough in the coming months, when his hand is unmistakable, Sam had begun to realize what was wrong with his brother's newspaper, and tried bravely if amateurishly to supply it with humor, vivacity, and local interest.

Orion still longed to get his hands on the old Hannibal *Journal,* which was not doing well since "Big Joe" Buchanan had deserted it in the spring of 1850 to seek the Golden West. Shortly before the first of September 1851 Orion took it over from young Buchanan and Sam Raymond, and on September 4 from his old office on Bird Street he brought out the first issue of his consolidated *Journal and Western Union.* Six months later he reduced this dropsical title simply to the *Journal.* Mark Twain states that his brother borrowed $500 from an old farmer named Johnson, at ten per cent interest, and so bought the plant and its good will.[37] Orion remembered the approximate date because around that time he saw the wedding procession of an old sweetheart, Jo Smith, on its way to the boat that would carry her to her new home at Louisiana, Missouri. "I was pleased to observe that there were not many carriages and it was a small affair, while there was a pitiful attempt to put on style." [38] In his vainglory Orion no doubt imagined himself on the threshold of a professional future that would make her sorry she had refused him. The Clemens family had its wedding too, on September 20, when in far-off Green County, Kentucky, Pamela married Will Moffett. Aged twenty-four and perilously verging upon the status of old maid, she had gone to visit her Aunt Pamelia, and there had agreed to marry her old Hannibal neighbor, who was also making a round of family visits. "No radical," as his grandson Sam Webster describes him,

Will took his bride off to Niagara Falls on their honeymoon, and then brought her to settle in St. Louis, where he ran a thriving commission business. Orion's paper reported the news on October 2. For Pamela the piano and guitar lessons and the pinched economies of Hannibal were over.

Even Orion thought he was doing a little better. With the honored name of the *Journal* at his masthead he had consummated his father's ambition for him. Orion also obtained some printing contracts from Marion County. In late September he was dallying with the idea of launching a monthly magazine, "devoted chiefly to Miscellanies, Poetry, and Polite Literature." Nothing came of it, but Orion did his best through the following months by printing excerpts in the paper from Kennedy's *Swallow Barn* and Dickens' *Bleak House* — incidentally trying vainly to interest Sam in Dickens — and later in angling for original work by authors like Emerson and Holmes, offering each celebrity a pittance of five dollars that was bluntly ignored.[39] He also continued to have trouble in getting telegraphic news, reporting on September 25 that the interests wanted to charge him "about four times too much," while the local telegraph line strung across the river from Illinois was of no use at all, since people were carrying off the wire piecemeal and a ferryman across the Sny had rigged himself a cable out of part of it. Still he could boast on November 6 that "we have a larger circulation, by *over one hundred,* than any other paper published in this section." Two months later, surveying his situation at the New Year, he reflected editorially that "the circumstances under which we took the Journal were anything but flattering," but through consolidation the circulation now compared "favorably with any paper out of St. Louis."

Orion's narrative, as vague in dates as Mark Twain's *Autobiography* is untrustworthy, states that "one day good news

came. Arnold Buffum sent me $150. After my father was
laid in his grave had come this first return for his investments
in Tennessee land." A Dutchess County farmer, breaking
the stubborn jinx, had bought eight hundred acres at twenty-
five cents an acre, from which the agent Buffum no doubt
deducted his commission.[40] The news seemed too good to
believe. And so it was. On reaching Fentress County the
New York farmer began to complain, saying that his tract
was not the best land, "wanted three times as much to make
him even," and started to make large entries upon the land
the Clemenses had held for twenty years. "Here was business
to attend to!" writes Orion, with wistful vanity. "People
might despise me as a poor manager of a newspaper, but
what would they think of me when they learned that I had
gone to Tennessee to attend to seventy thousand acres of
land belonging to my father's estate?" And so he engaged
Dr. Hugh Meredith — just back from California — to edit
the paper. "He was a man of steady habits, advanced in
life, and would preserve the solemnity of the editorial
columns. His son [Charles] was learning the trade of printing with me. I appointed Sam to the position of foreman.
He was then fourteen years of age." Here obviously Orion
is in error, since Sam had entered his employ around or
soon after his fifteenth birthday, which fell at least a year
before this trip. Orion then describes how he used a third
of Buffum's $150 "to pay the interest on my note," doubtless
the first year's interest on farmer Johnson's loan at ten per
cent, spent $50 more laying in stock "for the approaching
winter," and used the last $50 on his journey to Tennessee,
traveling to Glasgow, Kentucky, by stage. He walked the
six miles out to the farm of Uncle Isaac Settle, who had married John M. Clemens' sister Caroline. A lover of the romantic surprise, as Orion had proved himself several years earlier

when he had wound up in bed with Dr. Meredith's old-maid sister, on reaching the farm he "sat sometime before the fire in the simulated character of a stranger. When I divulged the ponderous secret of my identity Aunt Caroline nearly upset the coffee-pot as she sprang from the table to clasp me in her fleshy arms." So ends this fragment of his narrative, but it is clear from other circumstances — as well as from Orion's predestination to failure — that his trip to Tennessee was as fruitless as his father's had been ten years before, and that the high hopes for the "Tennessee Land" were to crumble in the years ahead.[41]

That this bootless errand occurred in midwinter 1851–52 is suggested by the files of Orion's newspaper. Unlike later absences of Orion, this leave gave Sam — under the thumb of Dr. Meredith's editorial "solemnity" — little opportunity for showing his mettle. One suspects Sam's touch in such a filler as this, on December 18:

> An old lady in Jersey —
> TO BE CONTINUED.

But on January 8 we read, "The Editor is absent," and again on January 15, "The Editor is still absent." And finally on January 22, the characteristic Orion flavor: "Well, we have got back — not that this is any very remarkable event, abstractly considered; but the fact is of some importance to ourselves," and in the same issue a sketch of social life among the young people of Kentucky and Tennessee, datelined "Near Glasgow, Ky., Dec. 29, 1851."

It was meet that Orion, harbinger of ill luck, should return in plenty of time to assist at a disaster that fate held in store for the printing shop. (He once printed an aphorism in the *Journal* saying that "some good people see in every misfortune that befalls themselves, a trial — in every one which happens to their neighbors, a judgment.") The issue of January 29, charred along the edges in the copy now preserved at the Missouri Historical Society, told the story under the headline "FIRE! FIRE!" Just after Orion's printers had finished one side of the paper, at 7 P.M., a big blaze was discovered sweeping through the office. The Liberty Boys with their buckets were Hannibal's chief defense against fire, but as Orion had remarked several months earlier, their "beautiful horizontal engine" christened "the Big Mo.," imported from St. Louis, was kept in the Market House and "could not be got out" in emergencies.[42] Whether from this or other causes, the fire did "considerable damage." In a neighborly spirit the rival papers helped to get the issue out which told the sad story. The *Messenger* lent its market reports, also its delinquent tax list, on which sadly enough Orion appears as owing a $10 tax on the assessed valuation of $200, on the Hill Street house. "We hope to get what is left of the office, righted up, and to be fairly under way again, in the course of a week or two." Orion the delinquent taxpayer took occasion to urge all delinquent subscribers to come across, "although the insurance money, payable in ninety days, will cover the damages." Orion collected $150 from insurance, and bought such replacements as were needed to continue the shop. Promptly he announced removal to "the room over Stover & Horr's Clothing Store, on Main Street." Paine however says that after the fire Orion set up his press in the parlor of the Clemens dwelling on Hill Street, while adding more space for living quarters by building a second story — publishing the *Journal* at home "for another two years." [43] Such a makeshift may have been adopted at some time during the paper's unprosperous career, but such refer-

ences as occur in the *Journal* itself show Orion keeping an
upstairs office on Main Street. One incident vividly remembered from Orion's catalogue of tribulations bears out the
legend of the shop domiciled in the parlor. This was the
night that a cow got into the office, upset a type-case, and
ate up a couple of composition rollers. Paine tells the story
as having happened just before the big fire, but it seems unlikely that an enterprising cow even in pioneer Missouri
could have climbed up to a second-floor office on Main Street.

About five weeks after removal to his new upstairs shop on
Main Street, Orion was once more in peril from fire. On
March 4 readers of the *Journal* again were confronted with
the headline "FIRE!" About daylight that morning Garth's
tobacco factory had burned, threatening the new printing
office nearby. But "the 'Liberty' fire engine was brought to
play upon [the fire], and fully re-established its lost character
as an efficient engine." The hero was none other than Sam's
former boss and Orion's Democratic rival, J. P. Ament of
the *Courier,* who in the expectation that the shop might
burn had moved out all the essentials, thus winning Orion's
gratitude "for his friendly and valuable aid." But lower in
the same column — probably written by Ament's future
satirist in this journal, and almost certainly before the incident of the fire — appeared this ungracious squib: "Our
neighbor of the *Courier* thinks he is 'pretty' — so he might
be, if he would shave off the kinky bristles which his vanity
flatters him are magnificent whiskers." Ament's divided state
of mind in perusing this medley of public thanks and abuse
may well be imagined.[44] Hannibal witnessed an even bigger
fire on March 29, when the livery stable of Shoot & Davis
roared up in flames, destroying thirty-one horses and other
valuable property. This time Orion escaped. His *Journal*

hinted broadly at the presence of a firebug in their midst, reporting that a stranger, "in an out-of-the-way place," was
heard laughing and saying, "Burn! G—— d——n you,
burn! I glory to see it!"

The month of March brought other if more remote excitement, in the visit to St. Louis of the great Hungarian
patriot Kossuth. Hannibal's mayor T. R. Selmes, genial proprietor of the Wild-Cat Store, headed a delegation of citizens
who went down the river, as Orion's paper reported on the
twenty-fifth, to invite him to "the second city of our own
Missouri . . . we yield to none in sympathy for your cause
. . . of king-ridden, down-trodden, bleeding Hungary . . .
Come with us and let us break bread together, and we will
do you good." As Selmes "well knew," Kossuth was leaving
immediately for New Orleans, but he favored the delegation with a flowery speech. Orion the Whig, it seems, took
no stock in this celebrity, writing an editorial on July 15
alluding to the imminent departure from our shores of "that
compound of arrogance and vanity, Louis Kossuth." But
many felt otherwise, and a few months later the paper remarked that all the fashionable ladies of Hannibal were
wearing either Kossuth hats or Jenny Lind bonnets.

Meanwhile Sam Clemens continued to feel the itch for
writing, as well as an impulse to brighten the wastes of village journalism. On April Fool's Day 1852, comic genius
may be fancied at work in the *Journal.* On the front page,
a discordant bit is sandwiched between the last installment
of "The White Fawn: Written Expressly for the Journal
& Union, by Marie," and the opening chapter of "The Pearl
of Rouen: Translated from the French by Anne T. Wilbur"
— the latter a *coup* which, Mark recalled after half a century,
was heralded with "immense noise" and added thirty-eight

subscriptions, "payable in turnips and cordwood." [45] Between the end and the beginning of these sugary romances, an epitaph is inserted:

> Weep, stranger, for a father spilled
> From a stage-coach, and thereby killed:
> His name John Sykes, a maker of sassengers
> Slain with three other outside passengers.

About the same time Sam must have mailed to a comic weekly in Boston, the *Carpet-Bag,* his first effort to win recognition outside the horizons of Hannibal. Its editor was B. P. Shillaber, creator of the famous "Mrs. Partington" whose sayings apparently later influenced Mark's delineation of Tom Sawyer's Aunt Polly. Shillaber himself eventually became a good friend of Mark Twain, but now he knew nothing of the personality behind the initials "S.L.C." signed to this sketch set in "the now flourishing young city of Hannibal." Shillaber's *Carpet-Bag,* specializing in homespun humor, was familiar to Orion's printing shop. On March 4, 1852, for example, from its pages the *Journal* had reprinted Jerusha Prym's "Familiar Letter on Art," embellished with crude woodcuts, and on April 1, Shillaber's jest about changing the inscription on a stone sent by Rome for the Washington Monument, to read: "Rome to America: 4000 Miles." A little later, on July 15, the *Journal* recommended that the military-minded youths of Hannibal take for their model "the 'Carpet Bag's' great hero, Ensign Jehiel Stebbings." Not the *Carpet-Bag* alone but the whole tradition it represented in rustic fun — the doings of shrewd Major Jack Downing, epic Mike Fink, shifty Simon Suggs, the clock-peddling Slicks, and a host of others — are cherished in the Hannibal newspapers of the time.[46]

From this stratum sprang Sam Clemens' first ideas of humor in print. The sketch he sent to Shillaber, "The Dandy Frightening the Squatter," pivoted upon a simple idea long familiar in the Southwest.[47] Its plot was no more original than that of his later and greater success "The Celebrated Jumping Frog." Along the Mississippi and in the backwoods they loved yarns about the bumpkin who gives a visiting coxcomb his come-uppance. Ament's *Courier,* for instance, on June 27, 1850, when Sam was still working for that paper, had printed " 'Doing' a Dandy," by one Fred Ballard, telling how a Yankee farmer had put a fop out of countenance by pretending to mistake him for the orangutang shown in Vermont "a spell ago." Sam's yarn related the discomfiture "about thirteen years ago" of a braggart "with a killing moustache" who, to show off before the ladies on a steamboat, with a brace of horse pistols had tried to intimidate "a tall, brawny woodsman" on the bank at Hannibal, and been pushed into the water for his pains. Such a tale, for all the clumsiness of its telling, salved the inferiority complex of the West.

On the basis of Mark's recollections in old age, Paine states that about this time the young printer also had two humorous anecdotes accepted by "the *Philadelphia Saturday Evening Post.*" Search of the files has failed to turn up evidence of any such contributions. But beginning in 1847 the Sons of Temperance, to whose junior affiliate Sam Clemens had belonged in 1850, published for some time in St. Louis an organ called the *Saturday Evening Post and Temperance Recorder.* Save for a single copy its files have perished. If Mark in old age confused its title with that of the more famous Philadelphia weekly, it would be one of the lighter errors of a memory almost perversely fallible.[48]

CHAPTER SIXTEEN

"TO DESTINY I BEND"

IN DESCRIBING "My First Literary Venture" in the *Galaxy* for April 1871, Mark Twain made no mention of "The Dandy," which was forgotten altogether until exhumed by Franklin Meine twenty years after the author's death, nor of those early pieces in the *Journal* and the mysterious *Saturday Evening Post* which he recollected so vaguely. Far more vivid were his experiences in the early autumn of 1852 and again in the late spring of 1853 in "subbing" for Orion as the acting editor of the *Journal*. In squeezing the juice of humor from them to regale readers of the *Galaxy*, Mark took characteristic liberties with the facts. The lucky survival of the *Journal* files from those years alone enables one to disentangle fact from fiction. Mark states that his "uncle" left town for a week and trusted him to get out a single copy of the weekly. He did so with such picturesque results that the "uncle" returned very angry to find that Sam had set the town by the ears, and barely escaped murder at the hands of three readers — who had breathed fire and brimstone upon the green editor, but left the office "incensed at my insignificance." Two quite separate interludes of youthful indiscretion are thus telescoped into one.

Around mid-September 1852 Orion was absent for about a

week from Hannibal, probably in St. Louis. On September 9 Sam had begun to exercise his wits by printing a lively account of a "family muss" among the alcoholic Irish on Holliday's Hill.[1] In preparing the issue of September 16 Sam found himself in sole command. Scanning the village horizon for copy to enliven the *Journal,* he recalled that since midsummer the editor of Hannibal's second Whig paper, the *Tri-Weekly Messenger,* had excited himself through five issues about the mad-dog menace. He had begun on July 15 by speaking facetiously of "the dog Law" which from that day forth ordered all canines to be licensed at a dollar a head and wear a collar, "whether it shall be a 'standing' or 'turn down' collar . . . left . . . to the taste of the wearer." Nine days later he reported that a calf had been bitten by a mad dog, then began to remark upon the multitude of dogs without collars. A mock-serious proposal in the *Journal,* now lost, signed "A Dog-be-deviled Citizen," called for the extermination of all dogs. Ament's *Courier* seems also to have entered the fray in defense of dogs. In late August the *Messenger's* "Local" twice returned to twit his adversaries, hinting that the "Dog-be-deviled Citizen" was growing "hypochondric" [*sic*].

Into this dreary and pointless wrangle Sam stepped, after a three-week lapse, now that Orion was safely out of town. On September 16, under the headline " 'LOCAL' RESOLVES TO COMMIT SUICIDE," he reported that the *Messenger* editor, "disconsolate from receiving no further notice from 'A Dog-be-deviled Citizen,' " had hit upon suicide. Having failed in "ridding the country of a nuisance" by drinking himself to death, he resolved by night to "extinguish his chunk" in the waters of Bear Creek. Accompanying the gibe appeared the first of three "villainous cuts engraved on the bottom of wooden type with a jackknife," as the artist Sam Clemens later described them. This one showed a dog-headed "Local" sounding the stream with his walking-stick fearful lest he "get out of his depth." The *Messenger*'s response was instant and savage, sneering at "this newly arisen 'Ned Buntline' . . . who has not the decency of a gentleman nor the honor of a blackguard." Two days later, having no doubt ascertained Orion's absence, he added that his opponent's "ideas are of so obscene and despicable an order as to forever bar them against a gentlemanly or even decent discussion. . . . In justice to the Editor of the Journal . . . we believe him innocent of intentionally doing us an injury, and absolve him from all censure." Sam had another rod in pickle, and his second and third woodcuts appeared on September 23, showing "Local" excited after having discovered "something interesting" in the *Journal,* and below the same dog-headed caricature bowled over by the blast of an old swivel he had discharged at "the canine race," while the "Dog-be-deviled Citizen" walks quietly away in the distance. These Parthian thrusts were blunted by a mollifying letter, plainly from Orion upon his return, deprecating the squabble and praising the *Messenger*'s local editor as "a young man, recently come amongst us, with a design of occupying a respectable position in society, by industry and by propriety and straightforwardness of conduct." After further muttering about "blackguards" and "the feeble eminations [*sic*] of a puppy's brain," the *Messenger* accepted the truce.

Upon the face of it, the savagery of "Local's" retort upon Sam Clemens is hard to understand. As Mark remembered it, however, his adversary — whom after nearly twenty years he identified as a newcomer to Hannibal named "Higgins" — had been disappointed in love, left a suicide note, but

when found by an anxious friend was unheroically wading
back in the shallows of Bear Creek. Mark's story, told with
full awareness of the "wretched" sport he had made, is no
doubt based on truth. "Higgins" is probably J. T. Hinton,
certainly a newcomer to town, and described as formerly on
the staff of the *Messenger,* in the announcement made in
those columns on December 11, 1852, when he married Miss
Sarah Kehoe of Hannibal.[2] He seems to have been the son
of a well-known Baptist preacher in Quincy, and Orion's
placatory paragraph spoke of the writer's having known
him elsewhere "for the past eight or ten years." That something had gone wrong with his love life is pretty clear from
an editorial paragraph headed "Verdant," which appeared
in the *Messenger* for September 4, suggesting the outrage of
his raw sensibilities before Sam began to lampoon him with
woodcuts:

> We are partial to tricks when well played, but when they
> fail in their intent, they lose their zest, were it not that the
> laugh is turned. Some SMART young man, evidently taking
> us for a "green 'un," sereptiously [*sic*] left in our sanctum a
> matrimonial notice, accompanied by a cake. The notice we
> consigned to the depths of oblivion, but the cake, being ex-
> ceedingly palatable, we devoured with gusto, laughing in
> our sleeve at the verdancy of the donor. When next such
> a trick is attempted we would advise that some person,
> whose chin has felt a razor, be selected, for without a beard,
> who'd be so verdant to take a wife.

His sneer at the puppyhood of the perpetrator — a detail
that figures in the controversy, and in Mark's recollection of
it years later — leaves one to surmise that a well-known red-
headed practical joker in village printing circles may already
have been in his mind's eye as the culprit of the cake.

In his memorable issue of the *Journal* on September 16 Sam had stirred up other hornets. In a squib styled "Editorial Agility" he burnished up his old grudge against Ament, conveniently forgetting the *Journal*'s debt to that rival who had lent a column of fillers after the January fire and rescued its equipment in the March conflagration. He now relates on the testimony of "a youngster" — probably Sam himself — how at the recent exhibit of a panorama in Benton Hall a curtain caught afire. In the audience was a certain editor. "Now it is well known that the editor of the —— is a very quiet, well-behaved little fellow, and sits still, like a good boy, as he is, unless some unlooked for accident occurs, or Pierce and King are mentioned." This allusion to the Democratic ticket in the forthcoming election of '52 delicately stamped the editor as Ament. Fearing for his press and type, just across the street, " 'thar he sot,' pale as a sheet, shaking like double rectified ague; his eyes standing out from his head; his 'nail-grabs' grasping a pew like grim death." Then "this soft-soaper of Democratic rascality . . . this father of NOTHING" jumped clean over nine pews in his hasty exit. What Ament thought of these attentions is not recorded.

Mild in comparison is a last fillip which Sam added to the issue of September 16, headed "Historical Exhibition — A No. 1 Ruse," and signed "W. Epaminondas Adrastus Blab." It offers a rambling tale of a hoax played by Abram Curts, an old-timer in Hannibal, upon Jim C—— and others, whom he charged admission to see "Bonaparte Crossing the Rhine" — a bone laid across a bacon rind. Like the yokels in *Huckleberry Finn*, Jim mutters "Sold! — cheap — as — dirt!" Still another piece in this issue bore the same pseudonym, its fourth occurrence (if two substitutions of

"Perkins" for "Blab" are allowed) within a week testifying to Sam's infatuation with it. Fittingly called "Blabbing Government Secrets," it tells how the writer's surname was altered to "Blab" by a special session of the Missouri Legislature — "all at a cost of only a few thousands of dollars to the State!" Beyond gibes at Governor King and his "Democratic Legislators" it is the most innocuous of Sam's four efforts in this issue. Clearly he had done his boyish best.

Upon Orion's return, in the *Journal* for September 23, W. Epaminondas Adrastus Blab announced that "I have retired from public life to the shades of Glascock's Island," and this brassy ignoramus is heard from no more. Sam went into rustication also, but on November 4 pretty obviously returned in an unsigned sketch called "Connubial Bliss." It reports further antics of the drunken Irishman of Holliday's Hill whose family rows continued to fascinate him. Turning aside from heavy humor, Sam moralizes about the "bloating, reeling drunkard" in a manner to win approval from that cold-water crusader Orion. At last the contrast between honeymoon days and those of wife-beating leads Sam into a pun: "Well, we are all subject to change — except printers; they never have any spare *change*." Here too Orion might have taken notice.[3] But with wood at four dollars a cord, butter twenty cents a pound, and eggs twenty cents the dozen — "rates which, if predicted a year or two since, would have astonished the natives" — the ever cash-poor editor probably had little or nothing to offer Sam and Henry but bare subsistence.[4]

One January night in 1853 another of Hannibal's numerous fires broke out. This one offered no threat to Orion's shop, but did leave memories to haunt Sam's imagination with guilt for many years. This was the fire that destroyed

the calaboose, which stood in low ground near the mouth of
Bear Creek. "The jail was a trifling little brick den that
stood in a marsh at the edge of the village, and no guards
were afforded for it; indeed, it was seldom occupied," wrote
Mark in *Tom Sawyer,* before describing how Tom and
Huck visited the luckless Muff Potter there, and passed him
tobacco and matches through the grating. According to
Life on the Mississippi and the *Autobiography,* Sam
Clemens once met a whisky-sodden tramp wandering about
the streets "one chilly evening" — other sources show it
was a Saturday night in January — and touched by his
friendless state, under the teasing of a gang of bad little
boys, got him some matches for his pipe. Sam then went
home to bed, but the tramp was picked up by the marshal
and clapped into the calaboose. In the early morning hours
the church bells rang for fire, and along with other villagers
Sam turned out to find the calaboose in flames. The
drunken tramp had set his straw bed afire, and was now
tugging frantically at the bars, "like a black object set
against a sun, so white and intense was the light at his back."
The keys were missing, and an improvised battering-ram
failed to shatter the door until long after the screaming
victim was past help. But Sam, sick at heart and filled with
self-accusation in fancying himself the cause of this tragedy,
had turned away.[5] It was certainly Orion, not Sam, who
wrote the account, headed "A Lecture on Temperance," in
the *Journal* for January 27:

> Last Sunday morning, between three and four o'clock, the
> calaboose, in this city, was discovered to be on fire, and soon
> burned to the ground. It was a brick building, but the wood
> work was dry, burned rapidly, and had made some progress
> before it was seen by any person outside. But it was seen

inside, and the cries of its single occupant were not to be mistaken for any but those of distress . . . This man was an insane Irishman — made insane by liquor — who had been incarcerated about midnight for breaking down the door of a negro cabin with an ax, and chasing out the inmates. It is supposed he set his bed clothes on fire with matches, as he usually carried them in his pocket to light his pipe, and the fire, when first seen from without, was in the corner occupied by his bed. Attempts were made to obtain the keys, and also to break down the doors, both of which proved unavailing. The Marshal, who has charge of the keys, slept four or five squares distant. . . . Before they were obtained, the fire had progressed so rapidly as already to have destroyed the man's life. . . . To those outside . . . he seemed to be leaning against the door, shrieking and moaning, until, stifled by the smoke and heated air, he fell to the floor.

Before he was deprived of his intellect, he said his name was Dennis McDermid, and that he had a mother and brother living in Madison, Indiana. He worked about eight months for Elder John M. Johnson, near this city, and proved himself a very good-hearted, clever, honest man . . . last May went to work on the plank road, indulged in drinking too freely, and lost his senses. For several months past, he seems to have had on him a kind of perpetual delirium tremens.

A few pieces of burnt flesh and bones were gathered from the ruins, deposited in a box, and interred in the city burying grounds. Thus, living and dying alone and friendless, he suffered in life, met a tragic death, and at last sleeps in a grave that no man honors.

Even he might have found a better friend than whisky.[6]

In later years, Mark realized that his "trained Presbyterian conscience" had ridden him for a deed inspired merely by kindness. "The tramp — who was to blame — suffered ten minutes; I, who was not to blame, suffered three months." The horror of death by fire, which figures so often in his medieval fantasies and entered of course into his projected book on Southern lyncherdom, here early touched his personal experience, and later was re-enforced by steamboat tragedies like that of the *Pennsylvania,* in which his brother Henry perished in 1858. Following the tramp's death, as he tells in *Life on the Mississippi,* young Sam in his dreams "for a long time afterward" saw that agonized face at the grating. He relates how his habit of talking in his sleep led to anxiety that his bedmate Henry should unriddle the mystery, but how Sam's babblings about their playfellow Ben Coontz led Henry to conclude that it was he who had supplied the tramp with matches, and thus saved Sam on the brink of confession. This too furnished literary "copy." Tom Sawyer, it will be recalled, mutters in his sleep about Injun Joe's murder of Dr. Robinson, and fearing that his model half-brother Sid will plumb the secret, binds up his own jaws nightly with supposed toothache.

Meanwhile Orion's mishaps, mingled with grandiose hopes, followed the reliable pattern. His rival of the *Messenger* announced on March 5 that "an accident occurred in the office of the Journal a few days since, which prevented our friend from issuing his paper on last Thursday as usual." Several columns of type had been accidentally thrown down, but Orion assured his readers that to make up for the default all subscriptions would be extended an extra week. A few days later, undaunted, he extended himself by starting a *Daily Journal* in addition to the weekly issue. His reply to misfortune and pitiful returns was to increase his bid. In the new daily for April 29 two pieces appeared over the signature "Rambler," which thenceforth for several weeks

became indubitably the hallmark of Sam Clemens *redivivus.*
These first ventures under a new label are bits of local
news — one telling about a stagecoach that crashed through
a cellar, the other reporting that "some French gentleman
or gentlemen" stole "two hams only" from Brittingham's
pork house. On May 5 "Rambler" contributed three stanzas
of sentimental bosh called "The Heart's Lament: To Bettie
W——e, of Tennessee." These verses and similar ones soon
to come, fastened upon Sam Clemens by his new nom de
plume, disclose him now playing the sedulous ape to another sub-literary type as familiar in newspapers of the time
as vernacular humor. This was the saccharine poetry, sown
broadcast by gift books and annuals, which he later satirized
in *Tom Sawyer,* when at school exercises a "slim, melancholy
girl" arose and recited "A Missouri Maiden's Farewell to
Alabama." [7] Hannibal in the early fifties was a nest of
singing birds, or parochial poetasters. The *Messenger* a few
months before had offered a prize of "an elegant morocco
bound Annual for 1853" for the best New Year's poem of
not less than a hundred lines. How precociously Sam realized the absurdity of such claptrap can only be guessed.
But in view of his budding interest in the genre and in
poetic parody, as well as his early love for outlandish names,
he may be suspected as the author of "Lines Written on the
death of Miss Armacinda McCan, of Monroe County,"
which Orion's paper had printed in 1852, signed "M." [8] At
any rate, clear proof of his versifying was soon to come,
along with an avalanche of prose.

The opportunity for which Sam had been waiting, ever
since his indiscretions of the previous September, is announced in the *Daily Journal* for May 6, 1853: "The Editor left yesterday for St. Louis. This must be our excuse if

the paper is lacking in interest." Immediately below fol-
lows the Sam Clemens touch, unmistakably the same young
man who had concocted the double-barreled hoax of the
steamboat disaster against the Willis girls and John Briggs:

TERRIBLE ACCIDENT!
500 MEN KILLED AND MISSING!!!
We had set the above head up, expecting (of course) to
use it, but as the accident hasn't happened, yet, we'll say
(To be Continued.)

Going down the same column, we find him paying his
respects to the editor of the Bloomington *Republican* — a
critic of Hannibal — as "that ugly monstrosity"; scolding
merchants for leaving goods boxes on the sidewalk; reporting the success of a New York printers' strike for higher
wages; and casting a cynical gibe at women. The most
famous item on this page is "Rambler's" poem, dated "Hannibal, May 4th, 1853," captioned

LOVE CONCEALED
To Miss Katie of H —— l.

The mood of three sentimental stanzas is effectually dam-
aged by that subhead, which Sam regarded as "a perfect
thunderbolt of humor." Reviewing his literary apprenticeship long afterward in the *Galaxy* he stated that the poem,
mis-recalled as "To Mary in H——l," had been sent in by
a "gorgeous journeyman tailor from Quincy" who acidly
resented the sport thus made at his expense. Most probably
it was the work of Sam's alter ego "Rambler," who signed it,
but Mark's recollection improved the story. In successive
issues, on May 7, 9, 10, 12, and 13, the raillery continued,
with "Grumbler" protesting the notion of verses addressed

to "Katie in Hell," then "Rambler" pitying his ignorance in confusing Hell with Hannibal. "Grumbler's huffy re-joinder, a sally from "Peter Pencilcase's Son John Snooks," "Rambler's" denial of the charge that he is a "coxcomb," and at last a note by the returning Editor, commanding the peace in the manner of Judge Clemens: "Rambler and his enemies must stop their 'stuff.' It is a great bore to us, and doubtless to the public generally." Except for this quietus, probably all the "stuff" had been contrived by Sam as shadowboxing.

Paine's assertion that Sam had hit upon the abbreviation "H——l" because "the title was too long to be set in one column" is not borne out by the original.[9] Sam simply thought the idea excruciating, returning to it six months later during his travels, when he wrote Orion from Phila-delphia on October 26: "Tell me all that is going on in H——l." And still more dimly remembered, over the years, the jest lingered in the alternative of "hell or Hadleyburg" in Mark's greatest short story.

Between the start and the finish of this controversy in the *Daily Journal,* Sam had salted each issue with more season-ing from the same sophomoric wit. The quality of these pages is very different from that under Orion's editorship. Sam reveled in punning marriage verses, jokes about the little girl who thought the last name of Uncle Tom's Topsy was Turvy, and the black mammy who asked the steamboat captain to wait till her hen laid the last of a dozen eggs. With no sanction from Orion he argued that the whisky tax made drinking a patriotic duty. He liked conundrums parodying school arithmetic: "If eight men dig twelve days and find nothing, how long must twenty-two men dig to find just double this amount?" He clipped a lurid murder story about a husband who trussed up his drunken wife, then poured sulphuric acid down her throat and gloated over her till she died. Locally he reported that "on last Sunday's" boating excursion to the Sny, somebody put tartar-emetic in the whisky jug, and after taking a swig one of "the b'hoys . . . made an onslaught on a pile of raw potatoes, as a means of settling his stomach, but he could not get over one potatoe down before 'twould come roaring back again with a sound like some one hallooing "New York!' 'New York!' " [10]

Apparently just as Orion returned, on May 13 Sam printed his most polished effort, "Oh, She has a Red Head," a mock-heroic defense of all whose hair was the color of his own — with assurance that Jefferson had red hair, and the conjecture that so did Adam and Jesus Christ. His avowal that "*all* children, before their tastes are corrupted, and their judgments perverted, are fond of red," must have pleased his mother Jane, who like all red-headed Lamptons from whom she sprang took an almost ecstatic delight in that color. Orion too approved the article, and after Sam had left Hannibal, on June 9 remarked that it had "afforded much comfort to the red-headed portion of the community," while grumbling at the reprints which had failed to give his *Journal* due credit.

In fact Orion's homecoming, unlike his return eight months before, did not snuff out the flame of Sam's wit. Tardily he must have realized that in this younger brother he had an editorial asset. The lively jig continues, and Sam almost certainly is the fiddler. As if with a defiant glance over the shoulder at foes of the Dog-be-Deviled Citizen, he writes: "To prevent Dogs going mad in August: Cut their heads off in July." Helpfully he tells how "to check a

Runaway Horse: Throw an empty flour barrel at him. Green cotton umbrellas are also good, but not always so accessible." And, while Orion was grinding out a filler about his recent stay at the Planter's House and the provincial blunder he had made in addressing the clerk as "bar keeper," Sam was preparing to launch the lively chatter of "Our Assistant's Column." It began on May 23, an olla-podrida of quips, town topics, and comments on world affairs. He rushed with ardor into the perennial feud between Hannibal and its Illinois neighbor Quincy, that "one horse town with stern wheel prospects" as Orion's *Journal* liked to call it. Here and along the bottoms lived the long-limbed ungainly "Suckers," in their dingy yellow linsey-woolseys, who had hardly seen a railroad or learned about illuminating gas, Sam implied. Young Clemens of Missouri, a "Puke" in their vocabulary of retaliation, promised to teach them "manners." He also plunged with vivacity into a quarrel that had been brewing for some time between the *Journal* and the Bloomington (Missouri) *Republican,* edited by an irascible candidate for the legislature named Abner Gilstrap. Sam mysteriously promised to "tell that circus story on you," but refrained. In his first "Assistant's Column" he parodied "The Burial of Sir John Moore" to inter "Sir Abner Gilstrap" in six stanzas, of which a specimen will serve:

> No useless coffin confined his breast,
>   Nor in sheet nor shirt we bound him;
> But he lay like an Editor taking his rest,
>   With a Hannibal Journal around him.

In his *Galaxy* memoirs Mark states that the angry editor stormed into his sanctum, but taking the measure of his boyish adversary, subsided after a war whoop. Again embroidery may be suspected.

Sam's taste of independence no doubt increased his dissatisfaction with Hannibal and subservience to a ne'er-do-well brother. Hard work, often till late at night, month after month and year after year had left him in his eighteenth year richer in experience and self-confidence, but with empty pockets in his "poor, shabby clothes." Paine states that not long before Sam left Hannibal, he had asked Orion for a few dollars to buy a secondhand gun. Orion, vexed by his own chronic failure to make ends meet, denied the request and scolded him for such extravagant thoughts. Sam then confided to Jane Clemens his resolution to leave home, under Orion's lack of appreciation, and try his luck in the world. Pamela was living in St. Louis with her prosperous husband, and there Sam proposed to go and find a printer's job. His sights were really set upon a farther range. In the last "Assistant's Column" he wrote for Orion, on May 26, Sam had inserted a paragraph about the fifteen to twenty thousand persons who were "continually congregated around the new Crystal Palace in New York City," adding that "drunkenness and debauching are carried on to their fullest extent." The association of ideas might have been too much for his gentle mother. So Sam spoke only of St. Louis.

Sadly his mother helped Sam pack his meager gear. Then she took up a Bible and laid his hand beside hers. "I want you to repeat after me, Sam, these words," she said. "I do solemnly swear that I will not throw a card or drink a drop of liquor while I am gone." Dutifully he repeated the words, and she kissed him.[11] During the year of wandering that followed there is no reason to believe Sam broke his promise. It was not in his nature to take such things lightly.

Later, of course, the term expired. A certain annoyance at
the sentiment of such oaths and pledges superimposing upon
free spirits the moral codes of others, can be detected in
the days of his maturity. In 1870 he told readers of the
Galaxy how his "grandmother" had pledged him never to
chew before breakfast, never to gamble without a "cold
deck" in his pocket, and never to drink — water. He loved
to tell the yarn of an old sea captain who took the pledge in
candidacy for a temperance club, then sailed on a long and
grueling voyage, and returned after rigors of heroic abstinence to find that after all he had been blackballed. "How
I do hate those enemies of the human race who go around
enslaving God's free people with *pledges* — to quit drinking instead of to quit *wanting* to drink," Mark once wrote
Henry Ward Beecher, and in his last travel book observed
that "to make a *pledge* of any kind is to declare war against
nature, for a pledge is a chain that is always clanking and
reminding the wearer of it that he is not a free man." [12] It
is not difficult to believe that Jane Clemens' solemn require-
ment may have added more than a featherweight to her
son's lifelong rebellion against the principle implied in forg-
ing such shackles.

Orion's advertisement on May 27, "Wanted! An Apprentice to the Printing Business. Apply Soon," roughly
marks the date of Sam's departure from Hannibal. This appeal ran for two weeks. Missing Sam's skill, industry, and
merriment around the shop and home, Orion straightway
was filled with that self-reproach which came so readily upon
all the Clemenses. He upbraided himself as "gloomy,
taciturn, and selfish." Lacking Sam's steadying purpose,
Orion failed to get out the *Daily Journal* for a whole month,
between June 11 and July 11, 1853. Wryly he explained in

his weekly for June 30: "We shall recommence the publication of the Daily Journal in the course of a week or two — so soon as we can gather our hands together, who have gone off on a sort of 'bust.'" The spirit of dullness settled again upon all the output of his press, and in retrospect Orion saw how much Sam's labor as well as his exuberant clowning had helped.

The last verses that Sam wrote in Hannibal did not appear in Orion's *Journal*. They were cherished privately, in an autograph album where he had written them for the latest of his many girl friends, Ann Virginia Ruffner, just his own age:

> Good-by, good-by,
> I bid you now, my friend;
> And though 'tis hard to say the word,
> To destiny I bend.[13]

The good-bye Sam spoke to Hannibal that early summer was, in one sense, a final and absolute valediction. That he would not return to Hannibal save as a visitant transitory as his own Mysterious Stranger, he could not know. Sam Clemens emerged from his matrix to range the world as prentice printer, Mississippi pilot, miner, journalist, lecturer, and ultimately, author. But Mark Twain never said good-bye to Hannibal.

No major artist ever made more of his boyhood than did Samuel Clemens. He found himself better adapted to Hannibal than to any other environment he ever met. As adult life with its casuistries and introspections grew more complex, he worshipped this golden age all the more — achieving in *Tom Sawyer* and *Huckleberry Finn* the universal

Hannibal, the home town of all boys everywhere. Then, in the still later years when this complexity neared the peak of disaster and his creative strength waned, he began tragically to find his access to this avenue of escape more and more difficult, as a mass of unfinished, unpublished stories about Tom and Huck attest. And, while he never ceased trying to blast away this road block, in his despair he turned increasingly against a modern world he never made, in bitterness and disillusion. It might be said that a humorist by temperament, for example Benjamin Franklin, is a man serenely adjusted to his environment, while a wit like Jonathan Swift is not. Clemens himself — "Mark the double Twain," as Dreiser called him, all his engaging self-contradictions making him a "human philopena" like his own extraordinary twins, Luigi and Angelo — partook of both natures. And so, while one side of his creative nature lived and moved upon the level of his boyhood, in almost perfect control of his materials, the other battled with clumsy valor upon the darkling plain of his maturity. By instinct he knew what a boy was like, from having been one himself in a river town in the golden age before the War; but to the question, What is Man? his self-taught philosophy yielded no better answers than that Man is either a knave or an illusion, "wandering forlorn among the empty eternities."

ACKNOWLEDGMENTS

PARTICULAR acknowledgment is made to the trustees of the Mark Twain Estate and Harper and Brothers for permission to quote from the works of Mark Twain. Very deep gratitude is expressed to the following who have given invaluable help in the preparation of this book. Owing to posthumous publication, it is feared that there are inevitable omissions, which are regretted.

Mrs. W. E. Bach, Miss Ellen Barrett, George Beadle, Mrs. B. J. Bolin, the late George H. Brownell, Buffalo Public Library, Mrs. R. P. Burdette, Thomas D. Clark, Kenneth Crouch, Mrs. Marcella DuPont, Mrs. Katherine W. Ewing, Miss Clara Frazer, Mrs. Norman Frost, Mrs. E. L. Gibbon, Harvard College Library, Mrs. W. W. Hinshaw, Albert R. Hogue, E. E. Jones, Miss Barbara Kell, Karl Kiedaisch, Jr., Mrs. Erle O. Kistler, Miss Isabel Lyon, The Mark Twain Museum (Hannibal), Mrs. Margaret Norris, New York Public Library (Berg Collection), Miss Ruth Richart, the Reverend Harold Roberts, Samossoud Collection, Mrs. V. L. Savedge, John C. Schmidt, Floyd C. Shoemaker, Miss Mollie Smith, Earl G. Swen, Mrs. R. McB. Varble, D. P. Violette, Ulysses Walsh, Mrs. E. A. Watson, the late Mrs. Annie Moffett Webster, Mr. and Mrs. Samuel Webster, Miss Dora Lee Wright, G. Harry Wright, Yale College Library.

SHORT-TITLE INDEX

NOTES

CHAPTER ONE

[1] This book is preserved among the MTP. Paine, *Biography*, p. 1, makes this comment but, with Paine's unfailing habit of diluting the salt, waters down both Suetonius and Mark Twain.

[2] Samuel L. Clemens to O. B. Sears, July 16 (1902); original letter in Mark Twain Museum, Hannibal, Mo. The sketch of John Clemens appears in "Hellfire Hotchkiss" (MTP, DV 310b), in which Clemens appears in the guise of Judge James Carpenter.

[3] *Autobiography*, I, 121.

[4] C. H. Firth, "Gregory Clement," *Dictionary of National Biography*, XI, 32–33. In MTP is a letter dated Sept. 2, 1876, to Mark Twain from the Hon. Sherrard Clemens, ex-Congressional fire-eater from western Virginia, then of St. Louis, which begins: "I regret, very deeply, to see that you have announced your adhesion to that inflated bladder, from the bowels of Sardis Burchard, Rutherford Burchard Hayes. You come, with myself, from Gregory Clemens, the regicide, who voted for the death of Charles and who was beheaded, disembowelled, and drawn in a hurdle." Sherrard adds he would rather have an ancestor who was hanged than to vote for Hayes. Mark Twain's endorsement: "From a fool." See *Autobiography*, I, 87, for further comment on Sherrard.

[5] John Clement, *Sketches of the First Emigrant Settlers in Newton Township, West New Jersey*, pp. 267–76. A Geoffrey Clements, shareholder in the Virginia Company, is claimed as ancestor by certain Clements of Virginia; see "Clements of Surry Co., Va., & Baltimore, Maryland," *Tyler's Quarterly*, XVII, 125.

[6] In refuting the untrustworthy genealogical work of William M. Clemens, Mrs. N. E. Clement in "Clement, Clements, Clemans. With a Notice of Mark Twain's Ancestry," *Virginia Magazine of History*,

XXXII, 292–98, notes recurrences of the name Samuel Clements in eighteenth-century records of Surry County, Va., but many unfilled gaps remain. A Captain Francis Clemens, who led a colony of nine persons to Virginia in 1689, obtained a grant of 450 acres, occupied several important public offices in Surry County, and later moved into adjacent Isle of Wight County, is suggested as a forebear, but again the line is not verifiable, and no other has been established.

7 Clemens, "What Paul Bourget Thinks of Us," *Literary Essays,* pp. 163–64.

8 J. B. Boddie, *Seventeenth Century Isle of Wight County, Virginia,* p. 112. For the Reynoldses and Moormans, see S. F. Tillman, *The Rennolds–Reynolds Family of England and Virginia,* pp. 1–2, and R. H. Early, *Campbell Chronicles and Family Sketches,* pp. 460–65.

9 C. O. Paullin, "The Moorman Family of Virginia," WMQ, 2d ser., XII, 177. For the Clarks, see Edgar Woods, *Albemarle County in Virginia,* pp. 165–66.

10 As printed by J. P. Bell, *Our Quaker Friends of ye Olden Time,* p. 131, under date of March 9, 1767, which is an error for 1765, as W. W. Hinshaw's *Encyclopedia of American Quaker Genealogy,* VI, 260, makes clear, and since Bedford County Records cited below show that the will of Thomas Moorman, husband of Rachel, was probated late in 1766.

11 Paullin, "The Moorman Family of Virginia," p. 178. Manumission became effective only after Virginia in 1787 passed "an act to confirm the freedom of certain negroes late the property of Charles Moorman, deceased"; W. W. Hening, *The Statutes at Large,* XII, 613–16. In 1777 the South River Meeting, associated with the Moormans, had formed a Friends' Manumission Committee to urge and assist the freeing of slaves: Herbert Aptheker, "The Quakers and Negro Slavery," *Journal of Negro History,* XXV, 352.

12 The will of Mark Twain's great-great-grandfather Thomas Moorman is in Bedford County Courthouse, Will Book A–1, pp. 32–34, as noted by C. O. Paullin, "Mark Twain's Virginia Kin," WMQ, 2d ser., XV, 297; and transcribed in full for Dixon Wecter by Ulysses Walsh, Vinton, Va. Dated July 22, 1765, and probated on Nov. 25, 1766, it shows he left the plantation in Bedford County and five Negroes to his wife, and gave Pleasant and Charles, his sons, equal shares in a four-hundred acre tract "on Permunkey River in Louisa County."

13 For a photograph of the log cabin see Paullin, "Mark Twain's Virginia Kin," opp. p. 294.

14 MTP, Notebook File, under date of Jan. 2, 1904.

[15] Marriage bond is in Bedford County Courthouse, noted by Paullin, "Mark Twain's Virginia Kin," p. 295; and transcribed in full for Dixon Wecter by Ulysses Walsh, Vinton, Va. Wedding date from "Simon Hancock Family Bible," *National Genealogical Society Quarterly*, XVI, 20. Hinshaw, *Encyclopedia*, VI, 894, reports that Samuel and Pamelia were married by John Ayers.

[16] HMC, p. 915. The compiler of this volume on Aug. 29, 1883, had written Mark Twain for biographical information about his father, and Mark on Sept. 4 passed on the request to his brother Orion (correspondence in MTP, Letter File). Undoubtedly the final source of information was the long-widowed Jane Lampton Clemens, aged eighty, then living with Orion in Iowa, with apparently a fair memory at this time and keen interest in family history. An error or two in the resultant sketch — such as the confusion of Mason with Campbell County as the birthplace of J. M. Clemens — do not seriously impeach its accuracy respecting most verifiable details.

[17] The birth dates of all the children of Samuel and Pamelia Clemens, as well as of Pamelia's children by her second husband, Simon Hancock, were recorded by the latter in his family Bible; see "Simon Hancock Family Bible," p. 20. Samuel Clemens was apparently back in Bedford on Dec. 12, 1798, when he signed his name as surety to the marriage bond of his wife's sister to Obediah Tate.

[18] The indenture is preserved in MTP, Documents File; Mark's comment occurs in a letter owned by his great-nephew Samuel C. Webster. For his earlier request for family papers, see MTBM, p. 174. "Hailsford" is Hale's Ford, the crossing of this river, now celebrated as the birthplace of Booker T. Washington. "Stanton" is Staunton or Roanoke River, which bounds Bedford County on the south.

[19] Bedford County Deed Book K–11, p. 782; cited by Paullin, "Mark Twain's Virginia Kin," p. 295, and transcribed in full for Dixon Wecter by Ulysses Walsh.

[20] Records summarized by Paullin, "Mark Twain's Virginia Kin," pp. 295–96. The Clemens family retained this property until 1854; it is now part of the State Farm at Lakin, W. Va.

[21] "Emigrants to Ohio and Illinois," *Tyler's Quarterly*, VII, 87; the year is not supplied, but their departure from home on Monday, July 29, makes it clear.

[22] HMC, p. 914.

[23] Paine, *Biography*, pp. 44 and 73; *Autobiography*, II, 28.

[24] For quotation see Xantippe Saunders to A. B. Paine, June 6, 1907, MTP, Letter File. She was the granddaughter of Pamela and Simon

Hancock, as she explained more fully in a letter, n. d., to Mrs. Evelyn Singleton (typescript in Genealogy Division, Los Angeles Public Library). Bedford County Will Book B, p. 49, gives the will, probated Jan. 24, 1791, of Simon's grandfather of the same name. Samuel, Edward, John, and William appear as the elder Simon's sons, and young Simon appears as the son of William. Long afterward in Adair County (Deed Book W, p. 432) Simon and his wife, "late Pamelia Goggin," in 1833 gave power of attorney to Samuel Hancock of Bedford County in settlement of the Goggin estate, following Rachel's death.

[25] Early, *Campbell Chronicles,* pp. 377–78, lists the brothers and sisters of Pamela Goggin and their marriages. The confusion over the name "Jubal" may well result from the fact that Simon himself had a cousin of that name — grandson of the elder Simon and son of John — as shown in Hancock family correspondence transcribed for Dixon Wecter by a descendant, E. E. Jones of Bluefield, W. Va. In MS records of the Goggin family the name "Mary" appears, but "Polly" was probably the more familiar name or nickname. In the documents cited below from MTP in settlement of the estate of Samuel B. Clemens in 1820–21, the name of Alexander Gill occurs repeatedly as bondsman or trustee, and a scrap of genealogy labeled "Children of William Goggin" confirms that this Gill was Pamela's brother-in-law.

[26] For example, that of Jan. 1, 1821, whereby Simon and Pamela Hancock renounce all rights in this estate; MTP, Documents File. Paine's statements occur in the *Biography,* p. 2, and the account indebted to Orion's help will be found in HMC, p. 914. The theory that Mark Twain's puzzling middle name "Langhorne" might have come from his father's association with the Langhorne mill at Lynchburg does not hold water. Apparently the only iron foundry in operation at this time was the Oxford (or Ross) Furnace. The Langhorne mill of a later period was a grist or flour mill.

[27] Wedding date from "Simon Hancock Family Bible," p. 20. Their marriage bond appears in Adair County Records under date of May 20, 1808.

[28] Adair County Order Book A, July 4, 1809, and Deed Book B. of 1811, p. 404. "Patrollers," selected from the militia, were organized to enforce the laws regulating the conduct of the Negroes at night.

[29] The Adair County Court in its December Term, 1820, issued him a certificate to administer this estate, also appointing him guardian of the minor children Hannibal and Caroline; MTP, Documents File.

[30] This bill of accounts, dated Jan. 9, 1821, is in MTP, Documents File; the sequel of Betsy Clemens' visit to Virginia is reported by Paullin, "Mark Twain's Virginia Kin," p. 297.

[31] Receipts given by Hancock to Marshall Clemens dated July 6, 1821, and Jan. 5, 1822; MTP, Documents File.

[32] All these indentures are in MTP, Documents File. The sideboard is mentioned by Paine, *Biography*, p. 2.

[33] This license is in MTP, Documents File. His preparation for the bar is mentioned in HMC, p. 914.

[34] HMC, pp. 914–15; for the intellectual backgrounds, see Niels H. Sonne, *Liberal Kentucky, 1780–1828*.

[35] The marriage bond, in the Adair County Records, Columbia, Ky., was found recently by Mrs. B. J. Bolin of that town. Mark's statement (*Autobiography*, I, 87) that his parents were married in Lexington is not borne out by the facts. Orion's information supplied to Holcombe, HMC, p. 914, gives the wedding date as Tuesday, May 6, 1823, and the distance from Lexington to Columbia was well over a day's journey.

CHAPTER TWO

[1] Xantippe Saunders to A. B. Paine, June 6, 1907 (MTP, Letter File), in common with other sources remarks upon Jane's fame as a local beauty. The red hair was a Lampton trait, as noted by Samuel Webster, who inherits it himself; MTBM, p. 136.

[2] Untitled MS, a six-page fragment in Orion's hand, MTP, Documents File.

[3] Adair County Order Book D, Nov. 6, 1821, for Walker's appointment as county attorney and Feb. 3, 1823, as justice of the peace.

[4] Retold by Samuel L. Clemens to W. D. Howells, May 19, 1886, *Letters*, pp. 468–69. Original letter in Berg Collection, NYPL.

[5] Orion Clemens to Samuel L. Clemens, July 14, 1885, MTP, Letter File.

[6] Barrett appears in the Index of Medical Students at Transylvania College. For the sketch of his life, see J. Thomas Scharf, *History of Saint Louis City and County*, I, 677.

[7] The *Daily Gazette* (Burlington), Oct. 1, 1885, and the Burlington *Hawkeye*, Oct. 1, 1885, carry accounts of the reunion but make no mention of a Dr. Barrett.

[8] The "Villagers," an unpublished MS (MTP, DV 47), in which the doctor is named "Ray." In Samuel Clemens' dictation of Dec. 29, 1906, MTP, the doctor's name is recalled as "Gwynne." See also Paine, *Biography*, p. 4.

[9] Samuel L. Clemens, dictation of Dec. 29, 1906, MTP.

10 The quotation from Mark is drawn from MTP, DV 206. Paine, *Biography*, p. 3.

11 Lewis and Richard Collins, *History of Kentucky*, II, 472–73.

12 Untitled six-page fragment in Orion's hand, MTP, Documents File.

13 Collins, *History*, I, 12; and F. B. Heitman, *Historical Register of Officers of the Continental Army*, p. 118. Description of William Casey from Judge Rollin Hurt, "The Permanent Settlement of Adair County," *Adair County News* (1919); typescript in MTP.

14 Collins, *History*, I, 356, and II, 124 and 775; William B. Allen, *A History of Kentucky*, p. 382. Stories of Casey's prowess as an Indian fighter are told in Hurt, "The Permanent Settlement of Adair County," MTP.

15 Marriage bond in Green County Records (Greensburg, Ky.) dated March 17, 1801, containing signatures of both Mark Twain's great-grandfather, William Casey, and his grandfather, Benjamin Lampton. Photostat in MTP. The description of Benjamin is drawn from the untitled MS in Orion's hand, MTP, Documents File.

16 Lampton Bible, in Mrs. W. B. Ardery, comp., *Kentucky Records*, I, 156. The name Patsy was inherited by Mark Twain's aunt, Patsy Ann Lampton Quarles.

17 For a typical discussion of "claimants" see Clemens, *Is Shakespeare Dead?* The Tichborne scrapbooks are in MTP. For early Lampton backgrounds, note Clayton Keith, *Sketch of the Lampton Family in America, 1740–1914*, though often inaccurate; C. O. Paullin, "Mark Twain's Virginia Kin," WMQ, 2d ser., XV, 297–98; *Autobiography*, I, 120 ff.

18 Adair County Order Book A: June 28, 1802; July 4, 1803; May 7, 1804; March 4, 1805; and April 6, 1807. On Dec. 4, 1805, Benjamin obtained the farm on Russell's Creek from the estate of Arthur Hopkins, the tutor his father-in-law had employed and then paid by conveyance of land; Adair County Deed Book E, p. 730; and Hurt, "The Permanent Settlement of Adair County," MTP.

19 The untitled MS in Orion's hand in MTP, Documents File, gives Jane's birth date, and also gives Columbia as her place of birth, but there is no supporting evidence for the latter statement. Patsy's birth date of March 22, 1807, is recorded on her tombstone and is verified by family records. Present-day Lampton Lane is mentioned in *Kentucky, a Guide to the Bluegrass State*, p. 432.

20 Adair County Order Book B, April 1, 1811, and Jan. 6, 1812; this structure now forms part of the house occupied by Mrs. Thomas E. Paull.

21 License appears in Adair County Order Book B, Feb. 3, 1812, with Benjamin Lampton signing as security. Lewis operated the tavern for the next decade, as the county records show. His brother Joshua was licensed as publican in late 1818, Order Book D, Dec. 7, 1818. Hurt, "The Permanent Settlement of Adair County," MTP, describes the roistering.

22 Militia records in the Kentucky Historical Society at Frankfort recorded by Mrs. Rachel McB. Varble of South Fort Mitchell, Ky. The oath was found by Mrs. Ruth P. Burdette of Columbia, photostats in MTP. See *Acts Passed at the First Session of the Twentieth General Assembly for the Commonwealth of Kentucky*, pp. 178–80, for the oath required of military officers.

23 Adair County Deed Book C, p. 456, under date of Sept. 18, 1814.

24 The Casey house still stands, although the service wing is not the original. Built of dark brown Adair County brick, it has thirteen large rooms, two hallways and four fireplaces; information supplied by Mrs. B. J. Bolin of Columbia, Ky.

25 Adair County Will Book B, p. 235, dated Aug. 31, 1816, probated Jan. 6, 1817 (Cyrus Walker appears as one of the witnesses); Deed Book D, p. 339, under date of April 24, 1817.

26 This last transaction is recorded in Adair County Deed Book E, p. 773. Earlier records pertaining to the Lampton affairs, summarized above, are found in Deed Book D, pp. 329 and 339; Deed Book E, pp. 73, 232, 233, 286, 298, 317, 417, 593, 604, 668, 727, 770, 773, 812, and 818; and the Town Trustees' Proceedings Book under date of Jan. 22, 1822. The fire company roster is recorded in Order Book D. Lewis Lampton died in the early summer of 1824. Marriage bond of Benjamin Lampton and Mary M. Hays is in Adair County Records under date of Feb. 1, 1819.

27 Clemens, *Roughing It*, II, 15, in which Mark speaks also of the "national distinction" of this stock, alluding no doubt to Virginia's Congressmen Sherrard Clemens and Alabama's Senator Jere Clemens (*Autobiography*, I, 86), whose family connection however cannot be proved. For Jane's pride in the Clemenses see *Autobiography*, II, 91.

28 Paullin, "Mark Twain's Virginia Kin," p. 298.

CHAPTER THREE

1 *Autobiography*, I, 87, and an autobiographical summary in Clemens' hand, written for his nephew Samuel E. Moffett around 1900 and now in the Berg Collection, NYPL. Mark Twain's unfounded claim that his parents were married in Lexington has already been noted.

2 In old age John Field often told this story of Jane Casey's solicitude, "with tears," according to Judge Rollin Hurt, "The Permanent Settlement of Adair County," *Adair County News* (1919); typescript in MTP.

3 Paine, *Biography*, p. 5; HMC, p. 914; Federal Writers' Project, *Tennessee*, p. 445; Judge Hurt's memoir for Dr. Nathan Montgomery (typescript in MTP); and six-page fragment by Orion about his mother, MTP, Documents File.

4 From a five-page MS in Orion's hand, signed "Cumberland" and dated St. Louis, March 11, 1867, which he sent to the St. Louis *Times*; MTP, Documents File.

5 Adair County Order Book E, Oct. 14, 1829, refers to him as "Hannibal Clemens of Fentress County, Tennessee."

6 The spirit of boosterism in Fentress County, as Mark Twain has his father express it (*Autobiography*, I, 4), remained unchanged a generation later. This is reflected in Hermann Bokum, *The Tennessee Hand-Book and Immigrant's Guide*, p. 67.

7 From an unpublished MS in MTP, Documents File, entitled "The Tennessee Land." Such a house is redescribed in Samuel L. Clemens and Charles Dudley Warner, *The Gilded Age*, I, 17.

8 Fentress County Records covering the years 1828 to 1835, cited by A. R. Hogue, *One Hundred Years in the Cumberland Mountains along the Continental Line*, pp. 11–13. See also Hogue, *History of Fentress County, Tennessee*, pp. 12–13.

9 Fentress County Deed Book A, p. 244, under date of May 20, 1833. Deed Books A, E, G, H, and I, as well as the Entry Book, Register's Office, Fentress County Court House, carry continuous mention of John M. Clemens' land transactions during this period. *Autobiography*, I, 3–7, printed from an MS written in 1870 (MTP, Documents File) which shows that Mark originally conjectured the land's cost at $100, later altering the sum to $400. See also A. V. Goodpasture, "Mark Twain, Southerner," *Tennessee Historical Magazine*, 2d ser., I, 255–60.

10 *Autobiography*, I, 94. "Sellers," of course, refers to Colonel Sellers of *The Gilded Age*, modeled after "my mother's favorite cousin, James Lampton." See *Autobiography*, p. 89.

11 MTBM, p. 44.

12 HMC, pp. 914–15. U.S. Census of 1830 shows John Marshall Clemens, wife, and three children, with one slave, living with Hannibal Clemens and his young wife, at Jamestown.

[13] Dr. J. T. Jones, "The House Mark Twain's Father Built," *Prose and Poems,* pp. 45–48.

[14] Records of Appointments of Postmasters, Vol. 12A, p. 127, in the National Archives, in which John M. Clemens' appointment from April 3, 1832, to May 28, 1835, appears.

[15] Jones, "The House Mark Twain's Father Built," p. 45.

[16] Jones, "The House Mark Twain's Father Built," p. 47; MTBM, p. 14.

[17] Samuel L. Clemens and Charles Dudley Warner, *The Gilded Age,* I, 18 and 26.

[18] Wedding date from family records in the possession of Mrs. O. C. Herdman of Waco, Texas.

[19] Since the fifth child of the Quarleses, William Frederick, was born in Tennessee on Dec. 15, 1833, and yet they were well settled in Missouri months before the Clemenses were to arrive, early 1834 would seem a probable date. Clayton Keith, *Sketch of the Lampton Family in America,* pp. 10–11, prints the recollections of the Rev. Eugene J. Lampton, son of Benjamin Lampton's much younger brother Wharton Schooler Lampton, one-time jailor in Columbia, who joined them in Florida late in 1835, after the arrival of John Marshall and Jane Clemens. Eugene Lampton's accuracy in regard to dates leaves much to be desired, but the factual information here supplied in the lack of conflicting testimony may be taken as probably trustworthy. Mark Twain does not give, and probably did not know, the date at which his grandfather Ben Lampton reached Florida.

[20] *Autobiography,* I, 5; Ralph C. H. Catterall, *The Second Bank of the United States,* pp. 317–18.

[21] MTBM, p. 42.

[22] MTBM, p. 5, mentions the abandoned sojourn in St. Louis, as told by Jane Clemens to her granddaughter; for earlier details of the journey, Paine, *Biography,* pp. 10–11, is the chief source. The proposed history of lynching is discussed in letter of Samuel L. Clemens to Frank Bliss, Aug. 26, 1901; photostat in MTP, Letter File. Report of the actual lynching from the St. Louis *Missouri Republican,* April 30, 1836.

[23] MTP, Documents File, "The Tennessee Land."

CHAPTER FOUR

[1] The parallel to the yet unborn jumping frog of Calaveras County is obvious. T. V. Bodine, "A Visit to Florida," Kansas City *Star* (May 19,

1912). Clayton Keith, *Sketch of the Lampton Family in America,* pp. 13–14, tells the frog story also. The Rev. Harold Roberts, in an unpublished MS (typescript in MTP) about Clemens' boyhood days in Florida, Missouri, to which the present writer is much indebted, collects other stories traditionally told by Quarles. Parts of the MS were published in the *Twainian,* n.s., I, No. 2 (Feb. 1942), under the title "Sam Clemens: Florida Days." The complete manuscript version will henceforth be referred to as Roberts, MS in MTP. *Autobiography,* I, 8–9, describes the store.

2 *Autobiography,* I, 96. Bodine and Roberts comment upon his religion and community standing. Quarles's obituary, Paris (Mo.) *Mercury* (March 7, 1876), mentions his county judgeship; a deed acknowledged before him as justice of the peace, dated April 28, 1851, is now in the Mark Twain Museum, Hannibal.

3 Harold Roberts, "Sam Clemens: Florida Days," *Twainian,* n.s., I, No. 2 (Feb. 1942), pp. 1–2, after careful investigation offers evidence supporting the identification made during Mark's lifetime by old-timers like the late Merritt A. Violette, through whose civic enterprise the house has been preserved.

4 *Autobiography,* I, 95.

5 Columbia *Missouri Intelligencer,* April 16, 1831.

6 *History of Monroe and Shelby Counties,* pp. 151–53, pictures the transformation at that date, which present observation confirms.

7 Monroe County Records, Register of the Land Office, June 10 and 27, 1835, as cited by Roberts, MS in MTP.

8 T. J. J. See, "The Return of Halley's Comet," *Munsey's Magazine,* XLIII, 3–12, supplies the dates (in correction of Paine, *Biography,* p. 1576 n.), and gives an illustration of the comet's appearance as seen in 1835.

9 Unpublished MS in MTP, DV 326, "The Mysterious Stranger in Hannibal."

10 Dr. Chowning married in 1843 and died in 1854; the daguerreotype is owned by his granddaughter, Miss Ruth Richart of Florida, whose mother often told her that he was the obstetrician. Samuel Clemens, on his last visit to Hannibal in 1902, is reported to have confirmed this.

11 Cited by Roberts, MS in MTP, from *Centennial History of Missouri,* ed. Walter B. Stevens (6 vols., St. Louis, 1921), I, 121.

12 Paine, *Biography,* p. 13 n., names only three claimants, but the present superintendent of the Mark Twain State Park at Florida, Mr.

Schmidt, has extended the list. Clemens, *The Adventures of Huckle-berry Finn,* pp. 357–60.

[13] Paine, *Biography,* p. 13. J. M. Clemens' grandmother, Rachel Moorman, had an elder sister Mary whose descendants intermarried with the Langhornes in Virginia, from whom the present Lady Astor springs; "Mark and Joseph Anthony Families of Virginia, with Contributory Data on Capt. Christopher Clark and Moorman Families," by F. A. Swain: typescript, NYPL Genealogical Room. Langhornes are found in Campbell County, where J. M. Clemens was born; R. H. Early, *Campbell Chronicles and Family Sketches,* p. 447; and also in early nineteenth-century Kentucky, Lewis and Richard Collins, *History of Kentucky,* II, 771.

[14] Jane Clemens to Olivia Langdon Clemens, Jan. 7, 1885, MTP, Letter File. *Autobiography,* I, 108.

[15] MTBM, p. 45.

[16] Samuel L. Clemens and Charles Dudley Warner, *The Gilded Age,* I, 63–64.

[17] Told to the author by Mr. D. P. Violette of Florida, who often heard the statement from his grandmother, Eliza Damrell Violette (Scott).

[18] Paine, *Biography,* p. 17. In "Villagers" (MTP, DV 47) Mark states that his father "whipped her with a bridle."

[19] Lampton had purchased this house less than two months before for $1000 from John Bryant, who had built the house (Monroe County Recorder's Deed Record, Book B, p. 242, cited by Roberts, MS in MTP).

[20] *Autobiography,* I, 96, and Keith, *Sketch of the Lampton Family,* pp. 12–13.

[21] Paine, *Biography,* p. 20, tells a story of frustration in getting federal pork-barrel aid for Salt River navigation, which inspired the phrase, first ascribed to Quarles; but this is not borne out by the facts. See *Laws of the State of Missouri, 1st. Session of the 9th General Assembly,* pp. 229–34, for the incorporation; and Minnie M. Brashear, *Mark Twain, Son of Missouri,* p. 44, n. 34, for use of the phrase as early as 1837.

[22] *Laws of the State of Missouri* (1837), pp. 237 and 147.

[23] Monroe County Court Records, Vol. A, p. 142; his two fellow justices were Samuel Curtright and Jonathan Gore, later well-known names in local judicial history.

24 Clemens, *The Adventures of Tom Sawyer,* p. 41, and *Pudd'nhead Wilson,* p. 14.

25 *Revised Statutes of the State of Missouri . . . 8th General Assembly,* pp. 155–56, and *Revised Statutes of the State of Missouri . . . 13th General Assembly,* p. 331.

26 Monroe County Recorder's Deed Record, Book F, pp. 112–13. Both the second and third houses have been destroyed, but a photograph of the latter appears in Paine, *Biography* (1912 ed.), opp. p. 20.

27 Date from a letter of Samuel L. Clemens to John Robards, June 10 (1876), supplying date for the tombstone; MTP, Clipping File.

28 For the history of the Quarles farm Roberts (MS in MTP) refers to Monroe County Recorder's Deed Record, Book L, pp. 499–500.

29 For Quarles's success as a farmer, see Hannibal *Journal,* Aug. 19, 1847.

30 George I. Bidewell, "Mark Twain's Florida Years," *Missouri Historical Review,* XL, 160.

31 Paine, *Biography,* p. 22, probably from Orion's lost autobiography. A private but apparently trustworthy source asserts that most of Orion's narrative (save for scattered sheets in MTP) was lost before Mark Twain's death, when Paine's suitcase was stolen in the Grand Central Station — although Paine in fear of Mark's anger never confessed the loss. The exact date of Margaret's death is taken from her tombstone.

32 Stout's purchases from the Clemenses appear in Monroe County Recorder's Deed Record, Book E, pp. 298–99, and pp. 300–301; their purchase from him is in Marion County Deed Record, G-265.

33 HMC, p. 897. In Marion County Deed Records, G-265, Nov. 13, 1839, the property is described as "containing sixty-five and a half feet front on Second Street, and running back with Hill Street, one hundred and forty two feet to the alley, being the same now occupied by Mrs. Smith the Messrs. Shackleford & others."

34 Paine, *Biography,* p. 19.

35 Cf. Paine, *Biography,* p. 72, and *Autobiography,* II, 274, regarding Stout.

36 *Autobiography,* p. 5.

37 Orion's sentimental account, from his lost autobiography, is quoted by Paine, *Biography,* p. 24, who on p. 30 notes a later similar occurrence involving Sam. Mark Twain's own inaccurate memoir appears in "Chapters from My Autobiography," *North American Review,*

CLXXXIV, 450–51, and a variant story appears in "A Playmate of Mark Twain's," *Human Life* (May 1906), in a garbled interview with his cousin Tabitha Quarles Greening; MTP, Clipping File.

CHAPTER FIVE

[1] MTP, DV 47, "Villagers": "Ben Coontz — sent a son to W. Point." In MTP, DV 304, "Tom Sawyer's Conspiracy," Ben Coontz's name appears in miscellaneous notes with label "fool — ½ idiot."

[2] *Autobiography*, II, 272, and MTP, DV 244. His age and birthplace are drawn from the 1850 U.S. Census of Hannibal — a mine of information used frequently in the chapters that follow. His politics are mentioned, in the phrase quoted above, in Orion Clemens' Hannibal *Journal*, May 27, 1852, and his ministering to Sam appears in MTP, DV 206.

[3] Information from Mark Twain's niece, Annie Moffett Webster, Dec. 10, 1947.

[4] HMC, pp. 220–23, and 915.

[5] HMC, pp. 897 and 914, buttressed by local tradition, gives the name of this hostelry as the Virginia House, although Paine, *Biography*, p. 27, asserts that the Clemenses first lived in "Pavey's old Tavern" on Hill Street. Pavey's, however, was one block south of Hill near "Wild-Cat Corner," at Main and Bird, where T. R. Selmes later opened his locally-famous store at the sign of the wildcat (Hannibal *Journal*, Jan. 7 and Oct. 14, 1847). Later the name "Virginia House" seems to have been lost to an inn operated on Front Street by J. G. Toncray (Hannibal *Journal*, June 1, 1848).

[6] William Hyde and H. L. Conard, eds., *Encyclopedia of the History of St. Louis*, I, 407–8, give the origins and career of James Clemens, Jr. His eminence among the magnates of St. Louis is described in the phrase quoted above from Orion Clemens' Hannibal *Journal and Western Union*, Sept. 25, 1851.

[7] All of these debts are listed in Marion County Deed Records, H–375, after transfer of Oct. 13, 1841. For James A. H. Lampton see MTBM, pp. 17–18.

[8] Autobiographical sketch, Berg Collection, NYPL: typescript in MTP.

[9] In a brief description of the city, Hannibal *Gazette*, Feb. 25, 1847, from which the above summary has been drawn.

[10] Hannibal *Gazette*, Nov. 25, 1847.

11 Typescript in MTP, DV 243, from original in Buffalo Public Library. For early disapproval of the packing industry in the heart of town, Hannibal Municipal Records, I, 97, Oct. 1845.

12 Hannibal *Journal and Western Union*, June 12, 1851.

13 Clemens, "My Platonic Sweetheart," *The Mysterious Stranger*, p. 288.

14 Mark Twain to his family, June 21, 1866, text in MTP, Letter File, from original in Webster Collection; to Will Bowen, Feb. 6, 1870, in *Mark Twain's Letters to Will Bowen*, ed. Theodore Hornberger, p. 18.

15 Aug. 31, 1876, *Mark Twain's Letters to Will Bowen*, pp. 23–24. The original letter, which Clemens went to the "unheard of trouble of re-writing and saying the same harsh things softly so as to sugarcoat the anguish" before sending to Bowen, is the only text that survives.

16 Nov. 4, 1888, in *Letters*, p. 502.

17 Feb. 2, 1891, in *Letters of James Whitcomb Riley*, ed. W. L. Phelps, pp. 329–30; and to Mrs. Boardman (Jenny Stevens), March 25, 1887, original letter in Berg Collection, NYPL.

18 Samuel L. Clemens to Thomas Bailey Aldrich, Dec. 6, 1893, original in Harvard College Library.

19 W. D. Howells quoted by Lorena M. Gary, "Oh Youth! Mark Twain: Boy and Philosopher," *Overland Monthly*, 2d ser., XCI, 154.

20 Samuel L. Clemens to Miss Kate Staples, Oct. 8, 1886, original in Berg Collection, NYPL.

CHAPTER SIX

1 From Mark's unpublished novel version of "Simon Wheeler, Detective," in the Berg Collection, NYPL.

2 Information to the writer from Pamela's daughter, Annie Moffett Webster.

3 *Galaxy*, IX, 866, and X, 286. The yarns set within this framework, however, can hardly be taken as true — including a pun Sam made at the age of two, and a tale about his father's fondness for "Hiawatha," which was not published during the latter's lifetime.

4 Clemens, *Following the Equator*, II, 28–29. The traditions of the stern father, at this time and place, are also illustrated in *The Callaghan Mail*, ed. H. H. Haines, pp. 58–60.

⁵ MTP, DV 326, "The Mysterious Stranger in Hannibal."

⁶ MTP, DV 327, a discarded portion of the published *The Mysterious Stranger.* Thinly disguised references to the Quarles farm and to Hannibal villagers support the identification.

⁷ MTP, DV 310b, "Hellfire Hotchkiss," in which "Judge Carpenter" — the pseudonym also used in "Villagers" — bears the same unmistakable traits of sternness and irreligion (he had been to church only once in nineteen years of marriage).

⁸ MTP, Clipping File, from Hannibal *Courier,* accompanied by a letter from John Robards to Samuel L. Clemens, June 5, 1882.

⁹ HMC, p. 900; for the Clemenses' unprosperity, Paine, *Biography,* pp. 27 and 41–42.

¹⁰ *Bray & Bailey* v. *Ira Stout,* No. 2406, Marion County Circuit Court Records; as reported on Jan. 12, 1842, the case was ultimately settled out of court.

¹¹ Hannibal Municipal Records, I, 134, June 15, 1846; his offer seems not to have been accepted, although on July 8 he was appointed a district overseer.

¹² Hannibal *Journal,* March 11, 1847, and Hannibal *Gazette,* April 22, 1847. Unable to dispose of all his Hannibal holdings, he later let some go at public sale for nonpayment of taxes (Hannibal *Journal,* Feb. 1 and Oct. 5, 1849). His residing in Quincy is noted in Orion Clemens' Hannibal *Western Union,* Jan. 16, 1851.

¹³ Marion County Deed Records, J–315, for the complete transaction; on Feb. 2, 1842, Jane Clemens relinquished her dower rights in this property (0–539).

¹⁴ A useful résumé by an able Hannibal lawyer of today, Mr. Harrison White, appeared in the Hannibal *Courier-Journal,* April 19, 1947.

¹⁵ MTP, DV 47 and DV 206.

¹⁶ *Autobiography,* I, 124. Beebe "the nigger trader" appears thinly disguised in MTP, DV 326, "The Mysterious Stranger in Hannibal."

¹⁷ Marion County Circuit Court Records, No. 2685, *State of Missouri* v. *George Thompson, Alanson Work, and James Burr;* and HMC, pp. 256–59. Some five years later Governor Edwards pardoned the men.

¹⁸ MTP, DV 206. *Autobiography,* I, 101–2, tells the story in somewhat different words at a later date; and Paine, *Biography,* p. 42, retells it in still other words that Paine invented for himself, as his script reveals.

19 Clemens, *Following the Equator*, II, 28; and Paine, *Biography*, p. 1040.

20 Clemens, "The Private History of a Campaign That Failed," in *Merry Tales*, p. 10.

21 MTP, Letter File. Published in part in Paine, *Biography*, p. 43.

22 MTP, DV 206. In this memorandum Mark had just been speaking of his collaterals, the Earls of Durham.

23 MTP, Documents File.

24 John M. Clemens to Messrs. Coleman and Johnson, Nov. 2, 1844, original letter in Webster Collection. This letter suggests that Clemens' eagerness to collect this debt was bound up with his own indebtedness; he had entrusted a receipt for its collection to George Wooden, who in October 1843 had bought the corner lot of the old Clemens property in Hannibal, and directed that payment be made to Woods, Christy & Co., St. Louis merchants who had been among his early creditors.

25 MTP, DV 206.

26 MTBM, p. 6.

27 Presumably from Orion's lost autobiography, in Paine, *Biography*, p. 44.

28 *Autobiography*, I, 116; and MTP, DV 47, "Villagers." Both accounts have inaccuracies of date. In "Villagers" the notation of Ben's death is followed by the cryptic phrase, "The case of memorable treachery," and in further miscellaneous autobiographical notes (MTP, DV 71) occurs the entry, "Dead brother Ben. My treachery to him." What grounds for self-reproach a six-year-old might have for "betraying" an elder brother is unexplained, but the guilt complex is characteristic and familiar.

29 *Autobiography*, I, 308, and II, 28.

30 *Autobiography*, II, 27–28.

31 MTP, DV 303, "Huck Finn and Tom Sawyer Among the Indians," galley proof in MTP, but unfinished and unpublished.

32 Paine, *Biography*, pp. 26 and 85.

33 Paine, *Biography*, p. 28. In dictation of April 6, 1906, in a passage omitted from *Autobiography*, Mark Twain observes that Orion's occasional lapses from the utter frankness Sam had enjoined so vexed the latter that "I destroyed a considerable part of that autobiography."

34 MTP, DV 310b, "Hellfire Hotchkiss."

[35] MTP, DV 47, "Villagers."

[36] Original appointment of Orion as secretary, dated March 27, 1861, and signed by Lincoln and Seward, is preserved in MTP, Documents File.

CHAPTER SEVEN

[1] Unpublished fragment of *Autobiography*, MTP, DV 244, written in 1903.

[2] Marion County Circuit Court Records, No. 3347, *John M. Clemens v. William B. Beebe*, Feb. 24, 1844, with a leaf from his ledger submitted by the defendant.

[3] MTP, Box 16, a scrap labeled "Memory Eccentricities."

[4] MTW, "Boy's Manuscript," pp. 29–30.

[5] Interview quoted in Hannibal *Courier-Post*, March 6, 1935. The original interview with Tabitha Quarles Greening appeared in the St. Louis *Post-Dispatch* on Dec. 10, 1899.

[6] MTBM, p. 45.

[7] Certificate preserved in MTP, Documents File.

[8] Dictation of Aug. 15, 1906, MTE, p. 107.

[9] Family recollection, from Annie Moffett Webster, Nov. 6, 1948. For the customary stress laid upon this bit of etiquette, Everett Dick, *The Dixie Frontier*, p. 174. Mrs. Horr's husband, Benjamin W., is found in 1844 as security for John M. Clemens, defendant in a lawsuit (*Crow, Tives & McCrary v. Clemens*, April 10, 1844; Marion County Circuit Court Records).

[10] MTE, pp. 234 and 107–9, for these incidents. The spelling of the girl's name is here corrected from the announcement in Orion's Hannibal *Journal and Western Union*, Jan. 29, 1852, of Margaret Koeneman's wedding to Dr. C. Spiegel of Palmyra.

[11] The phrase is Mark's, from MTP, DV 47, "Villagers."

[12] A newspaper clipping captioned "Former Florida Neighbor of Clemens Family Head of School Attended by Mark Twain," in the Morris Anderson scrapbook now in Hannibal's Mark Twain Museum, and a similar article in the Hannibal *Courier-Post*, March 6, 1935, are the chief sources of information here given about Miss Newcomb. In 1852 she married the bookseller John Davies, "the Welshman" of Mark Twain lore, and died in 1894.

13 Feb. 6, 1870; *Mark Twain's Letters to Will Bowen,* ed. Theodore Hornberger, p. 19.

14 This comment occurs in the Hannibal *Journal* of May 16, 1850, but the observance of May Day in Hannibal had long been traditional, as newspaper files attest. The couplet is drawn from the Hannibal *Missouri Courier,* June 7, 1849.

15 Hannibal Municipal Records, I, 21.

16 MTP, MS autobiography, deleted by Paine in editing the *Autobiography,* II, 214, which thus falsifies the "one distinction" of Richmond in the original text. More reminiscence of the Old Ship of Zion occurs in Clemens, *Life on the Mississippi,* p. 405.

17 MTP, DV 47, "Villagers." Tucker description from a short history of the old Presbyterian Church, attached to its photograph in the Mark Twain Museum in Hannibal. For the conversion of Jane and Pamela, see MTBM, p. 24; and for the non-conversion of John M. Clemens, see Samuel L. Clemens, *Following the Equator,* II, 28.

18 Samuel L. Clemens to Livy Clemens, from Paris, Ill., Dec. 31, 1871; a letter in the Samossoud Collection published largely in Clara Clemens, *My Father, Mark Twain,* pp. 9–12. An earlier letter to Livy, from Lockport, N.Y., March 4 (1869), describes his meeting there with Mr. Tucker's successor as Hannibal's Presbyterian pastor, Mr. Bennett, "whose church and Sunday school I used to attend every Sunday twenty years ago. My mother and sister belonged to his church. . . . His visit has filled my brain with trooping phantoms of the past. . . . "

19 With the comment that the hasp phrase was "Awfully good but a little too dirty," William Dean Howells had persuaded Mark to drop it from the text of *Tom Sawyer* (MTW, pp. 13–14). Dictionary story in Owen Wister, "In Homage to Mark Twain," *Harper's,* CLXXI, 547–56.

20 MTP, DV 243, typescript of fragment in Buffalo Historical Society.

21 MTP, DV 47, "Villagers," identifies the other boy as Will Bowen; in later years Mark arbitrarily fastened the story upon the boyhood of Artemus Ward, in lecturing upon that humorist.

22 Hannibal *Journal and Western Union,* Sept. 4, 1851.

23 *Ralls County [Mo.] Record,* June 6, 1902, as reported by their companion, Col. Joe Burnett.

24 Hannibal *Tri-Weekly Messenger,* Dec. 23, 1852. Sam Clemens' early gibes at spiritism are reprinted in Minnie M. Brashear, *Mark Twain, Son of Missouri,* pp. 131 and 133.

25 MTP, DV 326.

26 Hannibal *Journal and Western Union,* Jan. 22, 1852; during this time of Sam's employment in publishing the paper, it reported further incidents of spiritual phenomena (May 27 and June 17, 1852), but counseled its readers, "better keep away" from all spirits (March 29, 1853).

27 MTP, DV 47, "Villagers"; the incident appears in Clemens, *Life on the Mississippi,* p. 397.

CHAPTER EIGHT

1 *Autobiography,* I, 96; on p. 109 he slightly contradicts himself by stating that the visits ended when he was "twelve or thirteen."

2 Paine, *Biography,* p. 30, who errs in calling Wharton Lampton Jane's brother.

3 MTBM, p. 13. For Tabitha (Puss) Quarles's recollections, interview in St. Louis *Post-Dispatch,* Dec. 10, 1899; and compare *Autobiography,* I, 119.

4 This favorite saying of Mark Twain about his mother was probably borrowed from Shillaber's Mrs. Partington, whose likeness to the real Jane Clemens and her fictitious recreation as "Aunt Polly" has been noted by Walter Blair and others. See Howard S. Mott, Jr., "Origin of Aunt Polly," *Publishers' Weekly,* CXXXIV, 1821–23.

5 Clemens, "Hunting the Deceitful Turkey," in *The Mysterious Stranger,* pp. 307–11.

6 MTP, DV 326 and 327, early versions of *The Mysterious Stranger.*

7 *Autobiography,* I, 109.

8 *Autobiography,* I, 8.

9 Clemens, *Huckleberry Finn,* p. 152.

10 *Autobiography,* I, 96. See Clemens, *Huckleberry Finn,* pp. 134 ff. and 284–85, for the house twice used.

11 MTP, DV 55a, purporting to be "the home of the widow Bennett and her family" but unmistakably the Quarles farmhouse, described also in *Autobiography,* I, 96 and 102–3. For an independent description of the old homestead I am indebted to the Rev. Harold Roberts.

12 *Autobiography,* I, 123.

[13] Palymra (Mo.) *Whig,* Nov. 11, 1843, "Runaway Come Back," relates the unhappiness in Canada of Hannibal's ex-slaves belonging to Messrs. Collins, Glasscock, Beebe, Ratcliff, and others.

[14] Clemens, *Following the Equator,* II, 29. A canceled passage in the *Autobiography* (MTP, DV 206) speaks more harshly of public opinion apparently about the same incident: " . . . everybody seemed indifferent about it — as regarded the slave — though considerable sympathy was felt for the slave's owner, who had been bereft of valuable property by a worthless person who was not able to pay for it."

[15] MTP, DV 309a, "Adam Monument," in which she figures as a servant in the household of an eccentric admiral who picks up waifs and strays. In *Autobiography,* I, 99, he calls the bedridden crone Aunt Hannah, but compare MTP, DV 20: "Describe Aunt Patsy's house, and Uncle Dan, aunt Hanner, and the 90-year old blind negress."

[16] Clemens, "Corn-Pone Opinions," *Europe and Elsewhere,* pp. 399 ff.; the original manuscript, alluding to the free silver campaign, must have been written about 1896.

[17] *Autobiography,* I, 100.

[18] Clemens, *Huckleberry Finn,* p. 287; *Tom Sawyer,* p. 250; and MTP, DV 326, "The Mysterious Stranger in Hannibal."

[19] In the summer of 1855, on his way from St. Louis to Keokuk, where Jane Clemens and Orion then lived, Sam stopped at Hannibal and went inland to visit his Uncle John, as notebook entries reveal: MTBM, p. 27. But Jane in these latter years cherished a prejudice against John because he drank and had somehow abused "Patsy" — perhaps by remarriage. MTBM, pp. 42 and 224, notes the prejudice.

[20] The Quarles farm was sold on April 29, 1852, to Samuel Anderson; Monroe County Recorder's Deed Record, Vol. L, pp. 499–500. Martha Ann Quarles's death on July 23, 1850, and that of her husband on Feb. 25, 1876, are recorded by their tombstones in the old Florida cemetery.

CHAPTER NINE

[1] Paine, *Biography,* p. 46; and MTP, DV 235. His mother, on the other hand, calmly learned to "discount him 90 per cent for embroidery," and was unruffled by these lapses from truth, *Autobiography,* I, 293–94.

[2] *Autobiography,* I, 125, reports that Judge Clemens built part of

the house in 1845 and settled his family there. Paine, *Biography,* p. 46, gives the date as 1844. Marion County Deed Records, N–16, under date given, although the indenture itself bears the date of Oct. 16, 1846. The lease was written for twenty-five years, at $28 a year for the first five, and $35 annually for the remaining twenty.

3 Paine, *Biography,* p. 44.

4 MTP, DV 47, "Villagers." Sam and Henry appear under the code names Simon and Hartley. In his Nevada days Sam remembered to send Margaret Sexton his picture, as a sort of valentine, MTBM, p. 78.

5 Paine, *Biography,* p. 41; the Palmyra (Mo.) *Whig,* Aug. 8, 1840, lists the seven candidates for this office in Hannibal (Mason Township) and Clemens is not among them. For the elections of 1842 and 1844 no Mason County listings appear in the files of this newspaper.

6 Clemens, *The Innocents Abroad,* I, 230–31, in which Mark, after describing his exit, states that the "man had been stabbed near the office that afternoon, and they carried him in there to doctor him" — an unlikely possibility since the office was on Bird Street and the actual murder took place on Hill, below Main, as will be seen. See also Clemens' lecture, "The American Vandal Abroad," represented in fragmentary form in MTP, DV 52.

7 Palmyra (Mo.) *Whig,* Sept. 9, 1843, and *State of Missouri* v. *Hudson,* Marion County Circuit Court Records, No. 3516. The name of John M. Clemens does not occur in the sparse records surviving from this case, although Campbell D. Meredith, as a justice of the peace, was responsible for the coroner's inquest, and Sam Clemens' sometime schoolmaster Samuel Cross was foreman of this jury. Court Records, Jan. 6, 1844.

8 Certain details in the St. Louis *Republican* story are inaccurate, such as its mention of R. F. Lakenan, although he did not come to Hannibal to practice law until two years after the alleged date of the incident. Other versions appear in HMC, p. 914, and Paine, *Biography,* p. 45. In MTP, DV 47, "Villagers," Mark Twain writes: "Judge Carpenter [Clemens] knocked MacDonald down with a mallet and saved Charley Schneider," and in another note refers to "McDonald the desparado (plasterer)."

9 Clemens, *Life on the Mississippi,* pp. 408–9.

10 The appointment of "John M. Clemens Esquire" to this position on Aug. 26, 1844, and his resignation on July 10, 1845 — short of the twelve-month period of his appointment — appear in Marion County Court Records, Vol. C, pp. 278 and 378 respectively. The duties of a

road districting justice are set forth in *Revised Statutes of the State of Missouri . . . 13th General Assembly*, p. 965.

11 *Autobiography*, I, 131, briefly relates the story set forth fully in Marion County Circuit Court Records, No. 3873, *State of Missouri* v. *Wm. P. Owsley*, for murder. These twenty-nine pages are recorded throughout in the hand of John M. Clemens, who signs them as a justice of the peace, along with his fellow justice, Richard T. Holliday, owner of Holliday's Hill. Compare with Clemens, *Huckleberry Finn*, pp. 190–94.

12 Clemens, "The United States of Lyncherdom," *Europe and Elsewhere*, p. 245. Original in MTP, Paine 219.

13 MTP, DV 47, "Villagers"; Marion County Circuit Court Records, under date given. Advertisements show however that he was still in business in Hannibal as late as 1853.

14 John M. Clemens to Pamela Clemens, May 5, 1845, in Webster Collection; the bearer was Dawes himself.

15 Paine, *Biography*, p. 43, assigns it to the period before his justiceship.

16 Aug. 24, 1845, in MTBM, pp. 9–10.

17 Samuel L. Clemens to J. W. Atterbury, Jan. 20, 1886; original in Mark Twain Museum, Hannibal. For John M. Clemens and the railroad see HMC, p. 901. In Clemens, *The Man That Corrupted Hadleyburg*, p. 72, the town's two richest men compete for the plums of railroad construction.

18 Hannibal *Gazette*, Nov. 26, 1846, and Feb. 11, 1847; Hannibal *Journal and Western Union*, Dec. 18, 1851, and later.

19 On Jan. 19, 1847, he was named one of a committee of three "to value such materials and property as may be subscribed": Hannibal *Gazette*, Jan. 21, 1847.

20 Hannibal *Gazette*, Dec. 31, 1846, and Feb. 4, 1847; Hannibal *Daily Journal*, March 29, 1853.

21 MTBM, pp. 10–11 and 17.

22 Marion County Circuit Court Records, No. 3347, *John M. Clemens* v. *William B. Beebe*, and, No. 3546, *Beebe* v. *Clemens*. Another suit brought by Clemens against Beebe's clerk, E. H. Townsend, to collect a debt of $300 (No. 3612), was settled on Dec. 4, 1847, with the award of $55 to Orion Clemens, administrator.

23 MTP, DV 326, "The Mysterious Stranger in Hannibal."

24 Hannibal *Journal,* Feb. 11, 1847. The Hannibal *Gazette* of just a week before had reported that the committee of Hannibal citizens, whose formation Judge Clemens had moved to confer with Palmyrans about the Masonic college, "were most grossly and unprovokedly assailed and insulted, in the meeting." Among some jottings about early days (MTP, DV 131) Mark Twain noted: "Palmyra and Han. boy-feud." Minnie M. Brashear, *Mark Twain, Son of Missouri,* p. 73 n., observes that Mark never celebrates Palmyra in his writings, as if out of loyalty to the old partisanship.

25 *Autobiography,* II, 274–75. Taking still greater liberty with the facts, Mark sometimes assumed, as in "Villagers," that his father had been "elected County Judge by a great majority."

26 *Life in Letters of William Dean Howells,* ed. Mildred Howells, I, 288. Mark's biographical sketch of Orion, entitled the "Autobiography of a Damned Fool" (MTP, DV 310), was never completed or published.

27 Orion's comment on the back of a letter which Sam had written him on Feb. 6, 1861, relating how a New Orleans fortuneteller had told him that "father's side of the house was not long-lived, but that *he* doctored himself to death"; MTBM, pp. 52–58.

28 MTP, Letter File; Jane Clemens' letter is undated, but written shortly after the death of Jennie Clemens on Feb. 1, 1864. Long afterward in the *Autobiography,* I, 108, Mark observed with characteristic irony that although Dr. Meredith "saved my life several times," yet "he was a good man and meant well."

29 Paine, *Biography,* pp. 74–75.

30 Hannibal *Gazette,* March 25, 1847; Hannibal *Journal,* March 25 and Aug. 5, 1847, the latter still lamenting that jealousy between Hannibal and Palmyra still outweighs "all political and party consideration."

31 Clemens, *Tom Sawyer,* pp. 90–96.

32 Original letter in Mark Twain Museum, Hannibal; published by C. J. Armstrong, "John RoBards — Boyhood Friend of Mark Twain," *Missouri Historical Review,* XXV, pp. 493–98. Mount Olivet Cemetery records for 1876 show that out of a $100 contribution sent by Mark Twain, $4 went for opening the graves on July 31, $12 for filling up the graves, and $39 for cost of the new lot, leaving a balance of $45 which by Mark's instruction was sent to his mother in Fredonia, N. Y. The old Baptist cemetery has long since become a Negro burying ground.

33 Clemens, "Some Rambling Notes of an Idle Excursion," in *Punch,*

Brothers, Punch!, p. 31. The phrase concerning death appears in the unpublished "Letters from the Earth," MTP, DV 33.

CHAPTER TEN

[1] Hannibal Municipal Records, I, 223, under date of Nov. 4, 1847; and letter from Orion to Pleasant Taylor, March 11, 1848, in Webster Collection.

[2] Hannibal *Gazette,* Sept. 23, 1847.

[3] "The Chances of Success in Mercantile Life," *Merchants' Magazine,* XV, 477.

[4] *Autobiography,* I, 6. Of Dr. Grant's house Mark said, "My father died in it in March . . . but our family did not move out of it until some months afterwards"; MTE, p. 125.

[5] Hannibal *Gazette,* July 8, 1847. He was also in town in early Sept. (Hannibal *Journal,* Sept. 16), and made a temperance address on Feb. 19, 1848 (*Journal,* Feb. 17); Orion may have taken temporary employment in Hannibal, such for example as at the job printing office opened by the *Journal* in midsummer 1847, but the absence of his name through most of 1848–49 from local activities favored by him, like the Odd Fellows and the temperance crusade, suggests that family tradition is correct in asserting his return to St. Louis.

[6] *Autobiography,* II, 272–74; and "Chapters from My Autobiography," *North American Review,* CLXXXIV, 177 ff. Some of the details are clearly incorrect or deliberately invented, such as the mention of "our brother Ben," long since dead. See also MTP, DV 310, "Autobiography of a Damned Fool."

[7] Information from Mrs. Webster, March 12, 1949.

[8] *Autobiography,* II, 276; Minnie M. Brashear, *Mark Twain, Son of Missouri,* p. 98; and see Clemens, "The Turning-Point of My Life," *What Is Man?,* pp. 127–40, in which Mark, still more improbably, dates his apprenticeship from his irresponsible behavior in contracting the measles, in 1844.

[9] Paine, *Biography,* p. 78; MTP, DV 240; and John DeLancey Ferguson, *Mark Twain: Man and Legend,* p. 33.

[10] Hannibal *Journal,* July 1, 1847. This Whig paper quoted one veteran: "I went out a Polk soldier, and returned a Taylor Whig."

[11] Hannibal Municipal Records, I, 194; Hannibal *Gazette,* April 15

and 22, 1847. For torchlight processions see MTW, "Boy's Manuscript," p. 27.

12 *Autobiography*, II, 216.

13 MTP, DV 47, "Villagers," and *Autobiography*, II, 96. The Hannibal *Tri-Weekly Messenger*, Dec. 2, 1852, speaks disparagingly of "the 'mantles de costume' that hang so ungracefully over the shoulders of delicate young men during their street peregrinations."

14 San Francisco *Golden Era*, Feb. 28, 1864: MTP, Notebook File.

15 The descriptions of Jane are drawn from MTP, DV 206; and Samuel and Doris Webster, "Whitewashing Jane Clemens," *Bookman*, LXI, 531–35.

16 "Ma, I perceive that you have a passion for funerals and processions yet," Sam wrote home from Carson City on April 2, 1862, (unpublished portion of MS in Webster Collection). Later in Fredonia she settled in a house at the intersection of three streets, "to watch the funerals pass."

17 Webster, "Whitewashing Jane Clemens," p. 532.

18 MTP, Letter File, undated letter of about March 1864.

19 MTP, DV 20, quoted in MTW, p. 80.

20 MTP, DV 310b, "Hellfire Hotchkiss."

21 MTP, DV 131.

22 *Autobiography*, I, 118; and MTP, DV 47, "Villagers." MTP, DV 243, adds the revealing note: "The Paveys. Aunt P. [Aunt Polly, the *Tom Sawyer* name for Jane Clemens] protects a daughter." No Corsican is listed in the 1850 census of Hannibal. A similar scene, of a bully routed by a brave woman's tongue, occurs in Clemens, *Roughing It*, pp. 247–48.

23 MTP, DV 327, a passage discarded from the published *The Mysterious Stranger*.

24 Pamela Clemens to Orion Clemens, April 6, 1850, Webster Collection.

25 Information from Mrs. Annie Webster; and see for example Sam's letter to Pamela on July 23, 1875, in MTBM, p. 133.

26 Webster, "Whitewashing Jane Clemens," p. 534.

27 MTBM, pp. 17 and 45.

28 MTBM, p. 322.

[29] Paine, *Biography*, p. 1592, letter written by Orion on Oct. 3, 1858: original in Webster Collection.

[30] *Autobiography*, II, 92–93; Clemens, *Tom Sawyer*, p. 4.

[31] MTP, DV 326, "The Mysterious Stranger in Hannibal." In the *Autobiography*, II, 257, Mark wrote: "When I was a boy there was not a thing I could do creditably except spell according to the book." And in the unpublished "Eve's Autobiography" (MTP), in which Eve and Abel can spell while Adam and Cain cannot, Mark modestly says, "the ability to spell correctly is a gift . . . and is a sign of intellectual inferiority. By parity of reasoning, its absence is a sign of great mental power." A few details about the schoolhouse are drawn from a memoir owned by Mrs. Norman Frost of Hannibal, written by her father James Burkett Brown, a younger classmate of Sam Clemens, who testifies that Sam was "universally liked by both the schollars and teachers."

[32] Paine, *Biography*, p. 69.

[33] Advertisement in the Hannibal *Journal*, April 8, 1847; "Dawson's School Room" had already been designated in March 1847 as a polling place for city elections (Hannibal Municipal Records, I, 183). Mark's identification of this school with that described in *Tom Sawyer* is made in *Autobiography*, II, 179.

[34] MTP, DV 327. For young Dawson, see *Autobiography*, II, 179, and Clemens, *Life on the Mississippi*, p. 406.

[35] MTP, Paine 40.

[36] MTW, "Boy's Manuscript," pp. 28–29.

[37] In Clemens, *Tom Sawyer*, pp. 72 ff., the louse becomes a tick, for greater propriety; the earlier version in MTW, "Boy's Manuscript," p. 39, bears Mark's note: "Every detail of the above incident is strictly true, as I have excellent reason to remember."

[38] MTW, "Boy's Manuscript," p. 37; and *Autobiography*, II, 179.

[39] Samuel L. Clemens to his mother and sister, Feb. 8, 1862, Webster Collection; this passage is one of several omitted from this letter by Paine, *Letters*, pp. 63–68.

[40] *Autobiography*, II, 218. Apparently the only Jewish family in Hannibal at the time of the 1850 census was that of William Cohen the watchmaker.

[41] Clemens, "Concerning the Jews," in *Literary Essays*, p. 251.

CHAPTER ELEVEN

[1] MTW, "Boy's Manuscript," p. 39; and MTP, Paine 40, dramatized version of *Tom Sawyer,* in which such an irruption occurs while Tom is supervising the job of whitewashing the fence.

[2] *Mark Twain's Letters to Will Bowen,* ed. Theodore Hornberger, pp. 3–4, notes that — in addition to Sam Clemens himself — tradition variously claims John Briggs, John Garth, and Joe Buchanan as the other prototypes.

[3] For an account of the epidemic, HMC, p. 900. In *Autobiography,* II, 219, Mark erroneously dated the incident in 1845, but in the secretary's notebook kept on his Mississippi River trip of 1882 assigned the year correctly; in "The Turning-Point of My Life," *What Is Man?,* pp. 127–40, he asserts still more wildly that this act of irresponsibility led his mother to apprentice him to a printer. In the unpublished "Tom Sawyer's Conspiracy" (MTP, DV 304) he tried to utilize it for fiction.

[4] The earliest and probably truest account is in Clemens, *The Innocents Abroad.* The date was probably 1847, to judge by the retelling dropped from *Life on the Mississippi* (ed. Willis Wager), p. 417. "I believe there were only four of us in that devilment, yet from all reports there was a gang of forty," Mark observed, in 1902: as reported by Col. Joe Burnett, *Ralls County [Mo.] Record,* June 2, 1902.

[5] *Mark Twain's Letters to Will Bowen,* p. 19. In the latter 1840's, as inspection records of the City Council show, Hannibal had about a dozen wells and pumps in the city.

[6] Their last meeting as reported by Burnett, *Ralls County Record,* June 6, 1902.

[7] MTP, DV 20a.

[8] "Recollections of Norval L. ('Gull') Brady," Hannibal *Courier-Post,* March 6, 1935.

[9] *Autobiography,* I, 135–38, and II, 213. Mark dates the incident "1848 or '49," but since Jim Wolfe apparently was then Orion's apprentice, it must have happened between Sept. 1850, when Orion opened his shop, and Sept. 1851, when Pamela was married. For the career of confectioner compared with that of pirate, see MTW, p. 42.

[10] *Autobiography,* II, 180, 185, and 218; Clemens, "The Private History of a Campaign That Failed," *Merry Tales,* p. 14; *Mark Twain's Letters to Will Bowen,* p. 18; MTP, DV 47, "Villagers."

[11] MTP, DV 47, "Villagers"; the same case is almost certainly touched

upon in Clemens, *Life on the Mississippi,* pp. 394–97, among the anonymous village failures.

[12] MTP, DV 47, "Villagers"; *Letters,* p. 419; *Autobiography,* II, 184.

[13] A year or so after its publication in the *Century* in Dec. 1885, Mark wrote to the Rev. John Davis in Hannibal: "Please give my warmest regards to the Garths, and say I was ashamed of putting that 'd' Un Lap' cruelty into that 'Century' article, and so I have stricken it out and it will not appear in the Century's war book. I think John Robards deserved a lashing, but it should have come from an enemy, not a friend." Yet the passage still appeared unexpurgated in *Merry Tales* (1892), as noted in the *Twainian,* n.s., VII, No. 2 (March–April 1948), pp. 2–3. The census of 1850 spells the name "Roberts," and so it was pronounced in those days.

[14] MTP, DV 47, "Villagers"; see also *Autobiography,* II, 66–67 and 183; and HMC, pp. 991–92.

[15] Clemens, *Tom Sawyer,* p. 47. "One of our oldest and most worthy citizens," Nash was appointed postmaster under President Zachary Taylor, as the Hannibal *Journal* reported on May 10, 1849. Stung by a notice chalked on the post office door demanding better service, he replied: "I have to say, that the office is a poor and miserably contemptible thing, and nothing but my poverty could induce me to keep it at all." A clue to the "better days" is afforded by Mark's note in MTP, DV 47, "Villagers": "His aged mother was Irish, had family jewels, and claimed to be aristocracy." On Sept. 4, 1844, Nash had "taken the bankruptcy law," as shown by the St. Louis Record Book of Bankruptcy now in Jefferson City.

[16] *Autobiography,* II, 97–99.

[17] In MTP, DV 326, "The Mysterious Stranger in Hannibal," Mark may have embroidered upon the facts in his note: "Tom Nash's mother took in a deserted child; it gave scarlet fever death to 3 of her children and deaf [*sic*] to 2."

[18] Hannibal *Tri-Weekly Messenger,* Feb. 12, 1853.

[19] Clemens, *Life on the Mississippi,* p. 401; MTP, DV 47, "Villagers." Fate of the Blankenship house as reported by a Hannibal newspaper in Sept. 1900 (Morris Anderson scrapbook in the Mark Twain Museum, Hannibal).

[20] Paine, *Biography,* p. 64, probably from the joint recollections of Clemens and Briggs; he errs in calling the young man "Ben," as both "Villagers" and the 1850 census show. The full name of the island was Sny Carta, corruption of the French "Chenal Ecarte," or lost

channel, so known because the Mississippi had silted up between the island and the Illinois shore.

21 The 1850 census lists the names and ages of the Blankenship progeny thus: Benson, 21, laborer; Martha, 19; Nancy, 16; Sarah, 14; Elizabeth, 12; Thomas, 19, no occupation; Mary, 6; Catharine, 5. Apparently Tom had a twin sister, and was four to five years older than Sam Clemens.

22 *Autobiography,* II, 174.

23 From an obviously autobiographical reminiscence of village custom in "Which Was the Dream?"; MTP, DV 301.

24 J. W. Ayres, "Recollections of Hannibal," dated Harriman, Tenn., Aug. 22, 1917, and published in the Palmyra (Mo.) *Spectator* (Morris Anderson scrapbook, Mark Twain Museum). Ayres became superintendent of schools in Marion County in 1866.

25 MTP, DV 310; *Autobiography,* II, 174–75; and *Mark Twain's Letters to Will Bowen,* p. 18.

26 Hannibal Municipal Records, I, 21; Marion County Court Records, Book C, p. 400; Clemens, *Life on the Mississippi,* p. 414. Probably wholly imaginary is a yarn in MTP, DV 30, about "the time poor old Jimmy Finn fell off Lover's Leap" and Ira Stout clocked his descent.

27 MTP, DV 326.

28 Clemens, "In Defence of Harriet Shelley," *North American Review,* CLIX, 108–19; 240–51; 353–68 (original draft is in MTP, DV 49), in which Mark is making sport of Shelley's angelic character in the light of the poet's "murder" of his wife Harriet. A similar scorn for village sentimentalists who mourned over Injun Joe, despite the fact that he was believed to have killed five citizens, appears in Clemens, *Tom Sawyer,* pp. 296–97.

29 *Autobiography,* II, 175. Mark insists, I, 134, that Injun Joe's death, evidence of Divine punishment, left young Sam in a mood of fitful repentance.

30 *The Callaghan Mail,* ed. Harold H. Haines, pp. 93–94, who knew him in boyhood; other old-timers in Hannibal likewise recall him. Mrs. Norman Frost, daughter of "Buck" Brown, states (letter to author, May 20, 1950) that his real name was Joe Douglas, that he married and helped his wife do laundry for the townspeople, and was "a staunch church member."

31 Hannibal *Journal,* Nov. 25, 1852.

32 Hannibal *Gazette,* July 8, 1847; Hannibal *Journal,* July 6, 1848.

The Municipal Records are filled with numerous proposals for curbing the traffic by heavy licensing fees. More drastically, the Hannibal *Tri-Weekly Messenger,* Jan. 8, 1852, reported that "a petition is being circulated by the ultra moral reformers of this good city, praying the Legislature to abolish the privilege of raising corn and rye, so as to entirely prevent the manufacture of cheap malt liquors." A few months later about fifty citizens of Hannibal petitioned the county court to grant no more licenses, but after these signatures were collected, somebody stole the petition from the counter at Selmes's Wild-Cat Store (Hannibal *Daily Journal,* April 2, 1853).

[33] *Autobiography,* I, 109, and II, 99–102; MTP, Paine 154, "Concerning a Reformed Pledge," dated Hartford, Christmas 1886; MTP, Paine 255, "Conversations with Satan," written in Vienna about 1898. His most explicit statement about the use and benign effects of tobacco, dated March 14, 1882, was written for *Study and Stimulants,* ed. A. Arthur Reade, pp. 120–22. The roster of the Cadets is preserved in the Mark Twain Museum in Hannibal; comment on the founding and Fourth of July parade in which Sam marched will be found in Hannibal *Journal,* April 25, 1850, and Hannibal *Missouri Courier,* July 11, 1850.

CHAPTER TWELVE

[1] MTP, DV 47, "Villagers"; *Autobiography,* I, 132; and MTP, DV 310b, "Hellfire Hotchkiss," in which they reappear unmistakably as Shad and Hall Stover. Paine, *Biography,* p. 47, refers to the attempted murder of the uncle. Richard Hyde married in 1849 (Hannibal *Journal,* May 13, 1849), and probably settled down. "Burt Mackay's clan" a little later gained the petty notoriety of hoodlums, shooting to scare, then robbing their victim (Hannibal *Journal,* June 2, 1853).

[2] Hannibal Municipal Records, I, 19.

[3] Hannibal *Journal,* July 15, 1847.

[4] Clemens, *Huckleberry Finn,* p. 187; MTW, p. 65 n.

[5] As related in Clemens, "To My Missionary Critics," *Europe and Elsewhere,* p. 290; and "The Watermelon Story" (MTP, DV 41), a favorite lecture anecdote about how he had restored a stolen green watermelon to a farmer and taken a ripe one, adding the "moral" that "when you have been doing wrong, you have only to reform and do right, and you always get your reward."

[6] Interview with Mrs. R. E. Ireland, in Hannibal *Courier-Post,* March 6, 1935.

[7] Marion County Court Records, Book C, p. 230; Hannibal *Journal,* July 6, 1848, and April 25, 1850; MTP, DV 47, "Villagers"; MTBM, pp. 26–27; Clemens, *Tom Sawyer,* p. 252.

[8] In MTP, DV 310b, "Hellfire Hotchkiss," the Judge sneers at the Widow's vanity: "Granddaughter of a Hessian corporal, whom she has painted up in a breastpin as an English general."

[9] MTP, DV 303, and MTBM, pp. 49–50 and 52. In 1894 the old Holliday house burned to the ground. Today the Memorial Lighthouse stands not far from the spot.

[10] In MTP, DV 303, "Huck Finn and Tom Sawyer Among the Indians," the possibility of the heroine's rape is suggested vaguely and squeamishly.

[11] *Autobiography,* I, 132–33. The typescript bears Mark's note "Used in 'Huck Finn,' I think."

[12] Notes accompanying MTP, DV 326, "The Mysterious Stranger in Hannibal."

[13] Statement to author from the late Annie M. Webster, who also remembered St. Louis stories about Dr. McDowell's body-snatching for the purpose of supplying his students. See Clemens, *Life on the Mississippi,* p. 413; and Hannibal *Gazette,* Feb. 25 and Nov. 4, 1847, for contemporary accounts of the corpse and the stored firearms.

[14] MTP, DV 326, "The Mysterious Stranger in Hannibal," under the fictitious name of "Dr. Terry, the great surgeon who hung his daughter in the cave," in projecting a plot in which the physician would be rescued by the Mysterious Stranger from a big snowstorm in Hannibal.

[15] MTP, DV 47, "Villagers"; Clayton Keith, *Sketch of the Lampton Family in America, 1740–1914,* quotes young Dr. McDowell's statement about his father's cruelty as the motive that led the Lamptons to "adopt" him. In St. Louis in the autumn of 1861 Dr. McDowell treated Orion's little daughter Jennie for intermittent fever, after Orion and Sam had left for the West (Mollie Clemens to Orion Clemens, Nov. 17, 1861, MTP, Letter File).

[16] *Autobiography,* I, 105.

[17] *Autobiography,* II, 215.

[18] "The Dandy Frightening the Squatter," relating an incident dated "about thirteen years ago," in the (Boston) *Carpet-Bag,* May 1, 1852, identified by Franklin Meine.

[19] MTP, DV 47, "Villagers," and Clemens, *Life on the Mississippi,* pp. 44–45 and 408. "Villagers" calls the expectant saddler "Old Pitts,"

but *Life on the Mississippi,* written earlier, refers to him as "Stavely." According to the 1850 census, the Clemenses' next-door neighbor was a saddler named Stabler.

20 Hannibal Municipal Records, I, 23, presents the first ordinance against gaming; and Hannibal *Gazette,* Sept. 2, 1847, mirrors typical editorial comment.

21 For a vivid description of one such Upper Mississippi River trip in 1848 see Henry Lewis' journal: Bertha L. Heilbron, ed., "Making a Motion Picture in 1848," *Minnesota History,* XVII, 151 ff.

22 MTP, DV 47, "Villagers."

23 MTP, DV 71, a series of notes apparently intended for autobiographical purposes. Samuel T. Glover is alluded to without name in Clemens, *Life on the Mississippi,* p. 396, and identified in MTP, DV 47, "Villagers." H. L. Conard, ed., *Encyclopedia of the History of Missouri,* III, 65–66, summarizes his career.

24 Clemens, *A Tramp Abroad,* I, 90–91.

25 Hannibal *Journal,* Nov. 29, 1849; Hannibal *Journal and Western Union,* May 29, 1851; *Weekly Journal,* April 28, 1853, for typical items. And compare W. J. Petersen, *Steamboating on the Upper Mississippi,* p. 364.

26 *Mark Twain's Letters to Will Bowen,* ed. Theodore Hornberger, p. 19; and MTP, DV 131.

27 Samuel L. Clemens to Miss Minnie Dawson, June 12, 1902, letter in Mark Twain Museum in Hannibal.

28 MTP, DV 310b, "Hellfire Hotchkiss."

29 Reproduced as frontispiece to Minnie M. Brashear, *Mark Twain, Son of Missouri.* See also M. N. Squires, "Henry Lewis and His Mammoth Panorama of the Mississippi River," *Missouri Historical Review,* XXVII (April), and Heilbron, ed., "Making a Motion Picture in 1848," *Minnesota History,* XVII (June).

30 *Mark Twain's Letters to Will Bowen,* p. 27, under date of June 6, 1900.

31 Autobiographical summary written for Samuel L. Moffett, in Berg Collection, NYPL; Samuel L. Clemens to H. H. Rogers, Jan. 1, 1895, in *Letters,* p. 621; and *Autobiography,* II, 185.

32 Paine, *Biography,* p. 49; MTP, DV 244; and MTP, DV 47, "Villagers."

[33] Recollection of the late H. C. Nash, as set down in a letter written to the local newspaper by the father of Mrs. Dean B. Frost of Hannibal. Lent to the author in May 1948.

[34] Clemens, *Life on the Mississippi,* p. 398; MTP, DV 47, "Villagers"; and Hannibal *Gazette,* Aug. 20, 1847.

[35] Clemens, *Tom Sawyer,* p. 38; Clemens, *Life on the Mississippi,* pp. 402–3.

[36] Hannibal Municipal Records, I, 20; MTP, DV 310b, "Hellfire Hotchkiss."

[37] Palmyra (Mo.) *Whig,* Jan. 4, 1840.

[38] *Autobiography,* I, 125–30; in the original manuscript he identifies "the large unoccupied house" where this incident took place as located "on the corner of Main and Hill Street," across from the Clemenses — obviously the pilastered Levering house in which his father had died two years before. Incidentally, the comment of his male companion, the little Negro named Sandy, about dried herring, that people "eats 'em guts and all" (as the story originally read in the *North American Review*), was eventually altered — out of deference to the same spirit of prudery — to "innards and all."

[39] MTW, p. 14. The naked figure however was retained in Clemens, *Tom Sawyer,* p. 189.

CHAPTER THIRTEEN

[1] MTP, DV 33, "Letters from the Earth."

[2] Bernard DeVoto, *Mark Twain's America,* p. 43, reviews this spirit, reflected in the lore and humor of the old frontier.

[3] MTP, DV 310b, "Hellfire Hotchkiss"; MTP, DV 304, miscellaneous notes for "Tom Sawyer's Conspiracy"; and record of Mary Nash's marriage in Orion Clemens' Hannibal *Western Union,* Jan. 23, 1851. Perhaps her "badness" was only incorrigibility, as in the case of a Mary Lacy mentioned in *Autobiography,* II, 213.

[4] Hannibal Municipal Records, I, 24, and Hannibal *Gazette,* Nov. 12, 1846.

[5] Hannibal *Journal,* Dec. 13, 1849.

[6] MTW, p. 84.

[7] Hannibal *Gazette,* Nov. 26 and Dec. 17, 1846.

8 Hannibal *Western Union,* Jan. 9, 1851, by "Whippoorwill." For the satirical obituary of his paper, see the Hannibal *Missouri Courier* for Sept. 29, 1853.

9 Hannibal *Journal,* May 13, 1847.

10 Possibly the "incorrigible" Mary Lacy of the *Autobiography,* II, 213, may have been something of a tomboy, but this is not clear. Mark's fascination with the type, however, is clear enough. In his published story "A Horse's Tale," in *The Mysterious Stranger,* pp.147–219, he created a little heroine whose love for horses and soldiering leads her "Mammy Dorcas" to suggest she is *"twins,* and that one of them is a boy-twin and failed to get segregated." In the fragmentary "The Mysterious Stranger in Hannibal" (MTP, DV 326) he planned to have the celestial stranger fall in love with Hellfire Hotchkiss: "He feels a strange and charming interest in her. By the books he gathers that this is 'love' — the kind that sex arouses. There is no such thing among his brothers and sisters. . . . Presently the passion for Hl grows — becomes absorbing — is mutual. . . . [He] sees that the happiness of hell — which is purely intellectual — is *tame compared to this love.* He has found more in this random visit to earth than he bargained for."

11 MTP, Paine 40, written apparently in June 1884. Clemens, *Tom Sawyer,* p. 79, describes Tom's gift to Becky of "a brass knob from the top of an andiron" which in a fit of jealousy she spurns.

12 Samuel L. Clemens to Margaret Blackmer, Oct. 9, 1908, original in Yale College Library. In the novel, Tom Sawyer offers Becky a peach on her first day at school; in the play the two children share an apple, "contentedly munching." And he teaches her to repeat, while counting apple seeds laid on the palm of a small hand —

> One I love, two I love, three I love I say;
> Four I love with all my heart, and five I cast away —

In an unpublished fantasy, "Which Was the Dream?" (MTP, DV 301), Mark undoubtedly recollected such a scene, after he had won the lass's heart by tossing up a marble with his toes, and she offered him "the last winter-apple": "I held it to her mouth, she took her bite, then I took mine, and munching we sauntered into the thicket, along the worn path [to school], I holding her by her left hand. And by the stream we sat down together, and took bites turn about, and contentedly munched and talked. . . . I told her how to dig fishing-worms, and how to make a pinhook, and what to do to keep awake in church, and the best way to catch flies."

13 Newspaper interview of April 21, 1910, and obituary notice in Hannibal *Courier-Post,* Dec. 26, 1928.

14 Information from the granddaughter, Miss Clara Frazer of Hannibal, May 11, 1950; newspaper clippings and the surgical case used by him in the war are now in the Mark Twain Museum in Hannibal.

15 Hannibal *Journal,* March 16, 1853; cf. *Autobiography,* II, 212–14.

16 Recollection of Sam Clemens' friend James Burkett ("Buck) Brown, furnished to the writer by Mr. Brown's daughter, Mrs. Norman Frost of Hannibal. Mrs. Frost, born in 1869, was a classmate of "the unsinkable Mrs. Brown" (nee Molly Tobin) who is alleged by Gene Fowler in *Timber Line,* p. 330, to have been a hoydenish playmate of Sam Clemens. Chronology of course makes that claim absurd.

17 Samuel L. Clemens to Livy Clemens, Dec. 4, 1871; and Clemens to Laura Hawkins Frazer, *ca.* 1909, letter published in the Hannibal *Courier-Post,* March 6, 1935, which enumerates a long list of villagers.

18 Hannibal *Daily Journal,* Aug. 4, 1853; MTP, DV 47, "Villagers."

19 MTP, DV 47, "Villagers" tells the fuller story here quoted; see also *Autobiography,* II, 181–82, and HMC, pp. 609–10. A grimmer domestic tragedy, the murder of Amos Stillwell, allegedly by his wife and her paramour Dr. J. C. Hearne — although a jury lacked evidence to convict them — took place in 1888, long after Mark Twain's departure from Hannibal, but the story fascinated him and he retold it from hearsay in "Villagers." This is probably the "notorious" Hannibal story whose writing Mark once discussed with Howells (Paine, *Biography,* p. 1177), See the account by his friend Minnie Dawson, *The Stillwell Murder, or A Society Crime.* Stillwell, miller, commission merchant, and pork packer, had moved to Hannibal in 1848, and had been a partner of Pamela Clemens' husband, Will Moffett.

20 MTP, DV 47, "Villagers."

21 Hannibal *Journal and Western Union,* Jan. 15, 1852.

22 Hannibal *Journal,* Dec. 16 and 23, 1847.

23 O. S. Coad and Edwin Mims, Jr., *The American Stage* (The Pageant of America, copyright Yale University Press), p. 152; HMC, p. 835, which also notes the presence of a strolling troupe occupying the theatre in this year.

24 MTP, DV 240. Orion's Hannibal *Journal,* Nov. 25, 1852, noted the publication of *The Cabin and the Parlor,* a reply to Mrs. Stowe.

25 Walter Blair's suggestion, adopted by DeVoto, in MTW, p. 68; see also p. 84 for an expurgated bit in which the duke "judged he could caper to their base instincts." The city ordinance appears in Hannibal Municipal Records, I, 20.

26 MTP, Notebook File; *Letters,* p. 170–71; and MTE, p. 361. Compare the Virginia City (Nevada) *Evening Bulletin* of Dec. 7, 1863, during Mark's Nevada days: "The GIASCUTUS — Everybody has heard of the rare and wonderful creature . . . natives of the ocean between Panatankastean and Japan. Sam Wasserman has a couple of these curious creatures on exhibition . . . neither males, females nor neuters." But in MTP, DV 310, "Autobiography of a Damned Fool," in the midst of early Hannibal reminiscences occurs the note *"Burning Shame."*

27 Hannibal *Journal,* April 30, 1853.

28 Samuel L. Clemens, dictation of Nov. 30, 1906; MTE, pp. 110 ff. The Hannibal *Journal,* Dec. 20, 1849, hailed the advent of North's Ethiopian Minstrels. Campbell's "celebrated troupe" was also a great favorite (Hannibal *Whig Messenger,* Oct. 19, 1852).

29 Clara Clemens Samossoud to Dixon Wecter, May 10, 1950, MTP, Letter File. An incomplete draft of *The Mysterious Stranger,* MTP, DV 328. The effect of a poignant old refrain was always powerful. In MTP, Notebook File, an entry *ca.* early Jan. 1897, in the midst of grief for his daughter Susy, Clemens wrote: "Many a time I said, 'The two most pathetic, most moving things in the Eng[lish] tongue to me are these: One is the refrain of a long ago forgotten song familiar to me in my earliest boyhood: 'In the days when we went a gypsying, a long time ago.' The other, 'Departed this life' — and now this will be written upon *her* gravestone."

30 Samuel L. Clemens to Billy Claggett, Sept. 9, 1862, MTP, Letter File; and MTP, DV 326. "The Mysterious Stranger in Hannibal," in the Stranger's reflections upon the local youth.

31 As described in Henry Lewis' river diary in 1848. See Bertha L. Heilbron, ed., "Making a Motion Picture in 1848," *Minnesota History,* XVII, 427–28.

32 Hannibal *Journal,* June 29, 1848. But on Aug. 31, 1852, Sam Clemens' foe "Local" in the Hannibal *Tri-Weekly Messenger* hailed him as "the unrivaled comic gester [*sic*] . . . let everybody unite and give Dan a warm welcome, for it may be the last time we shall be blessed with a sight of his familiar 'phiz.' " Minnie M. Brashear, *Mark Twain, Son of Missouri,* p. 135.

33 Hannibal *Daily Journal,* Sept. 13, 1853; P. T. Barnum to Samuel L. Clemens, Jan. 19, 1875, and later; MTP, Letter File. Barnum himself probably did not accompany his circus to Hannibal; see Phineas T. Barnum, *The Life of P. T. Barnum,* p. 141.

34 MTP, DV 47, "Villagers"; Hannibal *Journal and Western Union,* March 27, 1851.

35 Hannibal *Tri-Weekly Messenger,* Feb. 19, 1853.

36 Hannibal *Journal,* Feb. 3, 1848, and Nov. 1, 1849; Clemens, *Tom Sawyer,* pp. 204–5.

37 Hannibal *Journal and Western Union,* March 27, 1851, *et seq.;* Clemens, *Huckleberry Finn,* pp. 223–24, in a passage also doubtless influenced by Mark's having witnessed the appropriately described "funeral orgies of the dead King" of the Sandwich Islands (14th Hawaiian letter to the Sacramento *Union,* dated June 22, 1866).

38 MTE, pp. 118 ff.; MTBM, p. 46.

39 MTP, DV 343; the narrative goes on to describe several other episodes of Day's clairvoyance, involving citizens with authentic names like T. R. Selmes the merchant and Brittingham the druggist.

40 Another manuscript, MTP, DV 326, "The Mysterious Stranger in Hannibal," treats the village lunatic called Crazy Fields, whom the boys torment, adding the cryptic note: "Crazy's history and misfortunes and his family and lost boy — Ratcliff."

CHAPTER FOURTEEN

1 MTE, p. 303. To Senator John P. Jones on Jan. 20, 1891, Mark wrote of his own "9 years' experience as a practical printer"; MTP, Letter File.

2 Paine, *Biography,* p. 79, merely states that Sam's work was so efficient that it left him an ample margin of free time for youthful companionship and rambles.

3 Hannibal *Gazette,* May 3, 1848 (its last issue); *Journal,* May 18, 1848. On June 1 the latter newspaper reported having seen the first issue of Ament's new publication in Hannibal. In his Hannibal *Missouri Courier* for May 24, 1849, Ament reviewed the history of "Our Paper," which had been suspended for several months in the winter of 1847–48 before the transfer from Palmyra to Hannibal.

4 As noted by Edgar M. Branch, *The Literary Apprenticeship of Mark Twain,* p. 274.

5 Hannibal *Journal,* Nov. 25, 1852; and Hannibal *Tri-Weekly Messenger,* July 24, 1852.

6 *Autobiography,* II, 278.

7 MTP, DV 310, "Autobiography of a Damned Fool." In MTP, DV 326, "The Mysterious Stranger in Hannibal," the dentures belong to "the widow Guthrie, 56 and dressed for 25," whose original was Mrs. Holliday. In a purported true story of Hannibal, "A Sett of Teeth at the expense of a Husband," the Hannibal *Gazette* of Nov. 25, 1847, jested about the hazards of false teeth in courtship. Orion Clemens' Hannibal *Journal and Western Union*, Jan. 22, 1852, marveled at "a beautiful set of teeth, on highly polished gold plate, put up for a lady in this vicinity" by an Ohio dentist, on exhibition in Hannibal. Aunt Polly's vigorous amateur tooth-pulling (Clemens, *Tom Sawyer*, pp. 58–59) was doubtless much more familiar to the village than such arts of replacement.

8 MTP, DV 328, another text of *The Mysterious Stranger*.

9 In some miscellaneous notes attached to MTP, DV 310, we read: "Miss Newcomb is Bangs' [the printer's] wife and henpecks him, but doesn't get much the advantage. Spit curls."

10 MTP, DV 323, an untitled and apparently unpublished sketch.

11 Annie M. Webster to the author, Dec. 8, 1949.

12 Perhaps McCormick came in answer to Ament's advertisement in the Hannibal *Missouri Courier* of Nov. 8, 1849, for an apprentice; a similar appeal was made on May 9, 1850. Still another learner named Ralph left little save his name upon Mark's memory. His chief recollections of McCormick and McMurry appear in *Autobiography*, II, 276 ff.

13 Description of McCormick appears in MTP, DV 328. Hannibal *Journal*, Nov. 18, 1852, reported, "Elder Campbell preached here last Sunday & Monday to very large audiences."

14 After meeting him and Wales McCormick once more in Quincy, Ill., Mark thus described him to Livy on Jan. 23, 1885; Clemens, *The Love Letters of Mark Twain*, ed. Dixon Wecter, p. 233.

15 Hannibal *Journal*, Nov. 23, 1848. In 1853 he married a girl from Louisville (*Journal*, Aug. 15, 1853).

16 Clemens, *Speeches*, p. 140.

17 Quoted in Paine, *Biography*, p. 77.

18 *Speeches*, pp. 138–40; and MTP, DV 328.

19 Clemens, *Roughing It*, II, 16; and an account by Orion quoted in Paine, *Biography*, p. 85.

20 MTP, DV 328.

21 Paine, *Biography,* p. 78.

22 For Sam's fancy printing, see Paine, *Biography,* p. 78; the first verses signed "Mark" appear in the Hannibal *Missouri Courier* of June 21, 1849, and those signed "C." in the Hannibal *Journal and Western Union,* June 19, 1851. See also a damsel's reply "To Brother Mark" in the Hannibal *Journal* of July 19, 1849.

23 Conversation reported to the author in a letter from Sam Webster, April 4, 1949. Compare Paine, *Biography,* pp. 81–82. Oddly enough, this supposedly significant turning point is not mentioned in Clemens, "The Turning-Point of My Life," *What Is Man?,* pp. 127–40.

24 Paine, *Biography,* p. 1281.

25 See for example the Hannibal *Gazette* of June 10, 1847. This newspaper prematurely rejoiced that the pond was being drained, only to retract on July 1: "What we took for workmen, was only some boys out at sea on planks."

26 Clemens, *Life on the Mississippi,* p. 412.

27 See Bertha L. Heilbron, ed., "Making a Motion Picture in 1848," *Minnesota History,* XVII, 432 and 434.

28 Clemens, *Tom Sawyer,* pp. 119–21; and Paine, *Biography,* p. 53. But compare, for example, Hannibal *Journal,* May 17, 1849.

29 MTBM, pp. 15–16.

30 Clemens, *Life on the Mississippi,* pp. 319 ff.

31 Samuel L. Clemens to Frank Bliss, Aug. 26, 1901, photostat in MTP, Letter File. The fullest account of the crime occurs in Marion County Circuit Court Records, No. 5800, *State of Missouri* v. *Ben, a Slave,* November Term, 1849.

32 *History of the Expedition . . . of Lewis and Clark,* ed. Elliott Coues, I, 256. For this suggestion the author is indebted to Bernard DeVoto.

33 Palmyra (Mo.) *Whig,* July 30, 1845.

34 Hannibal *Journal,* May 3, 1849, supplies an extended list.

35 MTBM, p. 15. From San Francisco Dr. Meredith wrote his wife on Nov. 7, 1849, that his party was about to set out for the gold fields (Hannibal *Journal,* Feb. 7, 1850).

36 Hannibal *Missouri Courier,* April 11 and June 6, 1850.

37 HMC, p. 316. Hannibal, however, more than held its own; cf. p. 902.

38 Hannibal *Daily Journal,* April 29, 1853.

39 MTP, DV 47, "Villagers." The Hannibal *Journal,* Oct. 19, 1848, had applauded him as an "industrious" newcomer to town.

40 Two of these he clipped from the St. Joseph *Gazette;* see Minnie M. Brashear, *Mark Twain, Son of Missouri,* pp. 123–33 and 151.

41 See *Autobiography,* I, 132. The incident is repeated in a sheaf of miscellaneous Hannibal notes (MTP, DV 235): "All emigrants went through there. One stabbed to death — saw him," and in MTP, DV 47, "Villagers": "*The Stabbed Cal. Emigrant.* Saw him." Another stabbing occurred on Market Street in 1853, apparently in a drunken scuffle (Hannibal *Tri-Weekly Messenger,* Feb. 26, 1853). Knives were generally carried and often used lethally; the uncle of Sam's girl friend Kitty Shoot, L. B. Shoot, was fatally pierced by a man named Boon Helm . . . following a difficulty last winter, at a corn husking" near Paris, Mo. (Orion's Hannibal *Journal and Western Union,* Sept. 18, 1851). Helm later became a notorious desperado, and was hanged in the West.

42 MTE, p. 77.

43 Paine, *Biography,* pp. 59–60; cf. Bernard DeVoto, *Mark Twain's America,* p. 79.

44 Clemens, *The Man That Corrupted Hadleyburg,* p. 29.

CHAPTER FIFTEEN

1 So announced Big Joe in the Hannibal *Journal* of Feb. 10, 1848, offering to sell a half interest which was soon taken, for a few months, by Judge J. G. Easton.

2 MTBM, p. 15. "Big Joe" Buchanan had tried to sell the *Journal* and also his city property "at a great bargain" before leaving for California; see Minnie M. Brashear, *Mark Twain, Son of Missouri,* p. 102, n. 44.

3 MTBM, p. 17.

4 Announcement in Hannibal *Western Union,* Oct. 10, 1850.

5 Paine, *Biography,* p. 84, obviously from the lost portion of Orion's autobiography. Orion must have returned to Hannibal after his 25th birthday, on July 17, since the census-taker lists him there, aged 25, along with Jane, 46, Pamela, 23, Samuel L., 14, and Henry, 12, noting that the latter two "attended school within the year." These ages sug-

gest indeed that the census-taker called between Pamela's birthday (Sept. 13) and Sam's (Nov. 30).

6 Fentress County Deed Book E, p. 532. Arnold Buffum was the agent, Richard Francis the buyer. Compare MTBM, p. 17.

7 Vol. 1, No. 6, the first preserved in the Missouri Historical Society, is dated Oct. 10, 1850; Brashear, *Mark Twain*, p. 102, is in error.

8 Orion's Hannibal *Journal*, Nov. 25, 1852, notes Ament's sale of the *Courier*, although he did not leave town immediately (Ament's own statement in the Hannibal *Tri-Weekly Messenger*, Dec. 7, 1852). On April 23 and 28, 1853, the *Journal* welcomed him back to Marion County, to go into the Land Office in Palmyra.

9 MTP, DV 310a, "The Albert-Orion Story."

10 Fragment of Orion's autobiography, pp. 696–705, in MTP, Documents File.

11 MTP, DV 310b, "Hellfire Hotchkiss."

12 Paine, *Biography*, p. 85, quoted from Orion's autobiography.

13 *Autobiography*, II, 271–72.

14 MTP, DV 326, "The Mysterious Stranger in Hannibal."

15 Hannibal *Journal*, June 3, 1852, an argument that all men will be saved, signed "Imprimatur," but almost certainly by the editor. His lecture at the Baptist Church (Sept. 5, 1853) was largely about temperance, though attacking the anti-nicotine crusade ("Tobacco don't kill people"). His brother's best satire on Orion's fickleness appears in MTP, DV 310, "Autobiography of a Damned Fool."

16 Fred W. Lorch, "Adrift for Heresy," *Palimpsest*, X, 372–80.

17 Hannibal *Daily Journal*, Aug. 8, 1853. After several more paragraphs of invective, Orion lamely adds that "we should have noticed this subject long since, but have not had time to write or think about anything . . . the type [has been] 'set up' at case, without copy. . . . No printers to be got hold of for 'love or money.'" This was shortly after Sam had left the shop to seek his fortune.

18 See for example the Hannibal *Journal* of Nov. 25, 1852, and May 27, 1853, the latter twitting the churchless Catholics for their lack of "religious zeal," and the rejoinder of a still more militant Protestant on June 2 inquiring why anyone should egg on the promotion of a faith so bigoted and "the sworn enemy to popular rights."

19 MTP, Paine 40.

[20] Paine, *Biography*, p. 84, quotes Mark's probable exaggeration in saying "it was the most earnest ambition I ever had."

[21] Samuel L. Clemens to Frank Walden, March 4, 1870, letter printed in Hannibal *Courier-Post,* March 6, 1935. At the same time he directed the publisher Bliss to honor his request for a free copy of *Innocents*; typescript in MTP, Letter File.

[22] In MTP, DV 326, "The Mysterious Stranger in Hannibal," the village Bob Ingersoll is named Ira Jepson — "vain of it — just as the ex-Cath priest (very few Irish) was vain of his desertion and courage, and was around telling the secrets of the priestly charnel-house to crowded (gratis) houses."

[23] See Thomas Bailey Aldrich, *Marjorie Daw and Other Stories*; this tale probably predated MTP, DV 47, "Villagers," although certainty is hard to establish. The Hannibal press of Orion's day not infrequently plays upon the theme that Poe had popularized; for example the *Tri-Weekly Messenger,* Dec. 21, 1852, describes how gas released by decomposing bodies is often responsible for sounds resembling groans and for the disarrangement of bodies found at exhumation. Mark's "Blennerhasset" was the surname of a noted criminal lawyer in St. Louis in the mid-years of the century; in 1849 he appeared as State's Counsel in Marion County, in the well-known trial of John S. Wise for the murder of Thomas B. Hart. This Richard, second cousin of the Herman Blennerhasset best known to history, died of apoplexy on Christmas Day, 1857, apparently with no gruesome aftermath. See *The Bench and Bar of St. Louis . . . and Other Missouri Cities,* p. 100.

[24] *Autobiography*, II, 272.

[25] Hannibal *Western Union,* Jan. 16 and 23, 1851. His fellow-Whig editor of the *Journal* still more vigorously assailed abolitionists as thieves, and sarcastically remarked that one "never knew an abolitionist to put a negro into his best bed" (May 16, 1850).

[26] Paine, *Biography,* p. 168; and MTP, DV 310, "Autobiography of a Damned Fool."

[27] If the tone be thought condescending, compare an item in the Hannibal *Journal* of Feb. 7, 1850, before Orion's day: "A drunken negro fell down the stairway of the telegraph office on Tuesday, which jostled his snuff-colored carcus into the shape of a pork barrel. His recovery is very doubtful."

[28] Fragment of Orion's autobiography, p. 696, MTP, Documents File; Orion Clemens to Miss Wood. Oct. 3, 1858, in Paine, *Biography,*

p. 1591, in which Orion also recalls the delegation of Sam, "though unwilling, yet firm," as the destroyer of unwanted cats.

29 Clemens, "The Late Benjamin Franklin," *Sketches New and Old,* p. 212. His ridicule of Orion's attempt to apply the maxims appears endlessly in MTP.

30 *Autobiography,* II, 285.

31 From Orion's narrative, quoted in Paine, *Biography,* p. 91.

32 Interview with Tabitha Quarles Greening, St. Louis *Post-Dispatch,* Dec. 10, 1899. Mark's early story "Jim Wolfe and the Tom Cats" (*Californian,* Sept. 21, 1867) states that "Me and Henry was always pestering him and plastering hoss bills on his back and putting bumble-bees in his bed." MTE, pp. 136–42, tells stories of Jim Wolfe and the wasps, in his trouser legs and in bed.

33 Paine, *Biography,* p. 92. On page 1674 he incorrectly dates it 1852–53. Orion continued to do business at the old stand, as files for the remainder of 1851 bear witness.

34 Unpublished MS of "Simon Wheeler, Detective," Berg Collection, NYPL.

35 Fragment of Orion's autobiography, pp. 696–97, in MTP, Documents File.

36 A few weeks later, the first issue of Orion's Hannibal *Journal and Western Union* printed a poem by "Fanny" beginning, "Unmentionables are my theme, of Bloomerdom I sing."

37 *Autobiography,* II, 285, ascribes the incorrect date of "about 1849 or 1850" to this deal.

38 Fragment of Orion's autobiography, p. 697, MTP, Documents File.

39 MTE, pp. 235–36.

40 A more modest earlier sale of 200 acres on May 3, 1850, for $50 to one Richard Francis had been made. Orion's narrative hereafter cited is the fragment in MTP.

41 Paine, *Biography,* p. 89, confirms this assumption. See *Autobiography,* p. 93, for eventual disposition of the land.

42 Hannibal *Western Union,* May 15, 1851. See also Mark's note in MTW, p. 65.

43 Paine, *Biography,* p. 92.

[44] Equal inconsistency may be remarked in the Hannibal *Journal*'s retraction in this issue of its many months of praise for an extinguishing device: "Phillips' Fire Annihilators won't do."

[45] MTE, p. 236; he remembered the translator, paid at Orion's usual rate of five dollars, as "a Philadelphian, Homer C. Wilbur."

[46] Edgar M. Branch, *The Literary Apprenticeship of Mark Twain*, pp. 4–7. One of Sam's early *jeux d'esprit*, on Sept. 16, 1852, refers to Ensign Jehiel Stebbings ("Blabbing Government Secrets").

[47] Branch, *The Literary Apprenticeship*, p. 7, which republishes "The Dandy Frightening the Squatter"; and Fred Lorch, "A Source for Mark Twain's 'The Dandy Frightening the Squatter,'" *American Literature*, III, 309–13.

[48] The launching of this St. Louis publication is noted in the Hannibal *Gazette* of May 6, 1847. Compare Paine, *Biography*, p. 90, and the *Twainian*, I, No. 1 (Jan. 1939), p. 2, and No. 2 (Feb. 1939), p. 3.

CHAPTER SIXTEEN

[1] Signed "W. Epaminondas Adrastus Perkins," a pseudonym changed the following week to "W. Epaminondas Adrastus Blab." Minnie M. Brashear, *Mark Twain, Son of Missouri*, p. 116, notes only the follow-up story on Sept. 16.

[2] Mark recalled that after the lampoon he "dropped in with a double-barreled shot-gun. . . . When he found that it was an infant (as he called me) . . . he simply pulled my ears and went away; but he threw up his situation that night and left town for good." The files show that "Local" ceased to write for the *Messenger* after Oct. 2, 1852, and thereafter Sam Raymond, neither a newcomer nor a bachelor, took over the title "Local Editor." But Hinton, "an excellent practical printer . . . a good writer" returned to Hannibal journalism in late Nov. 1852 as one of three co-purchasers of Ament's *Courier* (*Courier*, Nov. 25, 1852).

[3] The same issue of the Hannibal *Journal* contains an advertisement: "I want to hire a negro boy, between twelve and fifteen years of age. O. Clemens."

[4] Comment of *Tri-Weekly Messenger*, Dec. 18, 1852, on the high cost of living. The general prosperity of Hannibal, however, particularly in tobacco and pork, as well as a new "clothing manufactory, which keeps 30 or 40 male and female operatives constantly employed," is discussed in the *Journal* on Nov. 25, 1852.

5 Clemens, *Tom Sawyer*, p. 115. Mark's account, remarkably true to the facts, will be found in Clemens, *Life on the Mississippi*, pp. 414–15, and *Autobiography*, I, 130–31.

6 "He was the same man who undertook to set fire to the calaboose last Fall," adds the narrator in the Hannibal *Journal*, Jan. 27, 1853. The *Tri-Weekly Messenger*, Jan. 25, 1853, gives his name as Dennis McDavid: "It is supposed that he had matches about his person, and fired the building to procure his release. . . . It may however have been the result of an accident."

7 Clemens, *Tom Sawyer*, p. 199.

8 Possibly related to the "Mark" who indited those sugary verses previously noted in the *Courier*, for which Sam was working in 1849. This poem, printed on Feb. 26, 1852, begins excruciatingly enough for parody:

> Death has laid low the lovely form
> That we have loved so fondly;
> She is gone, like the misty morn,
> And left her parents, lonely.

"Rambler's" tribute to "Bettie W——e," more certainly by Sam Clemens, and other specimens are reprinted by C. J. Armstrong, "Mark Twain's Early Writings Discovered," *Missouri Historical Review*, XXIV, 485–501.

9 Paine, *Biography*, p. 90. Compare the facsimile in Brashear, *Mark Twain*, opp. p. 122.

10 Hannibal *Daily Journal*, May 10, 1853.

11 Paine, *Biography*, p. 93.

12 Clemens, "History Repeats Itself," *Galaxy*, X, 878; *Letters*, p. 459; *Following the Equator*, I, 20.

13 From the album owned by Ann Virginia Ruffner's son, F. W. Hixon of St. Louis. Printed in Julian Street, *Abroad at Home*, p. 252.

BIBLIOGRAPHY

WORKS OF SAMUEL L. CLEMENS

All references to published work are in *The Writings of Mark Twain* (Author's National Edition), 25 vols., New York and London, 1907–18, unless otherwise noted.

The Adventures of Huckleberry Finn.

The Adventures of Tom Sawyer.

"Chapters from My Autobiography," *North American Review,* CLXXXIV (1907), 114–19; 449–63.

"Concerning the Jews," in *Literary Essays.*

"Corn-Pone Opinions," in *Europe and Elsewhere.* New York, 1923.

"The Dandy Frightening the Squatter," *The* (Boston) *Carpet-Bag* (May 1, 1852). Identified by Franklin Meine.

Following the Equator. 2 vols.

The Gilded Age, with Charles Dudley Warner. 2 vols.

"History Repeats Itself," in *Sketches New and Old.*

"A Horse's Tale," in *The Mysterious Stranger, and Other Stories.* New York, 1922.

"Hunting the Deceitful Turkey," in *The Mysterious Stranger, and Other Stories.* New York, 1922.

"In Defence of Harriet Shelley," *North American Review,* CLIX (1894), 108–19; 240–51; 353–68.

The Innocents Abroad. 2 vols.

Is Shakespeare Dead? New York and London, 1909.

"Jim Wolfe and the Tom Cats," *Californian* (Sept. 21, 1867).

"The Late Benjamin Franklin," in *Sketches New and Old.*

Life on the Mississippi, Author's National Edition, and Heritage Press Edition, edited by Willis Wager, New York, 1944.

The Love Letters of Mark Twain, edited by Dixon Wecter. New York, 1949.

The Man That Corrupted Hadleyburg, and Other Stories and Essays.
Mark Twain, Business Man, edited by Samuel C. Webster. Boston, 1946.
Mark Twain in Eruption, edited by Bernard DeVoto. New York, 1940.
Mark Twain's Autobiography, edited by Alfred Bigelow Paine. 2 vols. New York, 1924.
Mark Twain's Letters, edited by Albert Bigelow Paine. New York, 1917.
Mark Twain's Letters to Will Bowen, edited by Theodore Hornberger. Austin, Texas, 1941.
["Memoranda"] *The Galaxy,* IX (1870), 866; X (1870), 286–87 and 878.
"My First Literary Venture," in *Sketches New and Old.*
"My Platonic Sweetheart," in *The Mysterious Stranger, and Other Stories.* New York, 1922.
The Mysterious Stranger. New York, 1916.
"The Old-Fashioned Printer," in *Mark Twain's Speeches.* New York, 1923.
"The Private History of a Campaign That Failed," *Merry Tales.* New York, 1892.
Pudd'nhead Wilson.
Roughing It. 2 vols.
"Some Rambling Notes of an Idle Excursion," in *Punch, Brothers, Punch!* New York, 1878.
"To My Missionary Critics," in *Europe and Elsewhere.* New York, 1923.
A Tramp Aboard.
"The Turning-Point of My Life," in *What is Man? and Other Essays.* New York, 1917.
"The United States of Lyncherdom," in *Europe and Elsewhere.* New York, 1923.
"What Paul Bourget Thinks of Us," in *Literary Essays.*

WORKS OF OTHER AUTHORS

Aldrich, Thomas Bailey, *Marjorie Daw, and Other Stories.* Boston, 1885.
Allen, William B., *A History of Kentucky.* Louisville, Ky., 1872.
Aptheker, Herbert, "The Quakers and Negro Slavery," *Journal of Negro History,* XXV (1940), 331–62.
Ardery, Mrs. W. B., comp., *Kentucky Records.* 2 vols. Lexington, Ky., 1926.
Armstrong, C. J., "John RoBards — Boyhood Friend of Mark Twain," *Missouri Historical Review,* XXV (1931), 493–98.
—— "Mark Twain's Early Writings Discovered," *Missouri Historical Review,* XXIV (1930), 485–501.
Barnum, Phineas T., *The Life of P. T. Barnum, Written by Himself.* London, 1855.

Bell, James P., *Our Quaker Friends of ye Olden Times.* Lynchburg, Va., 1905.

The Bench and Bar of St. Louis . . . and Other Missouri Cities. St. Louis, 1884.

Bidewell, George I., "Mark Twain's Florida Years," *Missouri Historical Review,* XL (1946), 159–73.

Boddie, John B., *Seventeenth Century Isle of Wight County, Virginia.* Chicago, 1938.

Bokum, Hermann, *The Tennessee Hand-Book and Immigrant's Guide.* Philadelphia, 1868.

Branch, Edgar M., *The Literary Apprenticeship of Mark Twain.* Urbana, Ill., 1950.

Brashear, Minnie M., *Mark Twain, Son of Missouri.* Chapel Hill, N.C., 1934.

Catterall, Ralph C. H., *The Second Bank of the United States.* Chicago, 1903.

"The Chances of Success in Mercantile Life," *Merchants' Magazine,* XV (1846), 475–77.

Clemens, Clara, *My Father, Mark Twain.* New York and London, 1931.

Clement, John, *Sketches of the First Emigrant Settlers in Newton Township, West New Jersey.* Camden, N.J., 1877.

Clement, Mrs. Nathaniel E., "Clement, Clements, Clemans. With a Notice of Mark Twain's Ancestry," *Virginia Magazine of History,* XXXII (1924), 292–98.

"Clements of Surry Co., Va., & Baltimore, Maryland," *Tyler's Quarterly,* XVII (1935), 125–27.

Coad, O. S., and Edwin Mims, Jr., *The American Stage* (Vol. XIV, The Pageant of America Series). New Haven, 1929.

Collins, Lewis, *History of Kentucky . . . Revised . . . by . . . Richard H. Collins.* 2 vols. Covington, Ky., 1874.

Conard, Howard L., ed., *Encyclopedia of the History of Missouri.* 6 vols. New York, 1901.

Coues, Elliott, ed., *History of the Expedition under the Command of Lewis and Clark.* 4 vols. New York, 1893.

Dawson, Minnie, *The Stillwell Murder, or A Society Crime.* Hannibal, Mo., 1908.

DeVoto, Bernard, *Mark Twain at Work.* Cambridge, Mass., 1942.

—— *Mark Twain's America.* Boston, 1932.

Dick, Everett, *The Dixie Frontier.* New York, 1948.

Early, Ruth H., *Campbell Chronicles and Family Sketches.* Lynchburg Va., 1927.

"Emigrants to Ohio and Illinois," *Tyler's Quarterly,* VII (1925), 86–94.

Federal Writers' Project, *Kentucky, a Guide to the Bluegrass State* (American Guide Series). New York, 1939.

—— *Tennessee, a Guide to the State* (American Guide Series). New York, 1939.

Ferguson, (John) DeLancey, *Mark Twain: Man and Legend.* Indianapolis, 1943.

Firth, C. H., "Gregory Clement," *Dictionary of National Biography* (New York and London, 1887), XI, 32–33.

Fowler, Gene, *Timber Line.* New York, 1933.

Gary, Lorena M. "Oh Youth! Mark Twain: Boy and Philosopher," *Overland Monthly,* n.s., XCI (1933), 154–55.

Goodpasture, A. V., "Mark Twain, Southerner," *Tennessee Historical Magazine,* 2d ser., I (1931), 253–60.

Haines, Harold H., ed., *The Callaghan Mail, 1821–1859.* Hannibal, Mo., 1946.

Heilbron, Bertha L., ed., "Making a Motion Picture in 1848 [Henry Lewis' Journal of a Canoe Voyage]," *Minnesota History,* XVII (1936), 131–58 and 421–36.

Heitman, Francis B., *Historical Register of Officers of the Continental Army . . . 1775 . . . 1783.* Washington, 1893.

Hinshaw, William W., *Encyclopedia of American Quaker Genealogy.* 6 vols. Ann Arbor, Michigan, 1936–50.

History of Monroe and Shelby Counties, Missouri. St. Louis, 1884.

Hogue, Albert R., *History of Fentress County, Tennessee.* Nashville, Tenn., 1916.

—— *One Hundred Years in the Cumberland Mountains along the Continental Line.* McMinnville, Tenn., cop. 1933.

Holcombe, Return Ira, *History of Marion County, Missouri.* St. Louis, 1884.

Howells, William Dean, *Life in Letters of William Dean Howells,* edited by Mildred Howells. 2 vols. Garden City, N.Y., 1928.

Hyde, William, and H. L. Conard, eds., *Encyclopedia of the History of St. Louis.* 4 vols. New York, 1899.

Jones, Dr. J. T., "The House Mark Twain's Father Built," in *Prose and Poems.* Columbia, Ky., 1916.

Keith, Clayton, *Sketch of the Lampton Family in America, 1740–1914.* N.p., 1914.

Lewis, Henry, *see* Bertha L. Heilbron.

Lorch, Fred. W., "Adrift for Heresy," *The Palimpsest,* X (1929), 372–80.

—— "A Source for Mark Twain's 'The Dandy Frightening the Squatter,'" *American Literature,* III (1931), 309–13.

Missouri, State of, *Laws of the State of Missouri, 1st Session of the 9th General Assembly.* Jefferson City, 1837.

—— *Revised Statutes of the State of Missouri . . . 8th General Assembly.* St. Louis, 1835.

—— *Revised Statutes of the State of Missouri . . . 13th General Assembly.* St. Louis, 1845.

Mott, Howard S., Jr., "The Origin of Aunt Polly," *Publishers' Weekly,* CXXXIV (1938), 1821–23.

Paine, Albert Bigelow, *Mark Twain, a Biography* (Centenary Edition). 4 vols in 2. New York, 1935.

Paullin, C. O., "Mark Twain's Virginia Kin," *William and Mary College Quarterly,* 2d ser., XV (1935), 294–98.

—— "The Moorman Family of Virginia," *William and Mary College Quarterly,* 2d ser., XII (1932), 177–80.

Petersen, William J., *Steamboating on the Upper Mississippi.* Iowa City, 1937.

"A Playmate of Mark Twain's," *Human Life* (May 1906).

Reade, Alfred A., ed., *Study and Stimulants.* Manchester, Eng., 1883.

Riley, James W., *Letters of James Whitcomb Riley,* edited by W. L. Phelps. Indianapolis, 1930.

Roberts, Harold, "Sam Clemens: Florida Days," *The Twainian,* n.s., I, No. 2 (Feb. 1942), pp. 1–3.

Scharf, John Thomas, *History of Saint Louis City and County.* 2 vols. Philadelphia, 1883.

See, T. J. J., "The Return of Halley's Comet," *Munsey's Magazine,* XLIII (1910), 3–12.

"Simon Hancock Family Bible," *National Genealogical Society Quarterly,* XVI (1928), 20.

Sonne, Niels H., *Liberal Kentucky, 1780–1828.* New York, 1939.

Squires, Monas N., "Henry Lewis and His Mammoth Panorama of the Mississippi River," *Missouri Historical Review,* XXVII (1933), 244–56.

Street, Julian, *Abroad at Home.* New York, 1914.

Tillman, S. F., *The Rennolds-Reynolds Family of England and Virginia.* Washington, 1948.

The Twainian, I, No. 1 (Jan. 1939, p. 2), and No. 3 (Feb. 1939, p. 3); n.s., VII, No. 2 (March–April 1948), pp. 1–3.

Virginia, State of. General Assembly, *The Statutes at Large, Being a Collection of All the Laws of Virginia from the First Session of the Legislature in the Year 1619,* edited by W. W. Hening. 13 vols. Richmond, Va., 1819–23.

Webster, Samuel and Doris, "Whitewashing Jane Clemens," *The Bookman,* LXI (1925) 531–35.

Wister, Owen, "In Homage to Mark Twain," *Harper's,* CLXXI (1935), 547–56.

Woods, Edgar, *Albemarle County in Virginia.* Charlottesville, Va., 1901.

NEWSPAPERS

Columbia (Mo.) *Intelligencer*
Hannibal *Courier*

Hannibal *Courier-Journal*
Hannibal *Courier-Post*
Hannibal *Daily Journal*
Hannibal *Gazette*
Hannibal *Journal*
Hannibal *Journal and Western Union*
Hannibal *Tri-Weekly Messenger*
Hannibal *Weekly Dollar Journal*
Hannibal *Weekly Whig Messenger*
Hannibal *Western Union*
Palmyra (Mo.) *Whig*
Paris (Mo.) *Mercury*
Ralls County [Mo.] Record
Virginia City (Nevada) *Evening Bulletin*

UNPUBLISHED MATERIAL

COLLECTIONS

The Mark Twain Papers in the University of California Library, Berkeley, California.

The Mark Twain collection in the possession of Samuel C. Webster, New York.

Mark Twain material in the Berg Collection, New York Public Library.

The Mark Twain Museum, Hannibal, Missouri.

The Samossoud (Clara Clemens) Collection, La Jolla, California.

COUNTY AND MUNICIPAL RECORDS

As indicated in the footnotes, specifically, a search has been made of the Order Books, Deed Books, Will Books, Court Records, and general records of:

Adair County, Kentucky
Bedford County, Virginia
Fentress County, Tennessee
Green County, Kentucky
Marion County, Missouri
Monroe County, Missouri

and the Municipal Records of Hannibal, Missouri.

MISCELLANEOUS MANUSCRIPT RECORDS

United States National Archives. Records of Appointments of Postmasters, Vol. 12A, p. 127, "Pall Mall, Fentress County, Tennessee."

St. Louis Record Book of Bankruptcies, Sept. 4, 1844 (now in Jefferson City, Mo.).

INDEX

INDEX

References in bold face refer to whole chapters or sections. Ms. refers to un-published manuscripts. The names of fictional characters appear in quotation marks.